ULTIMATE COM

X-MEN

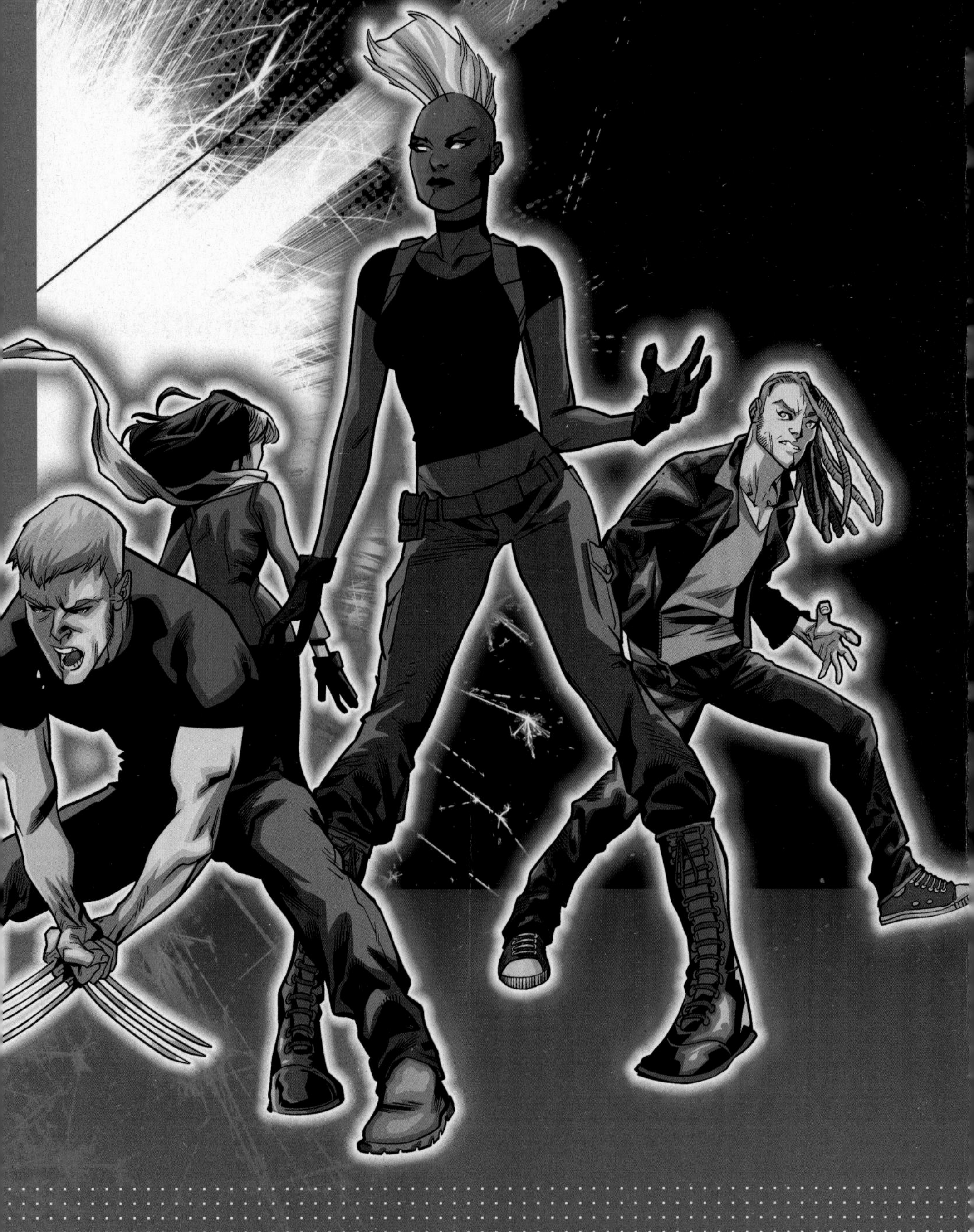

ULTIMATE COMICS X-MEN

WRITER: **BRIAN WOOD**

PENCILER: **MAHMUD ASRAR**

INKER: **JUAN VLASCO**

COLORIST: **JORDIE BELLAIRE**

LETTERER: **VC'S JOE SABINO**

COVER ART: **DAVE JOHNSON**

ASSISTANT EDITORS: **EMILY SHAW** & **JON MOISAN**

EDITOR: **MARK PANICCIA**

COLLECTION EDITOR: **NELSON RIBEIRO**

ASSISTANT EDITOR: **ALEX STARBUCK**

EDITORS, SPECIAL PROJECTS: **JENNIFER GRÜNWALD** & **MARK D. BEAZLEY**

SENIOR EDITOR, SPECIAL PROJECTS: **JEFF YOUNGQUIST**

SVP OF PRINT & DIGITAL PUBLISHING SALES: **DAVID GABRIEL**

BOOK DESIGNER: **RODOLFO MURAGUCHI**

EDITOR IN CHIEF: **AXEL ALONSO**

CHIEF CREATIVE OFFICER: **JOE QUESADA**

PUBLISHER: **DAN BUCKLEY**

EXECUTIVE PRODUCER: **ALAN FINE**

CS X-MEN BY BRIAN WOOD VOL. 2. Contains material originally published in magazine form as ULTIMATE COMICS X-MEN #24-28. First printing 2013. ISBN# 978-0-7851-6720-4. Published by WIDE, INC., a subsidiary of MARVEL ENTERTAINMENT, LLC. OFFICE OF PUBLICATION: 135 West 50th Street, New York, NY 10020. Copyright © 2013 Marvel Characters, Inc. All rights reserved. All red in this issue and the distinctive names and likenesses thereof, and all related indicia are trademarks of Marvel Characters, Inc. No similarity between any of the names, characters, persons, s in this magazine with those of any living or dead person or institution is intended, and any such similarity which may exist is purely coincidental. **Printed in CANADA.** ALAN FINE, EVP - Office Marvel Worldwide, Inc. and EVP & CMO Marvel Characters B.V.; DAN BUCKLEY, Publisher & President - Print, Animation & Digital Divisions; JOE QUESADA, Chief Creative Officer; TOM BREVOORT, ; DAVID BOGART, SVP of Operations & Procurement, Publishing; C.B. CEBULSKI, SVP of Creator & Content Development; DAVID GABRIEL, SVP of Print & Digital Publishing Sales; JIM O'KEEFE, VP of istics; DAN CARR, Executive Director of Publishing Technology; SUSAN CRESPI, Editorial Operations Manager; ALEX MORALES, Publishing Operations Manager; STAN LEE, Chairman Emeritus. ding advertising in Marvel Comics or on Marvel.com, please contact Niza Disla, Director of Marvel Partnerships, at ndisla@marvel.com. For Marvel subscription inquiries, please call 800-217-9158. etween 7/19/2013 and 8/26/2013 by SOLISCO PRINTERS, SCOTT, QC, CANADA.

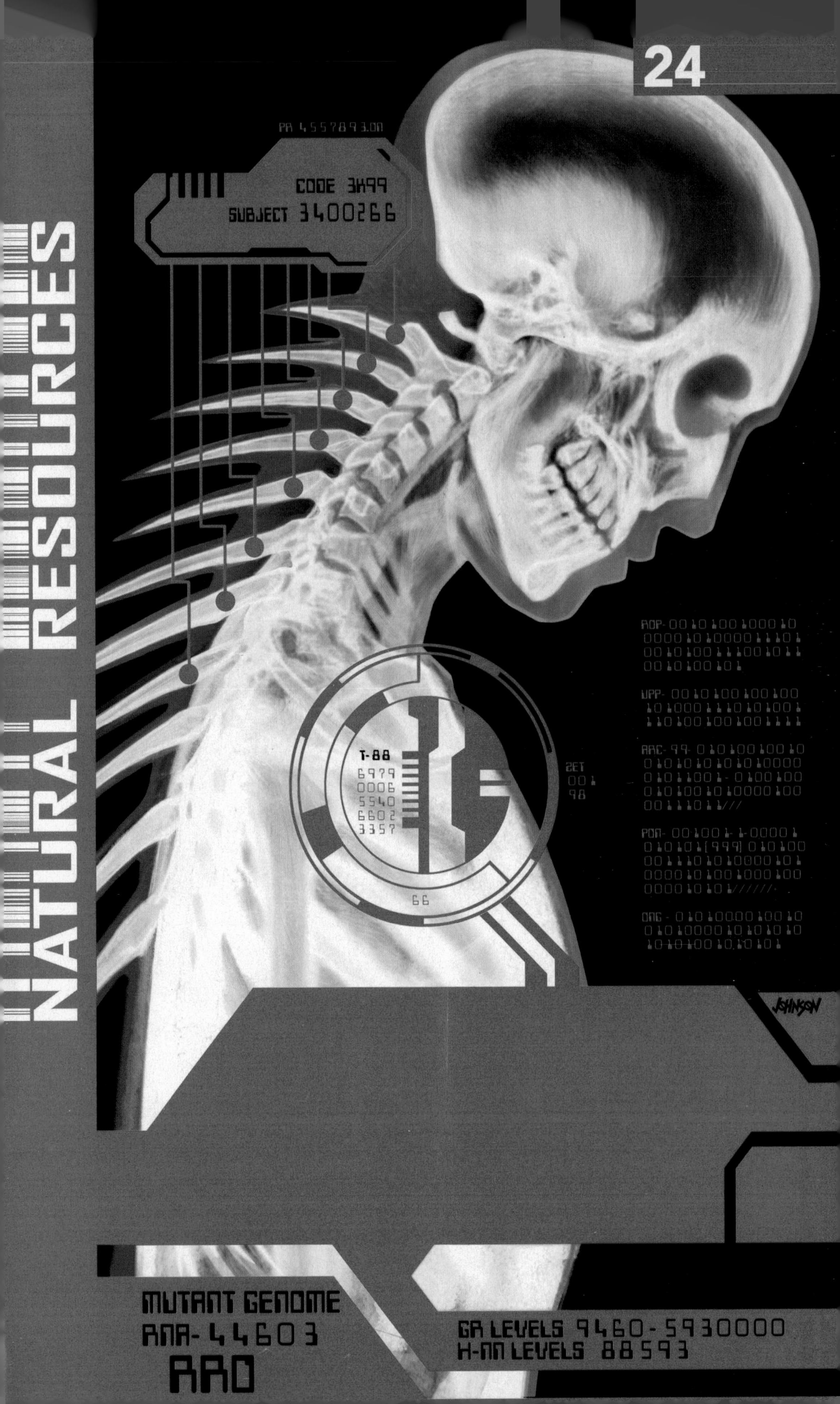

24
NATURAL RESOURCES
CODE 3K99
SUBJECT 3400266
T-88
6979
0006
5540
6602
3357
66
JOHNSON
MUTANT GENOME
RNA- 44603
RRD
GR LEVELS 9460-5930000
H-NN LEVELS 88593

LIVING IN A WORLD WHERE MUTANTS ARE HATED AND FEARED MORE THAN EVER, ONE GROUP OF YOUNG HEROES HAS BANDED TOGETHER TO FIGHT BACK.

ULTIMATE COMICS X-MEN

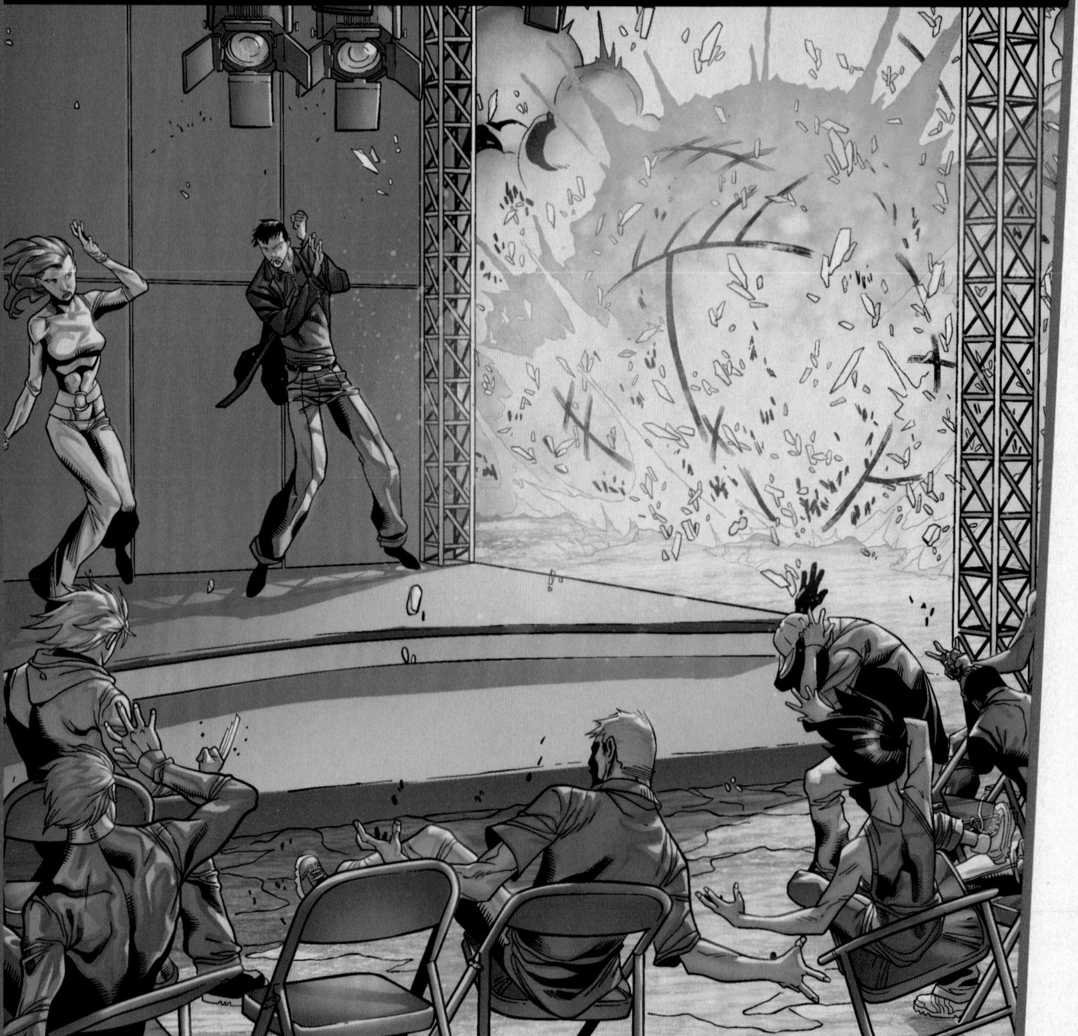

PREVIOUSLY:

The Sentient Seed, intended as the mutants' gift to mankind, was not the agent of peace that Kitty Pryde intended. Not only did the seed transform Utopia into a target for those looking to exploit its economic value but its existence divided the mutant homeland, as well.

Realizing that Utopia was in danger, Kitty Pryde and Tony Stark hatched a defense plan. They blew up the greenhouse, creating the illusion that the seed had been destroyed, while secretly distributing the seed to countries in need, free from the eyes of the media.

But following the explosion, Mach Two, having had enough of Kitty's goodwill towards the humans, took her followers and decamped from Utopia.

Between threats from the U.S. government, Karen Grant's spies from Tian, and now Mach Two's rebel faction, can Kitty Pryde and Utopia stand their ground?

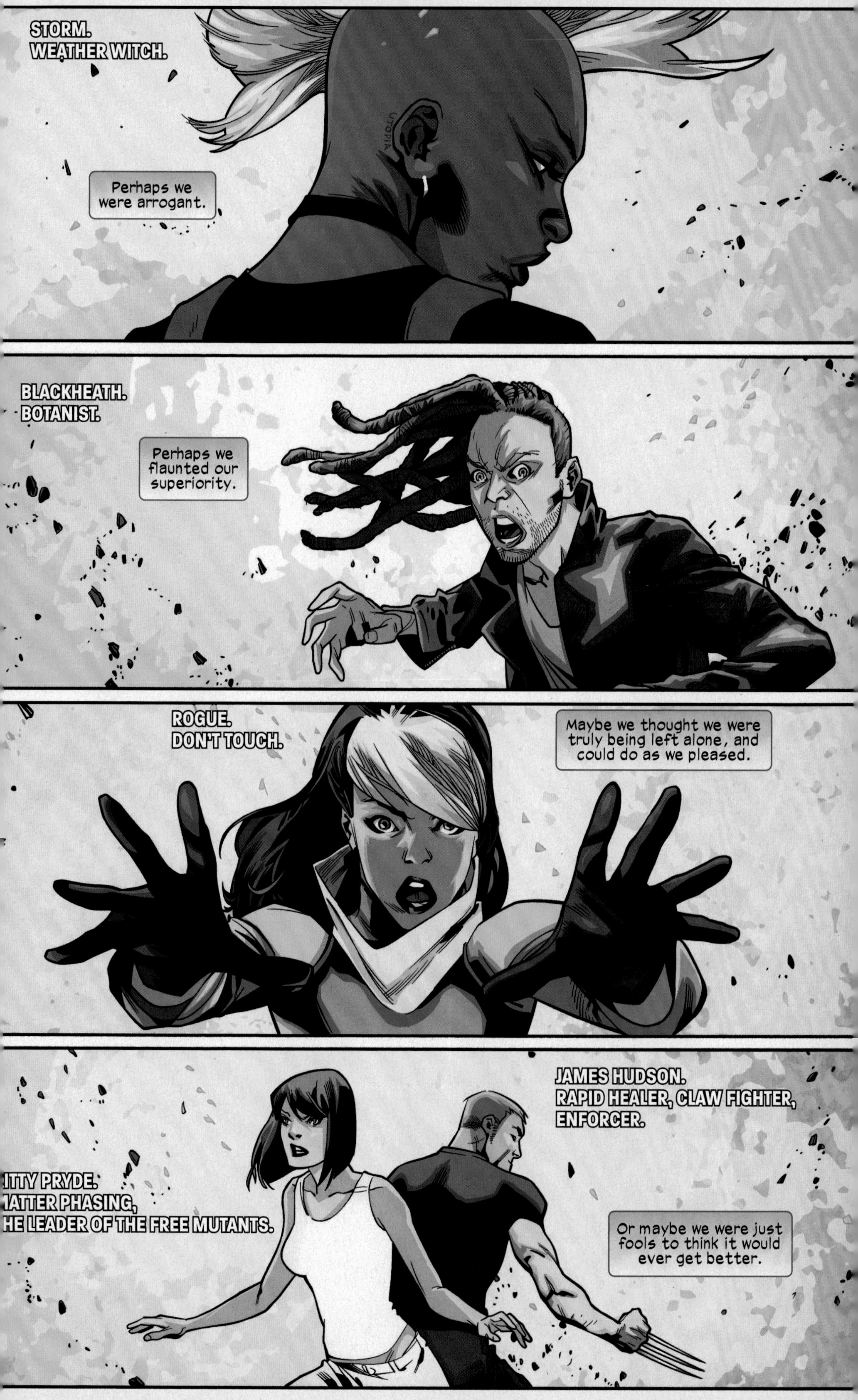

STORM.
WEATHER WITCH.
Perhaps we were arrogant.
BLACKHEATH.
BOTANIST.
Perhaps we flaunted our superiority.
ROGUE.
DON'T TOUCH.
Maybe we thought we were truly being left alone, and could do as we pleased.
ITTY PRYDE.
IATTER PHASING,
HE LEADER OF THE FREE MUTANTS.
JAMES HUDSON.
RAPID HEALER, CLAW FIGHTER,
ENFORCER.
Or maybe we were just fools to think it would ever get better.

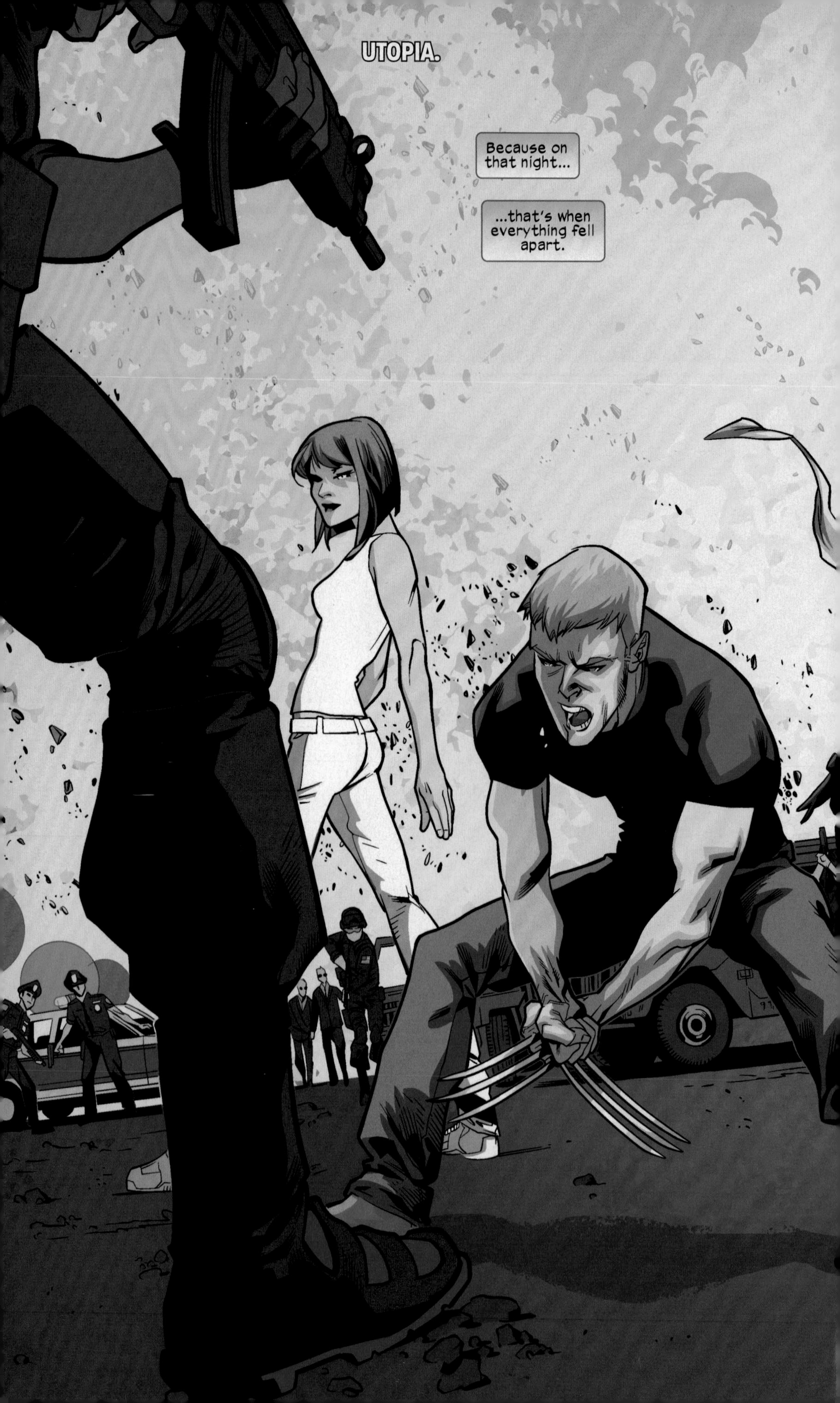
UTOPIA.
Because on that night...
...that's when everything fell apart.

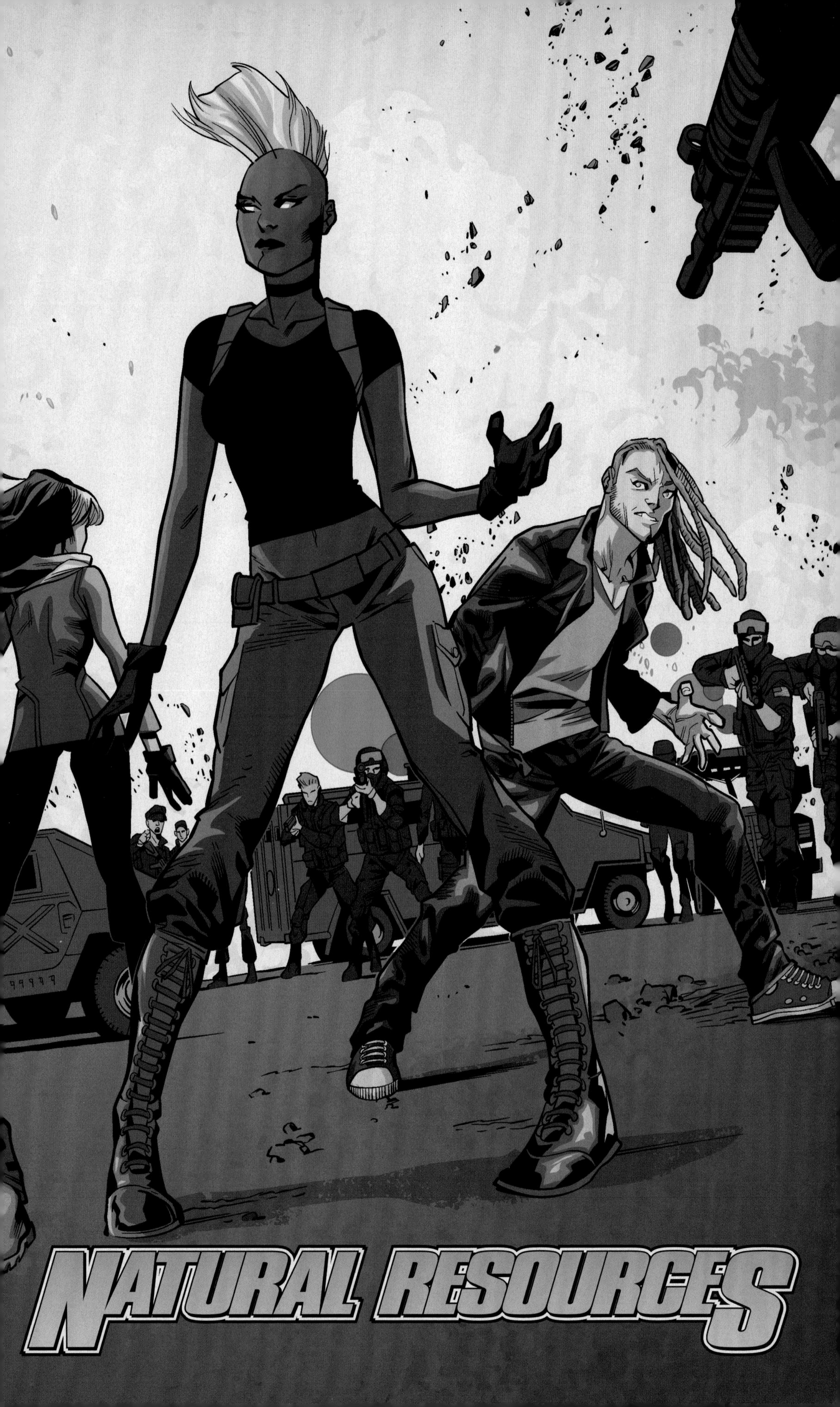
NATURAL RESOURCES

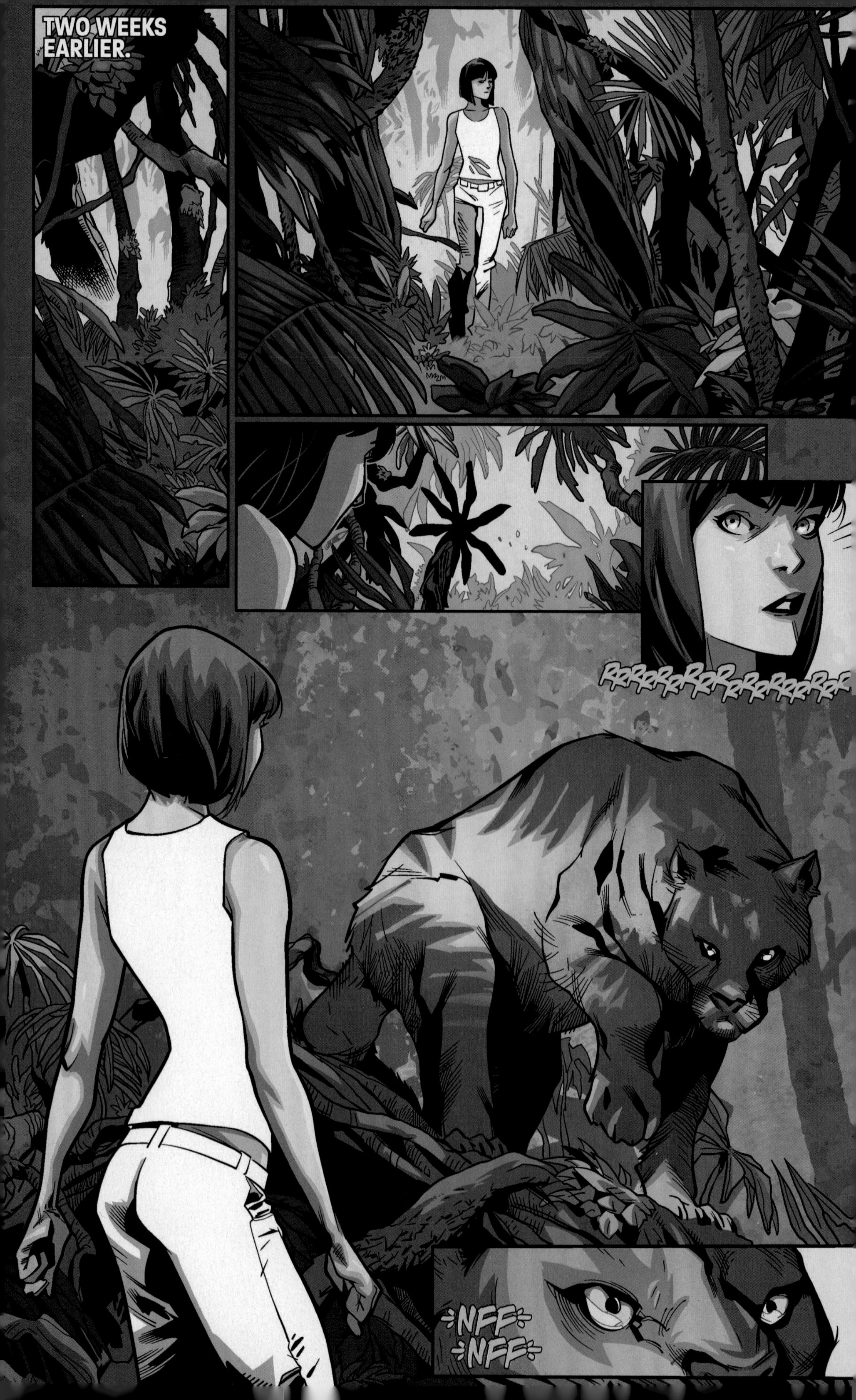
TWO WEEKS EARLIER.
RRRRRRRRRRRRRRRRRR
NFF NFF

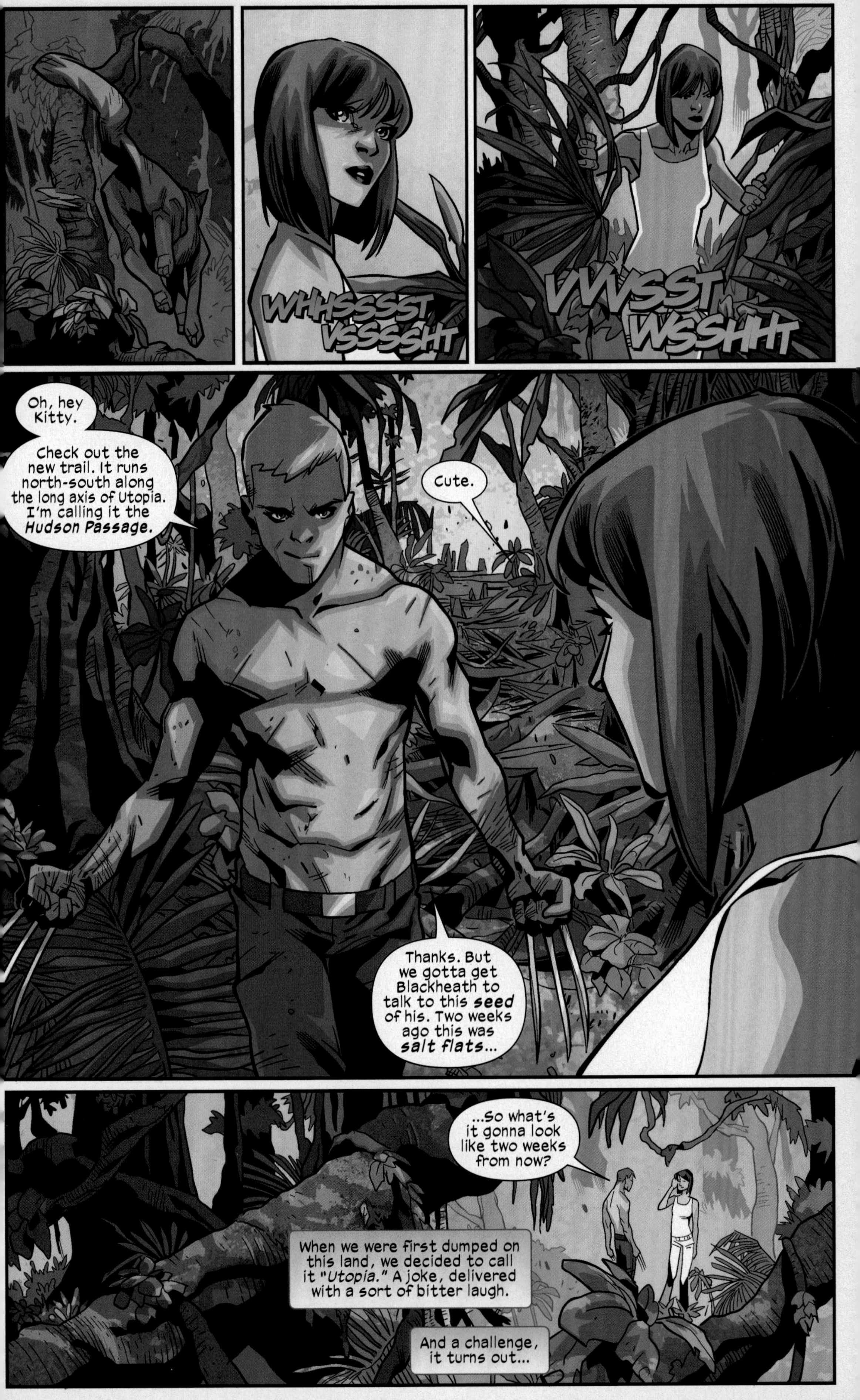
WHHSSSST VSSSSHT
VVVSST WSSHHT
Oh, hey Kitty.
Check out the new trail. It runs north-south along the long axis of Utopia. I'm calling it the *Hudson Passage.*
Cute.
Thanks. But we gotta get Blackheath to talk to this *seed* of his. Two weeks ago this was *salt flats*...
...So what's it gonna look like two weeks from now?
When we were first dumped on this land, we decided to call it "*Utopia.*" A joke, delivered with a sort of bitter laugh.
And a challenge, it turns out...

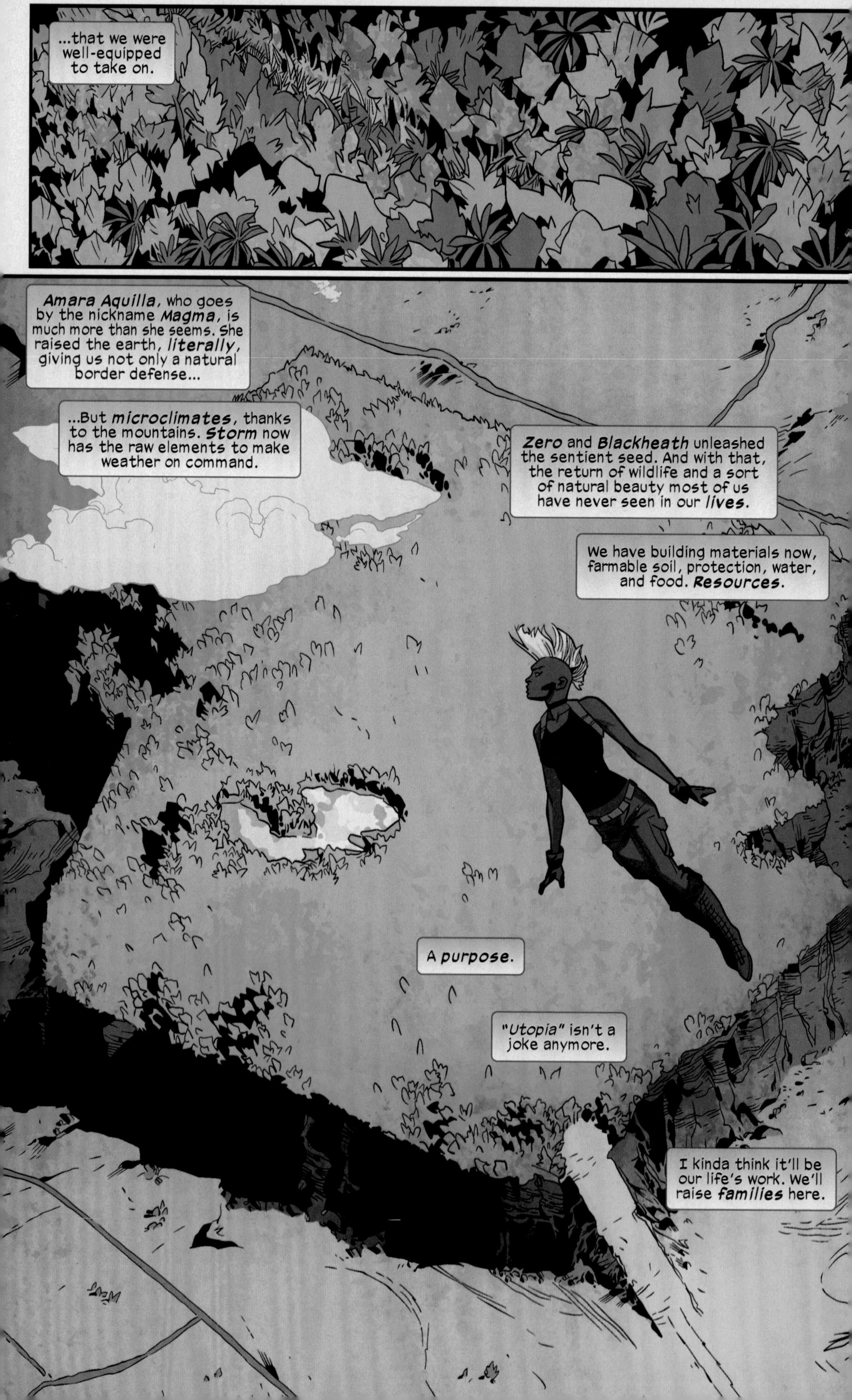

...that we were well-equipped to take on.
Amara Aquilla, who goes by the nickname *Magma*, is much more than she seems. She raised the earth, *literally*, giving us not only a natural border defense...
...But *microclimates*, thanks to the mountains. ***Storm*** now has the raw elements to make weather on command.
Zero and *Blackheath* unleashed the sentient seed. And with that, the return of wildlife and a sort of natural beauty most of us have never seen in our *lives*.
We have building materials now, farmable soil, protection, water, and food. ***Resources***.
A *purpose*.
"Utopia" isn't a joke anymore.
I kinda think it'll be our life's work. We'll raise *families* here.

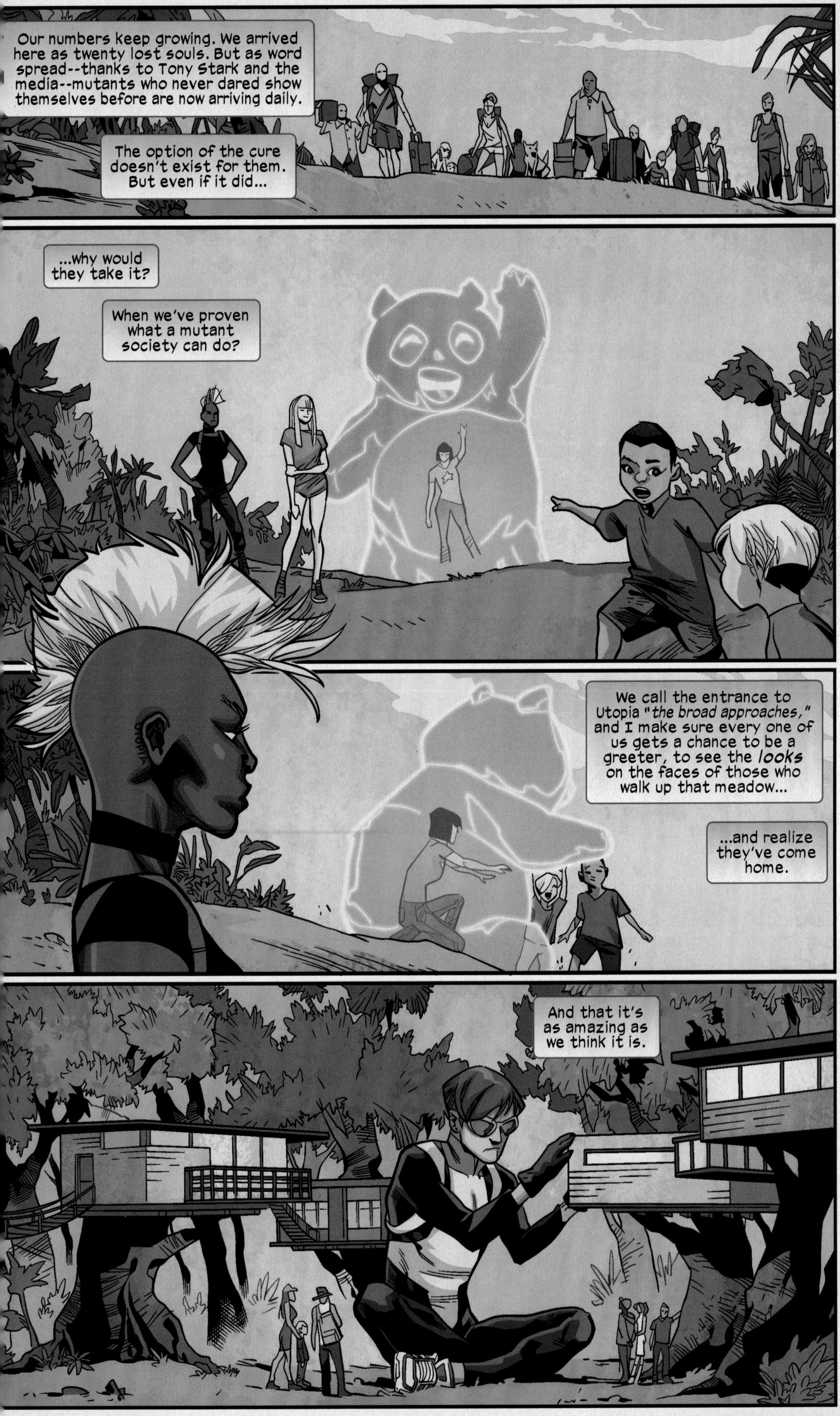

Our numbers keep growing. We arrived here as twenty lost souls. But as word spread--thanks to Tony Stark and the media--mutants who never dared show themselves before are now arriving daily.
The option of the cure doesn't exist for them. But even if it did...
...why would they take it?
When we've proven what a mutant society can do?
UTOPIA
We call the entrance to Utopia "*the broad approaches,*" and I make sure every one of us gets a chance to be a greeter, to see the *looks* on the faces of those who walk up that meadow...
...and realize they've come home.
And that it's as amazing as we think it is.

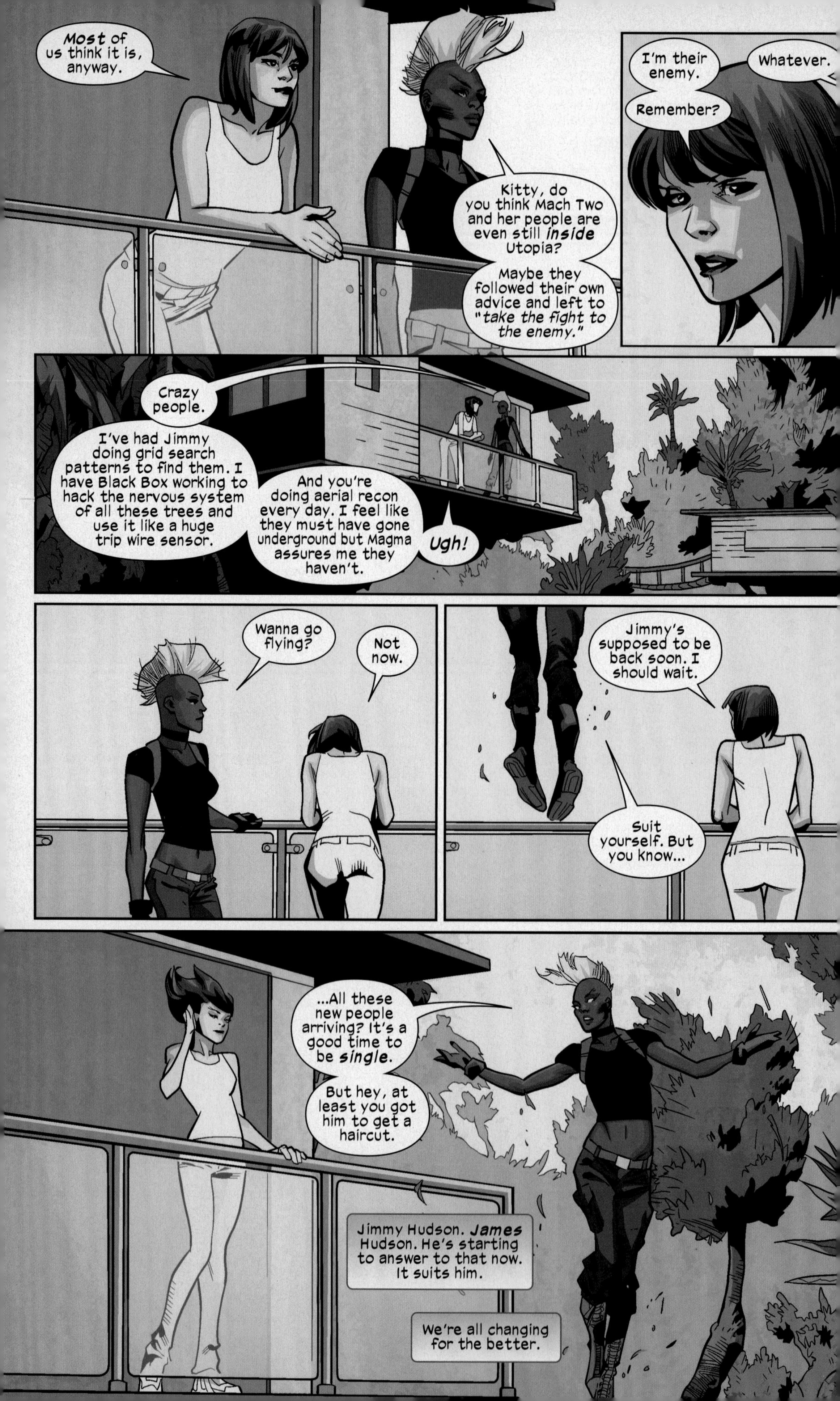

Most of us think it is, anyway.
Kitty, do you think Mach Two and her people are even still inside Utopia?
Maybe they followed their own advice and left to "take the fight to the enemy."
I'm their enemy.
Remember?
Whatever.
Crazy people.
I've had Jimmy doing grid search patterns to find them. I have Black Box working to hack the nervous system of all these trees and use it like a huge trip wire sensor.
And you're doing aerial recon every day. I feel like they must have gone underground but Magma assures me they haven't.
Ugh!
Wanna go flying?
Not now.
Jimmy's supposed to be back soon. I should wait.
Suit yourself. But you know...
...All these new people arriving? It's a good time to be single.
But hey, at least you got him to get a haircut.
Jimmy Hudson. James Hudson. He's starting to answer to that now. It suits him.
We're all changing for the better.

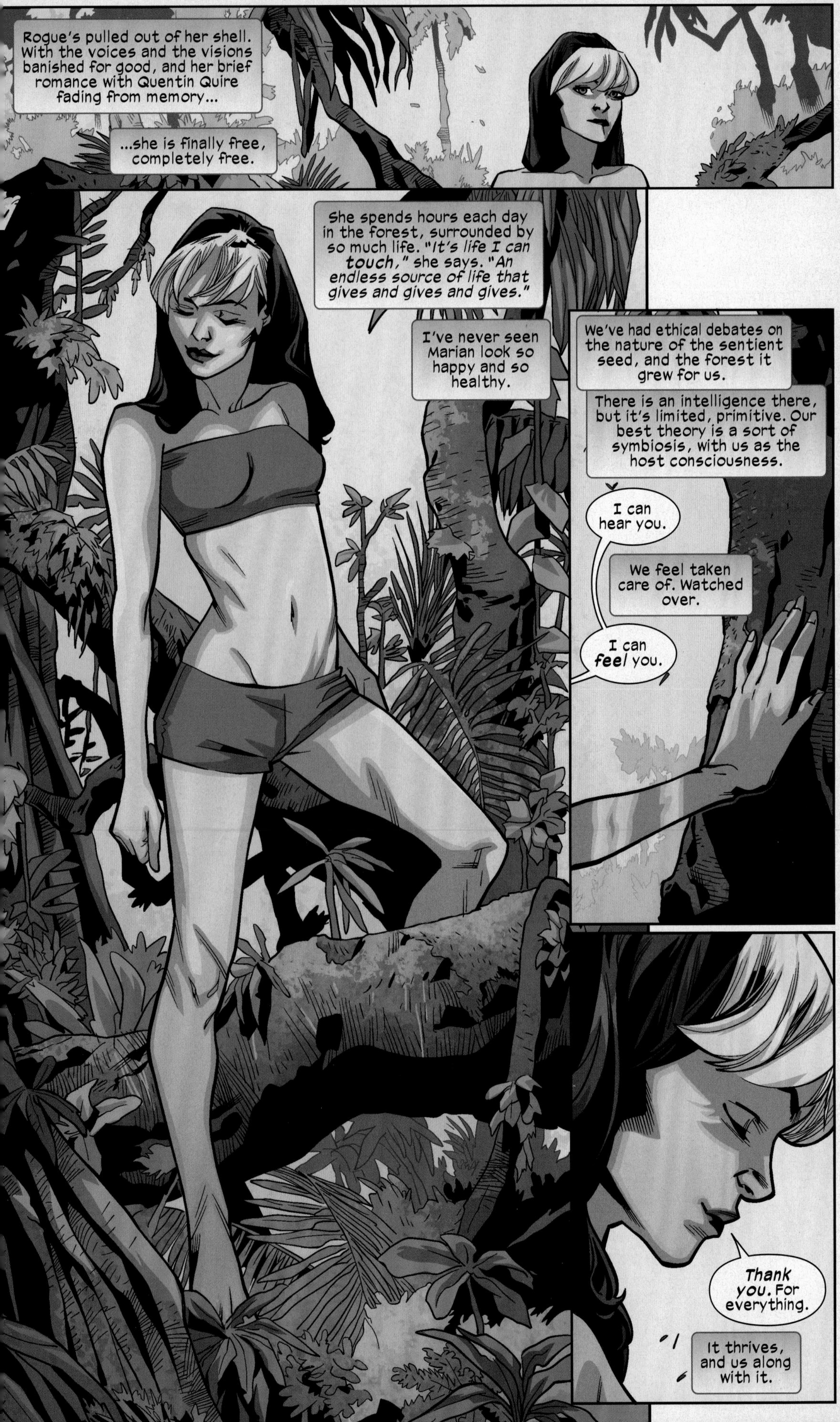

Rogue's pulled out of her shell. With the voices and the visions banished for good, and her brief romance with Quentin Quire fading from memory...
...she is finally free, completely free.
She spends hours each day in the forest, surrounded by so much life. "It's life I can touch," she says. "An endless source of life that gives and gives and gives."
I've never seen Marian look so happy and so healthy.
We've had ethical debates on the nature of the sentient seed, and the forest it grew for us.
There is an intelligence there, but it's limited, primitive. Our best theory is a sort of symbiosis, with us as the host consciousness.
I can hear you.
We feel taken care of. Watched over.
I can feel you.
Thank you. For everything.
It thrives, and us along with it.

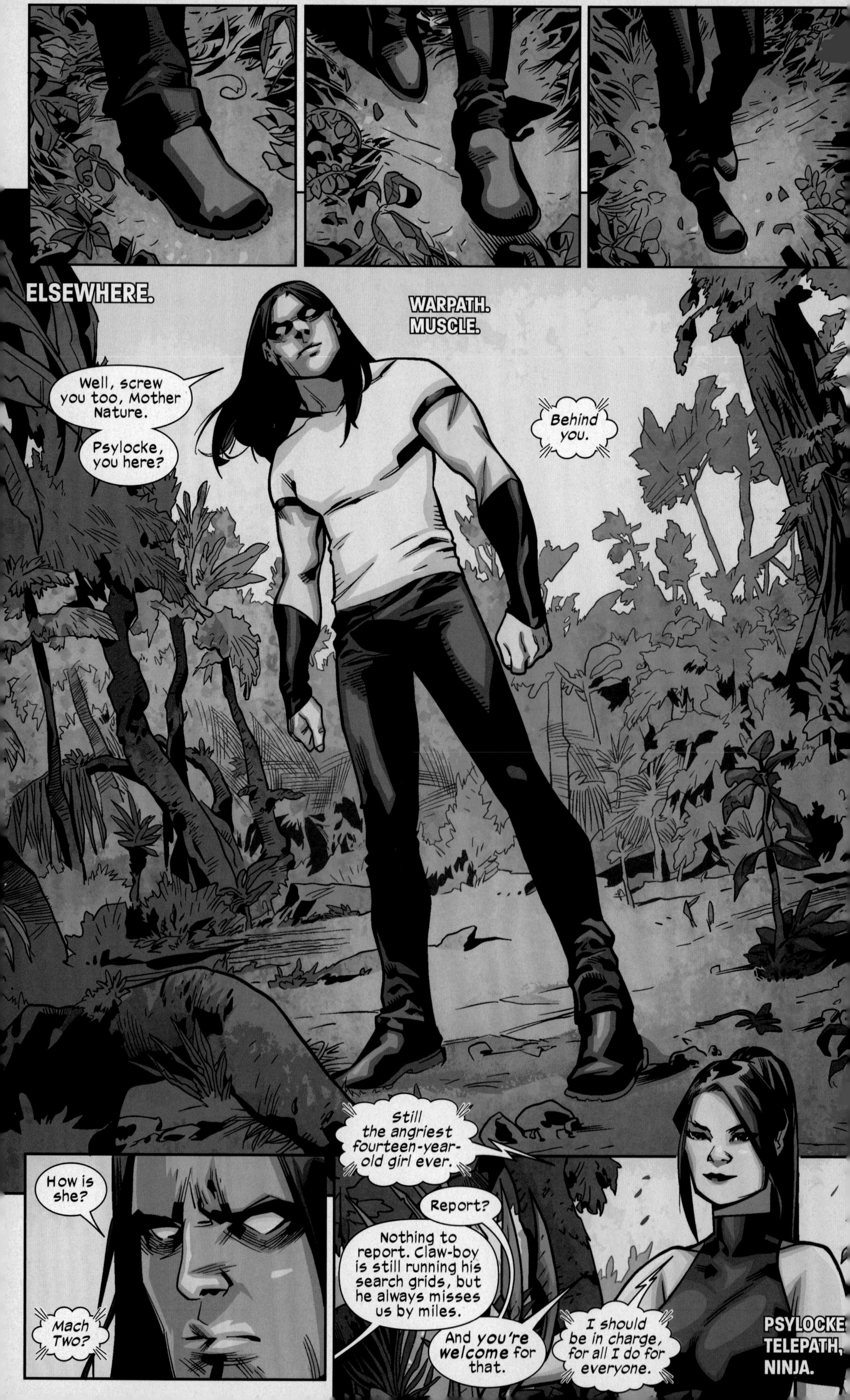
ELSEWHERE.
Well, screw you too, Mother Nature.
Psylocke, you here?
WARPATH. MUSCLE.
Behind you.
Still the angriest fourteen-year-old girl ever.
How is she?
Mach Two?
Report?
Nothing to report. Claw-boy is still running his search grids, but he always misses us by miles.
And you're welcome for that.
I should be in charge, for all I do for everyone.
PSYLOCKE TELEPATH, NINJA.

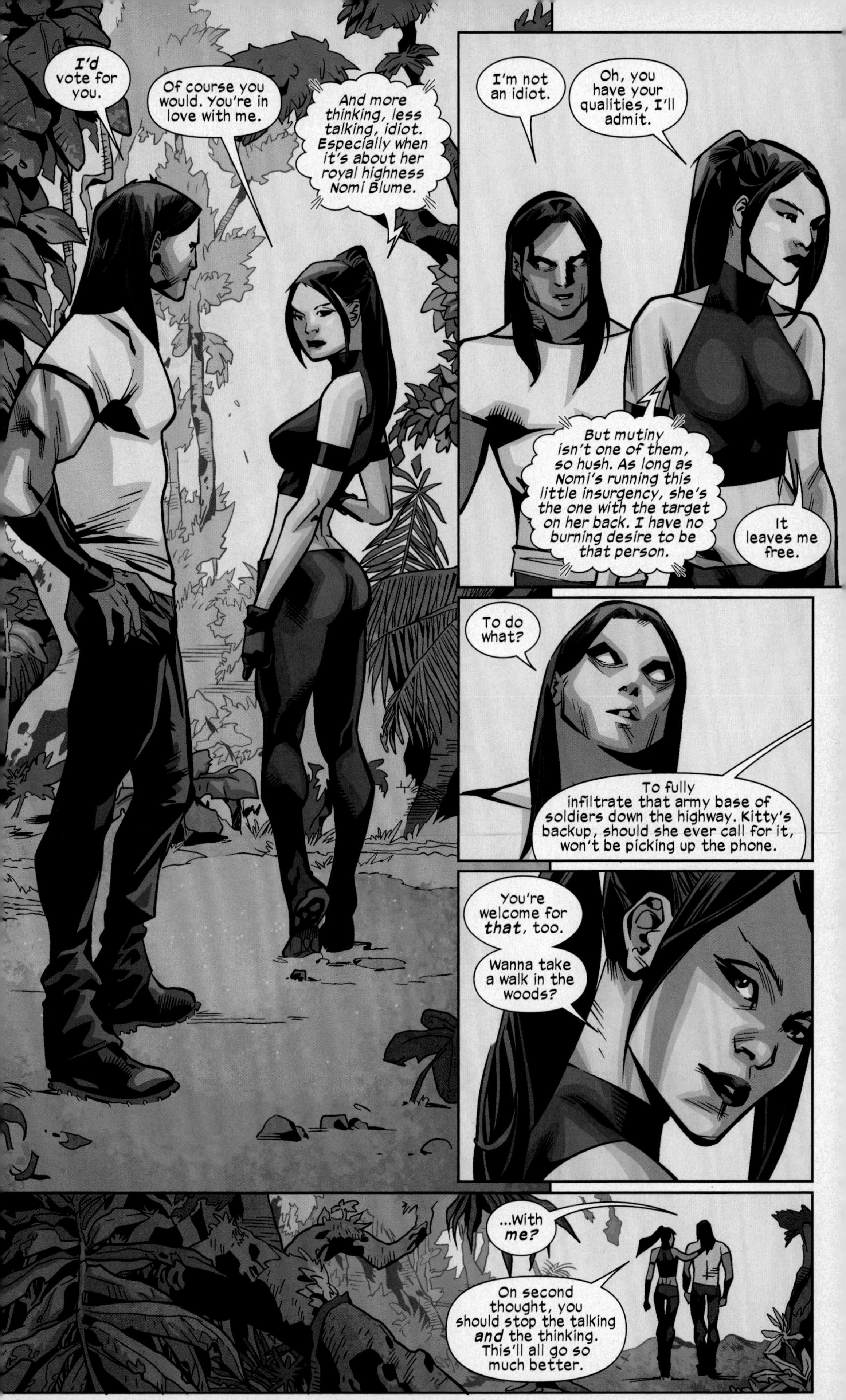

I'd vote for you.
Of course you would. You're in love with me.
And more thinking, less talking, idiot. Especially when it's about her royal highness Nomi Blume.
I'm not an idiot.
Oh, you have your qualities, I'll admit.
But mutiny isn't one of them, so hush. As long as Nomi's running this little insurgency, she's the one with the target on her back. I have no burning desire to be that person.
It leaves me free.
To do what?
To fully infiltrate that army base of soldiers down the highway. Kitty's backup, should she ever call for it, won't be picking up the phone.
You're welcome for that, too.
Wanna take a walk in the woods?
...With me?
On second thought, you should stop the talking and the thinking. This'll all go so much better.

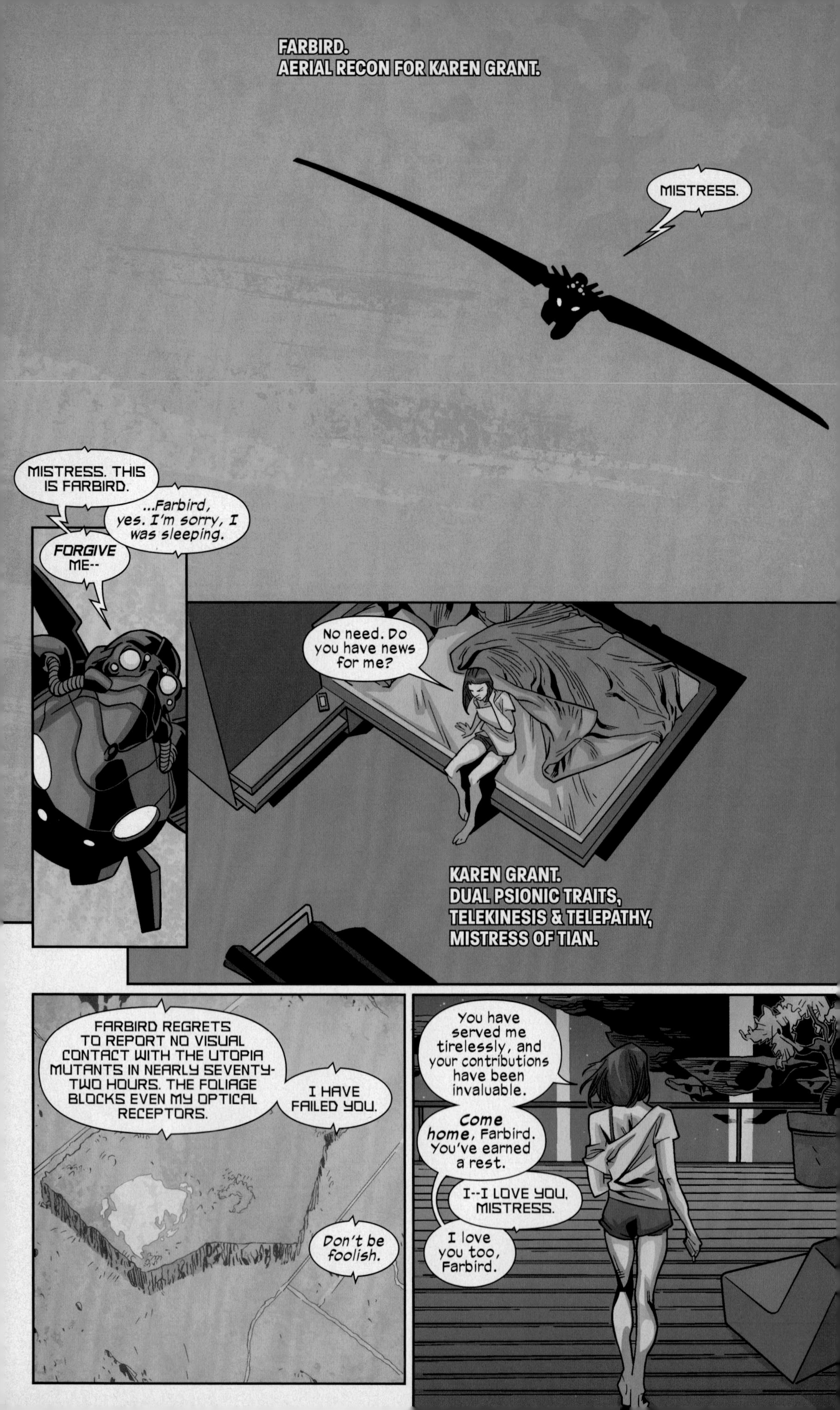

FARBIRD.
AERIAL RECON FOR KAREN GRANT.
MISTRESS.
MISTRESS. THIS IS FARBIRD.
...Farbird, yes. I'm sorry, I was sleeping.
FORGIVE ME--
No need. Do you have news for me?
KAREN GRANT.
DUAL PSIONIC TRAITS, TELEKINESIS & TELEPATHY, MISTRESS OF TIAN.
FARBIRD REGRETS TO REPORT NO VISUAL CONTACT WITH THE UTOPIA MUTANTS IN NEARLY SEVENTY-TWO HOURS. THE FOLIAGE BLOCKS EVEN MY OPTICAL RECEPTORS.
I HAVE FAILED YOU.
Don't be foolish.
You have served me tirelessly, and your contributions have been invaluable.
Come home, Farbird. You've earned a rest.
I--I LOVE YOU, MISTRESS.
I love you too, Farbird.

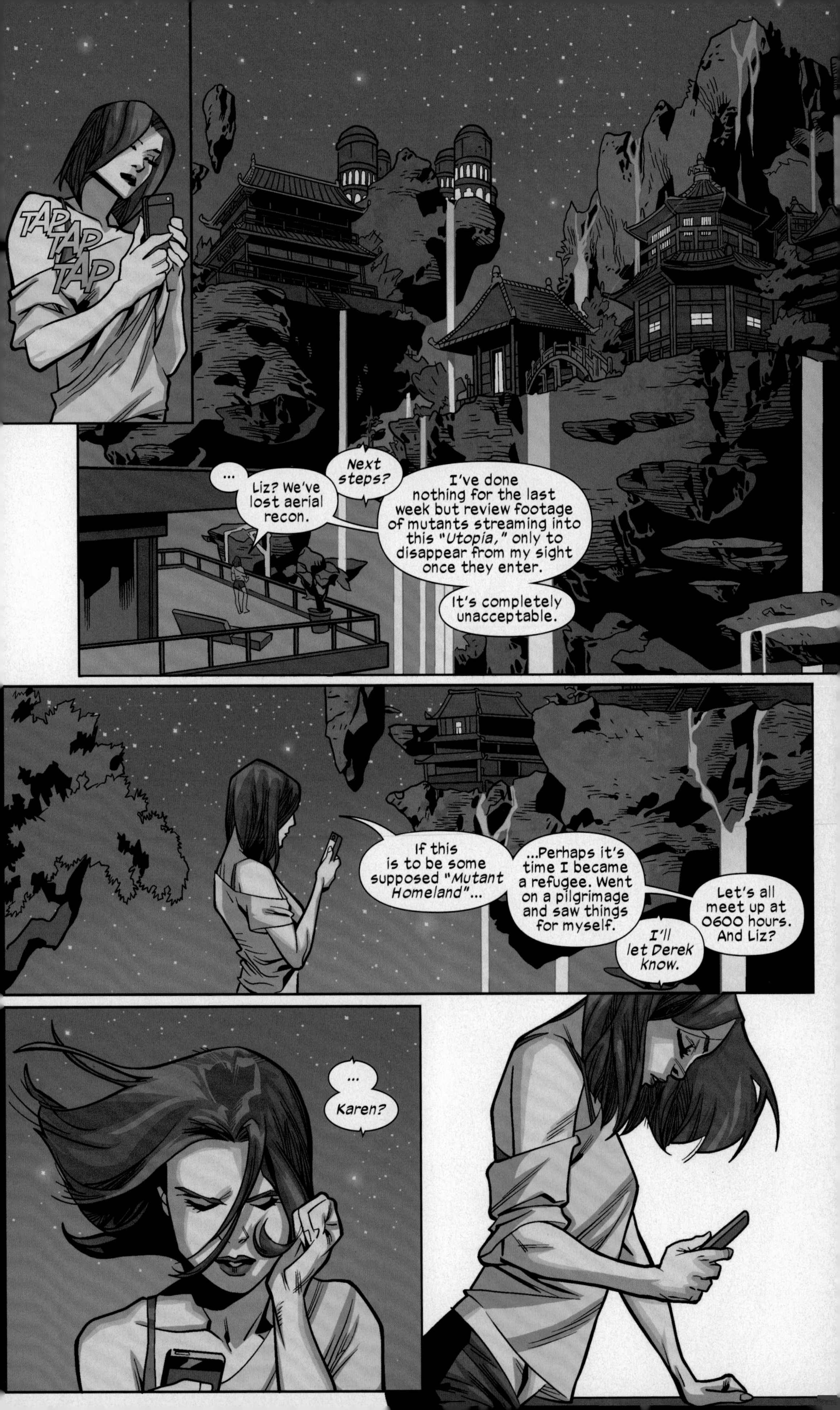
TAP TAP TAP
...
Liz? We've lost aerial recon.
Next steps?
I've done nothing for the last week but review footage of mutants streaming into this "Utopia," only to disappear from my sight once they enter.
It's completely unacceptable.
If this is to be some supposed "Mutant Homeland"...
...Perhaps it's time I became a refugee. Went on a pilgrimage and saw things for myself.
Let's all meet up at 0600 hours. And Liz?
I'll let Derek know.
...
Karen?

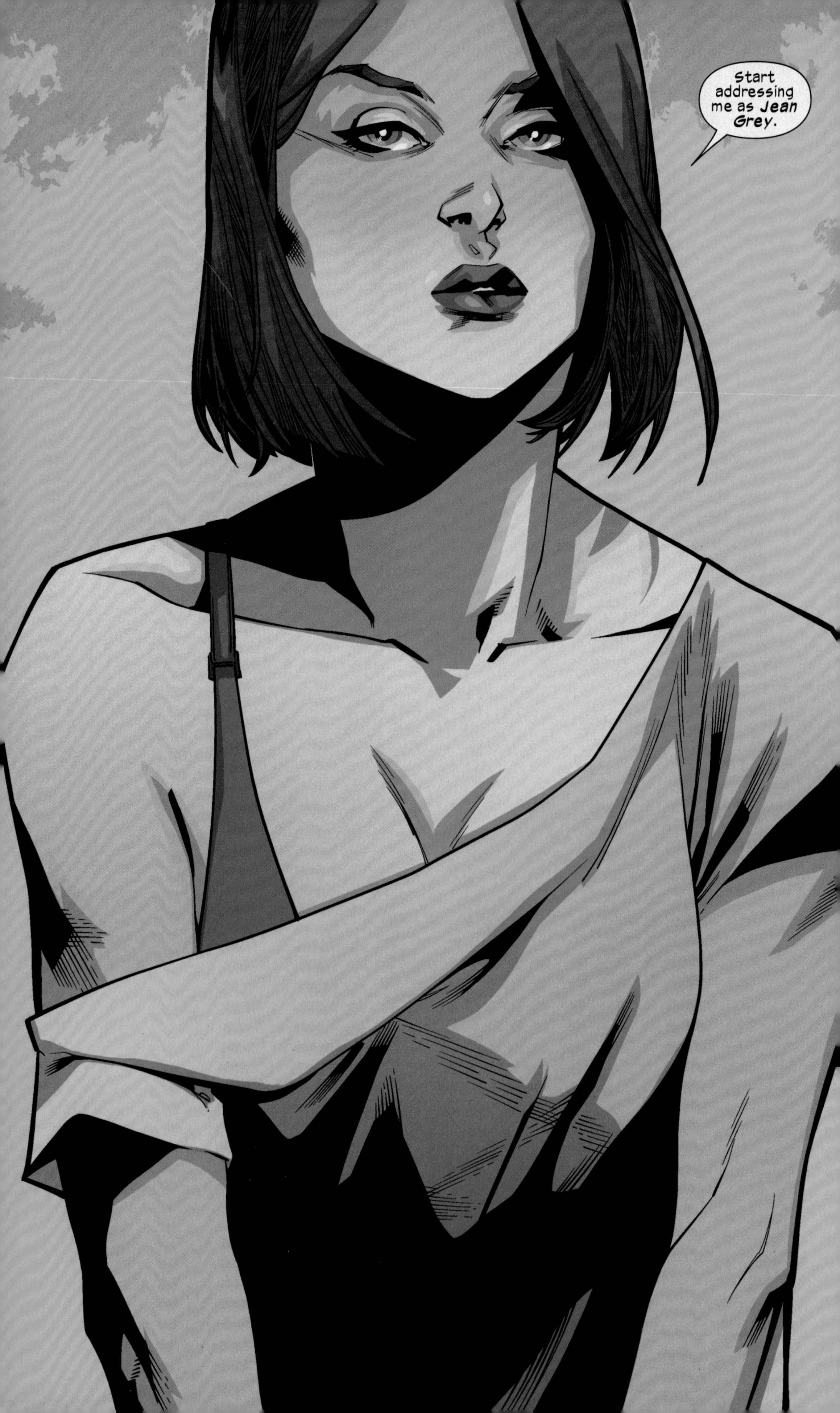
Start addressing me as Jean Grey.

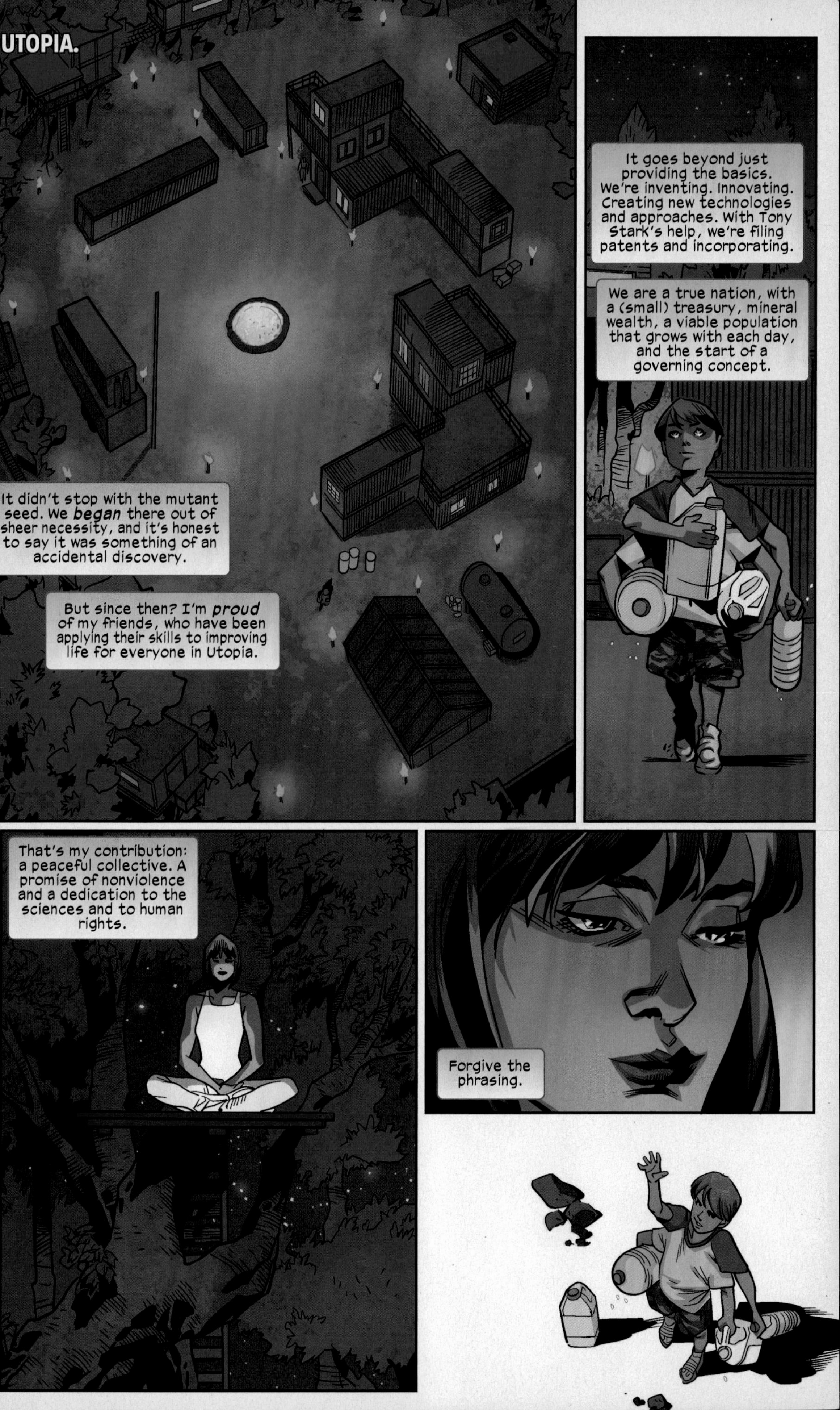

UTOPIA.
It didn't stop with the mutant seed. We *began* there out of sheer necessity, and it's honest to say it was something of an accidental discovery.
But since then? I'm *proud* of my friends, who have been applying their skills to improving life for everyone in Utopia.
It goes beyond just providing the basics. We're inventing. Innovating. Creating new technologies and approaches. With Tony Stark's help, we're filing patents and incorporating.
We are a true nation, with a (small) treasury, mineral wealth, a viable population that grows with each day, and the start of a governing concept.
That's my contribution: a peaceful collective. A promise of nonviolence and a dedication to the sciences and to human rights.
Forgive the phrasing.

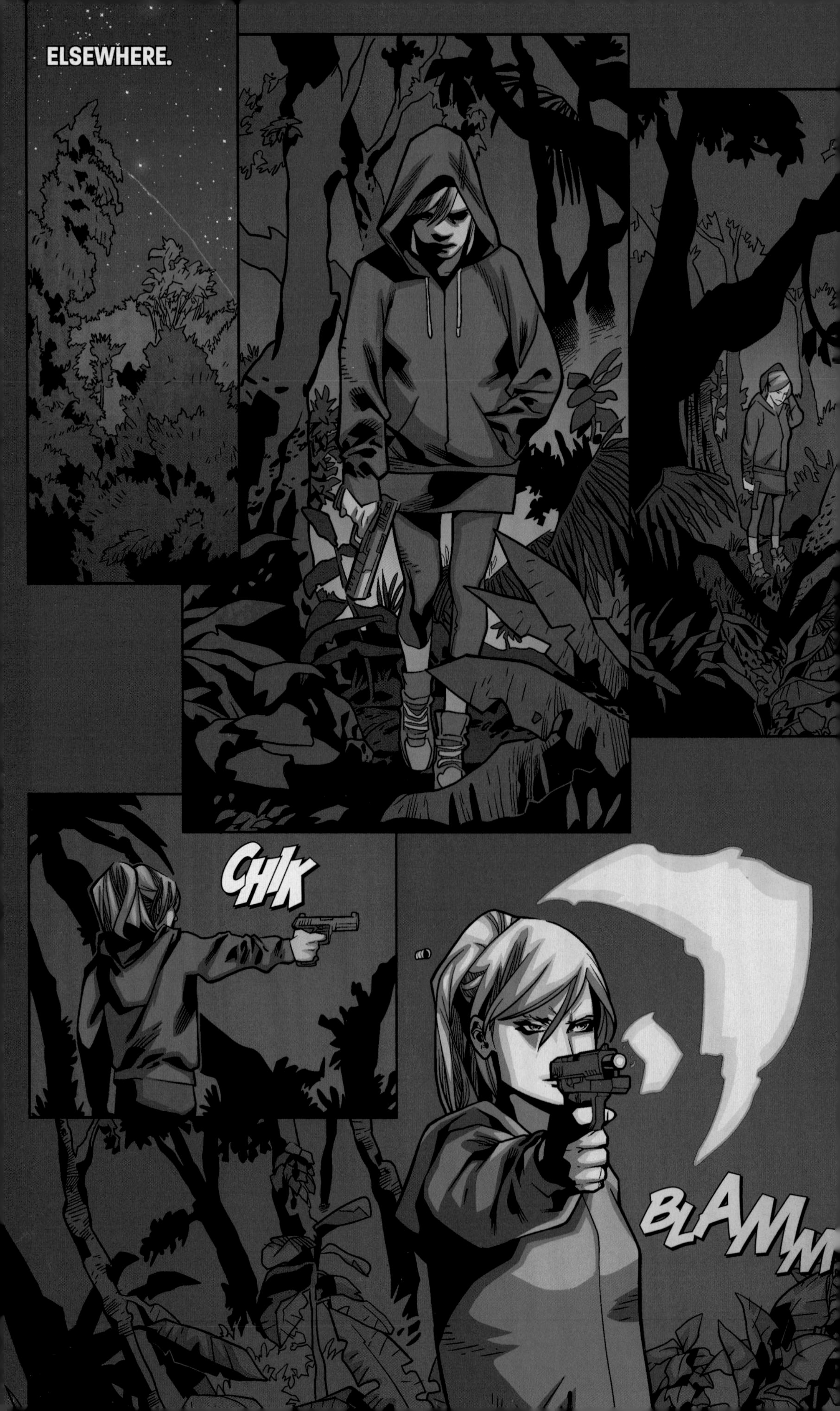
ELSEWHERE.
CHIK
BLAMM

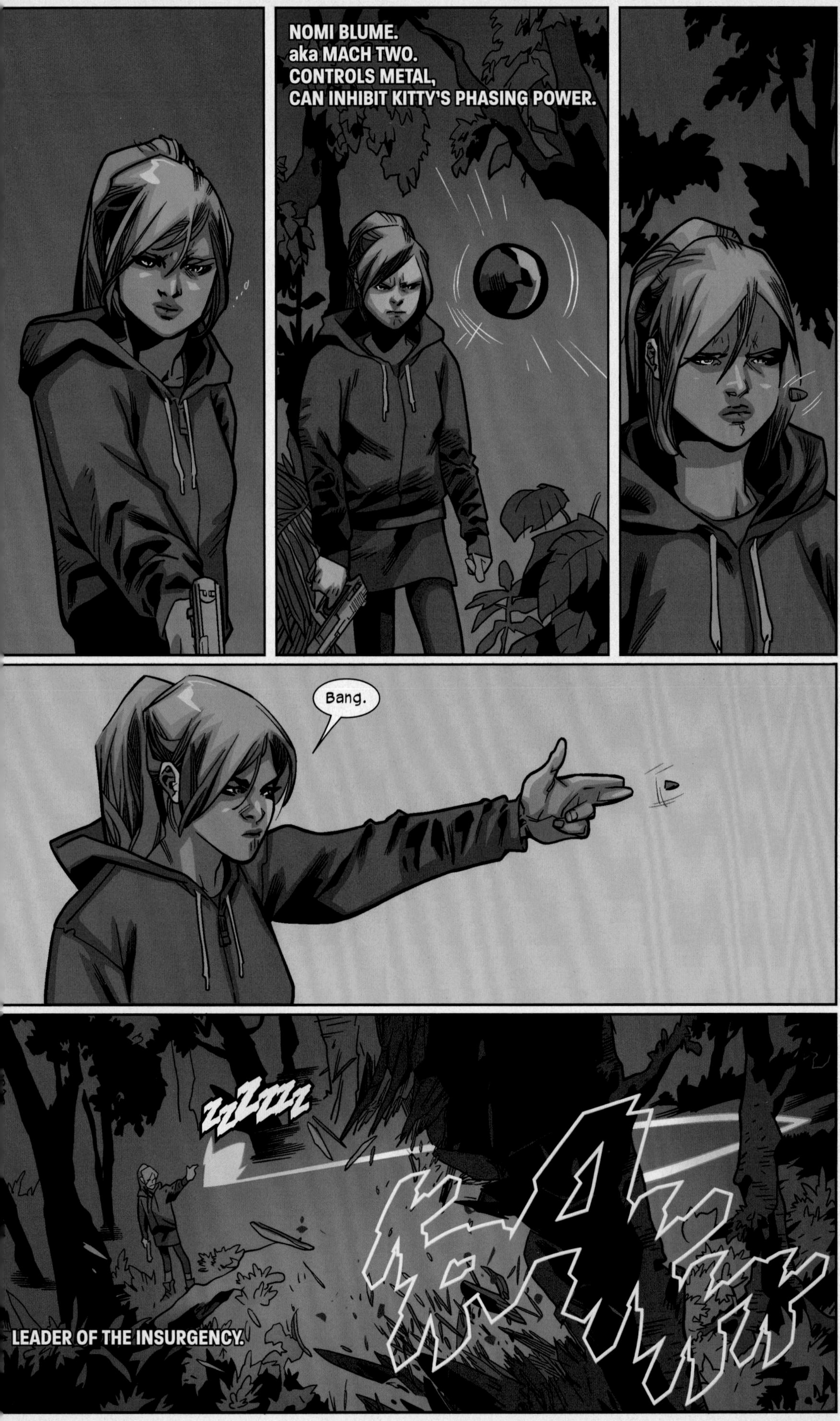

NOMI BLUME.
aka MACH TWO.
CONTROLS METAL,
CAN INHIBIT KITTY'S PHASING POWER.
Bang.
ZZZZZZ
LEADER OF THE INSURGENCY.

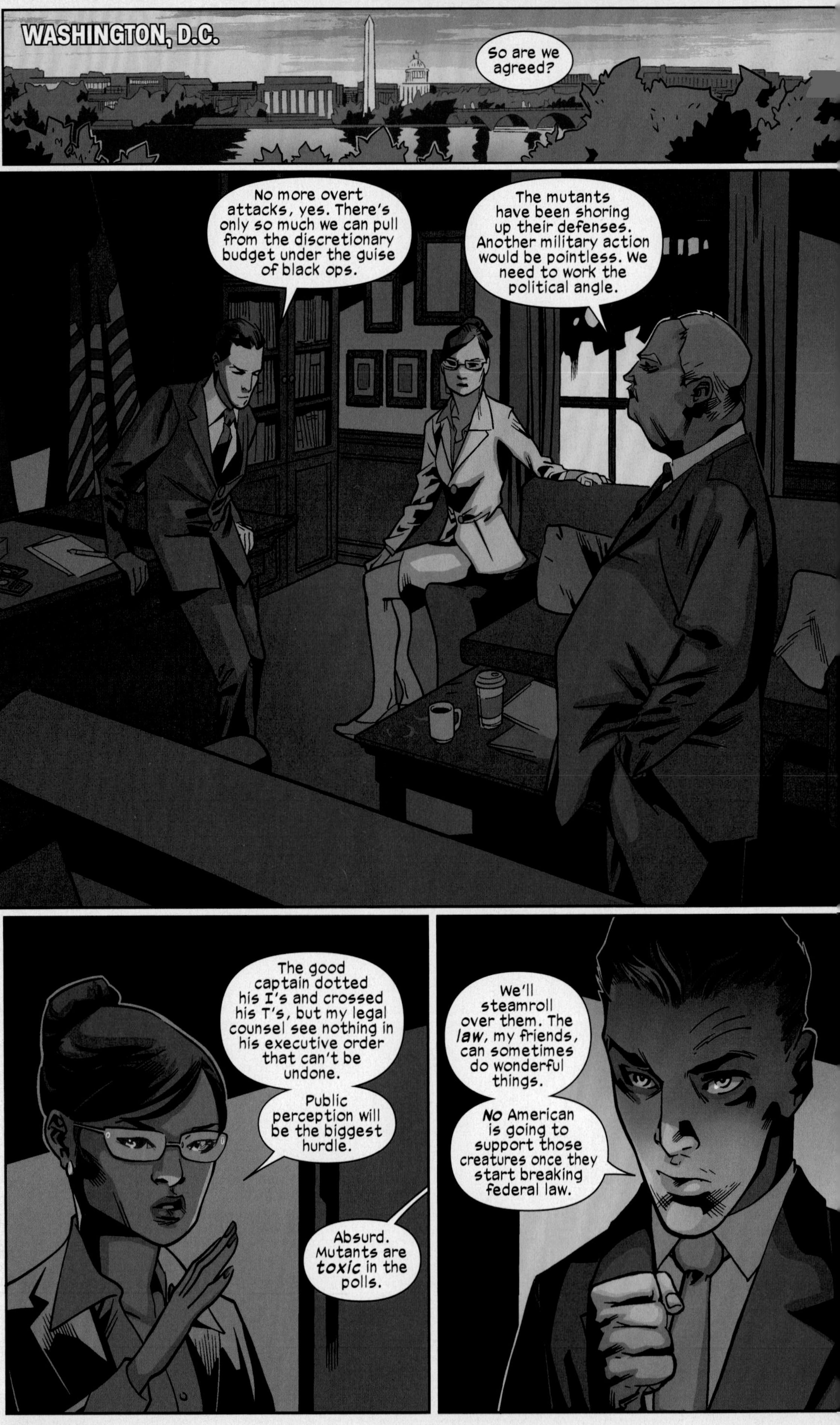
WASHINGTON, D.C.
So are we agreed?
No more overt attacks, yes. There's only so much we can pull from the discretionary budget under the guise of black ops.
The mutants have been shoring up their defenses. Another military action would be pointless. We need to work the political angle.
The good captain dotted his I's and crossed his T's, but my legal counsel see nothing in his executive order that can't be undone.
Public perception will be the biggest hurdle.
Absurd. Mutants are *toxic* in the polls.
We'll steamroll over them. The *law*, my friends, can sometimes do wonderful things.
No American is going to support those creatures once they start breaking federal law.

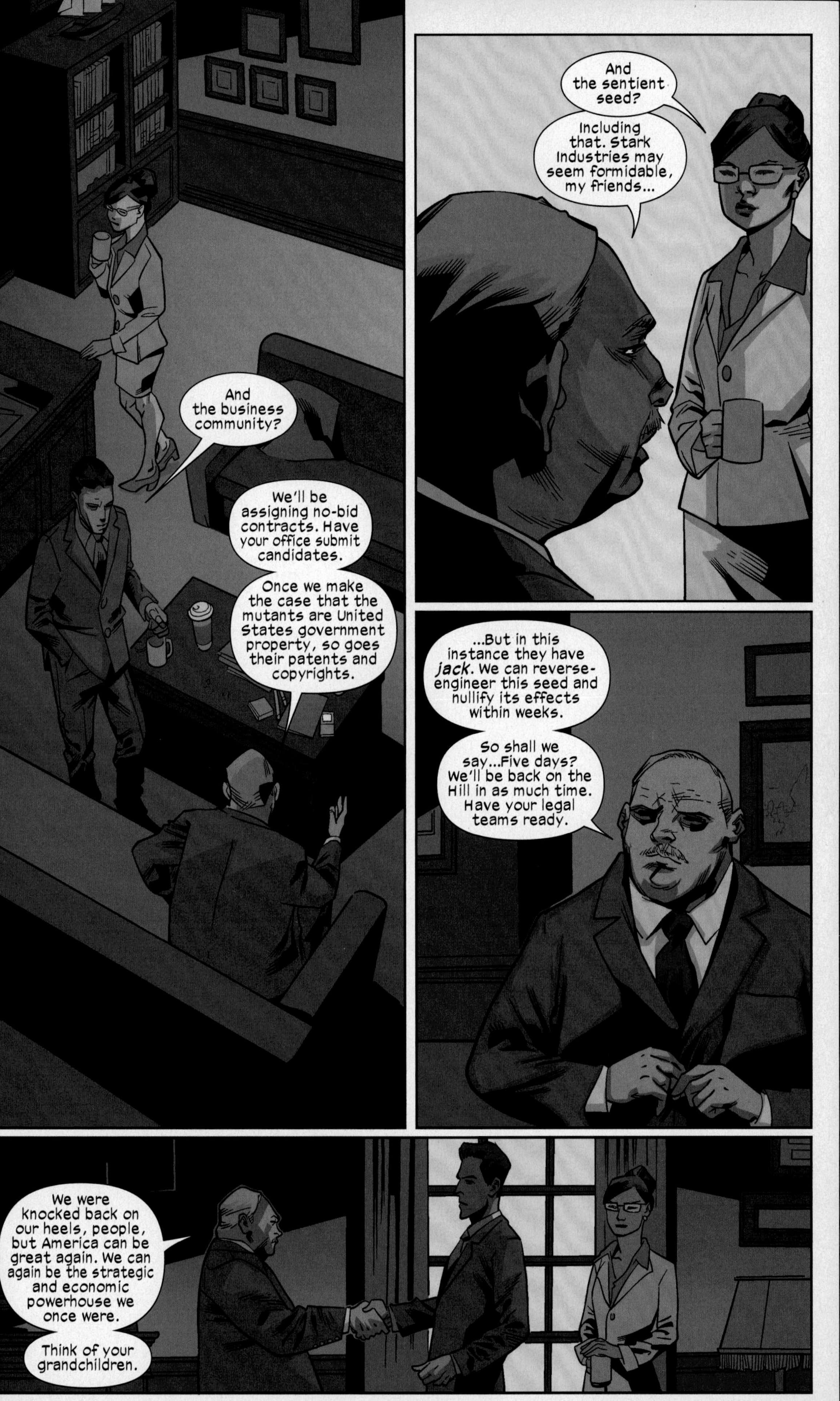
And the business community?
We'll be assigning no-bid contracts. Have your office submit candidates.
Once we make the case that the mutants are United States government property, so goes their patents and copyrights.
And the sentient seed?
Including that. Stark Industries may seem formidable, my friends...
...But in this instance they have *jack*. We can reverse-engineer this seed and nullify its effects within weeks.
So shall we say...Five days? We'll be back on the Hill in as much time. Have your legal teams ready.
We were knocked back on our heels, people, but America can be great again. We can again be the strategic and economic powerhouse we once were.
Think of your grandchildren.

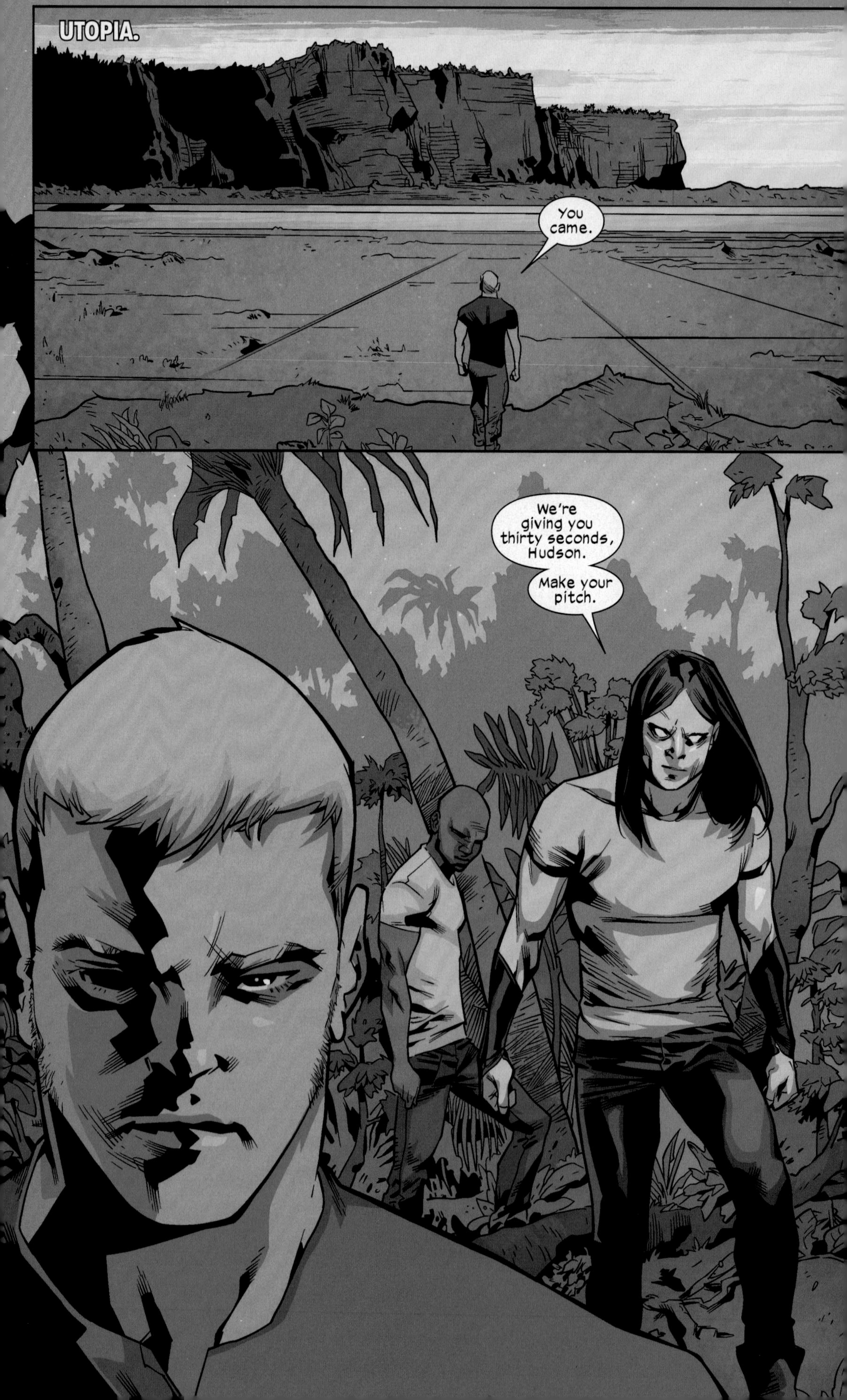
UTOPIA.
You came.
We're giving you thirty seconds, Hudson.
Make your pitch.

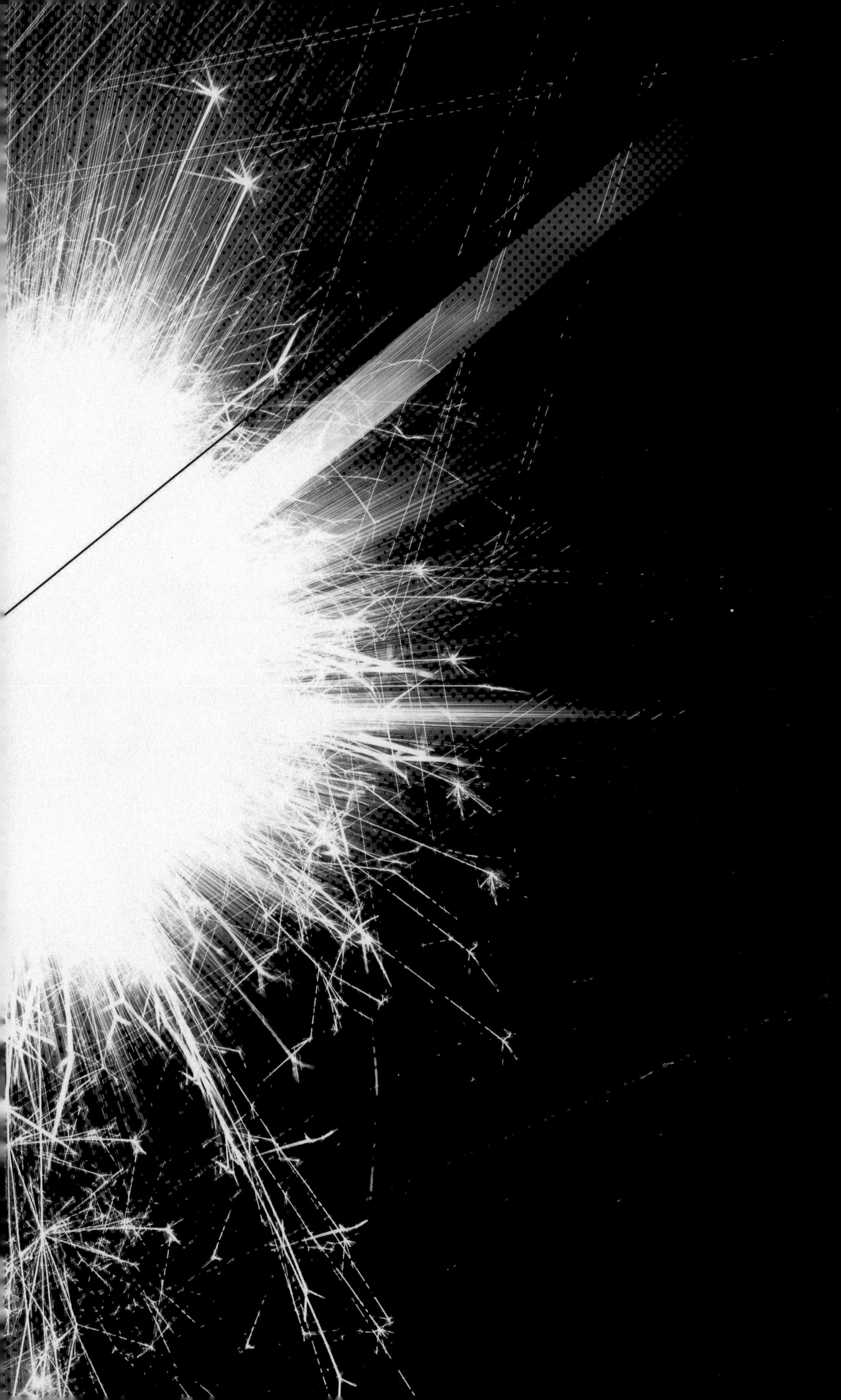

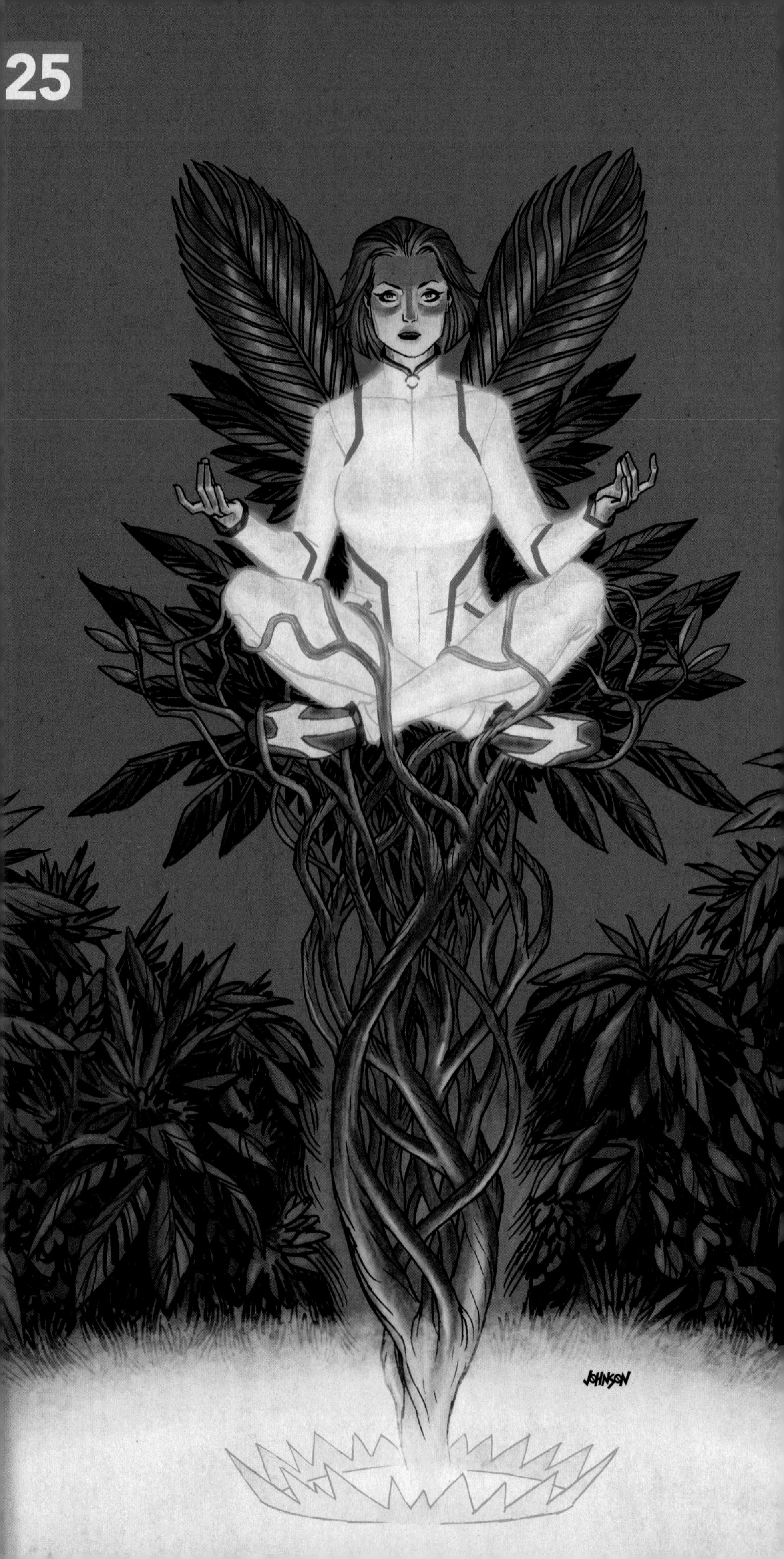
25
JOHNSON

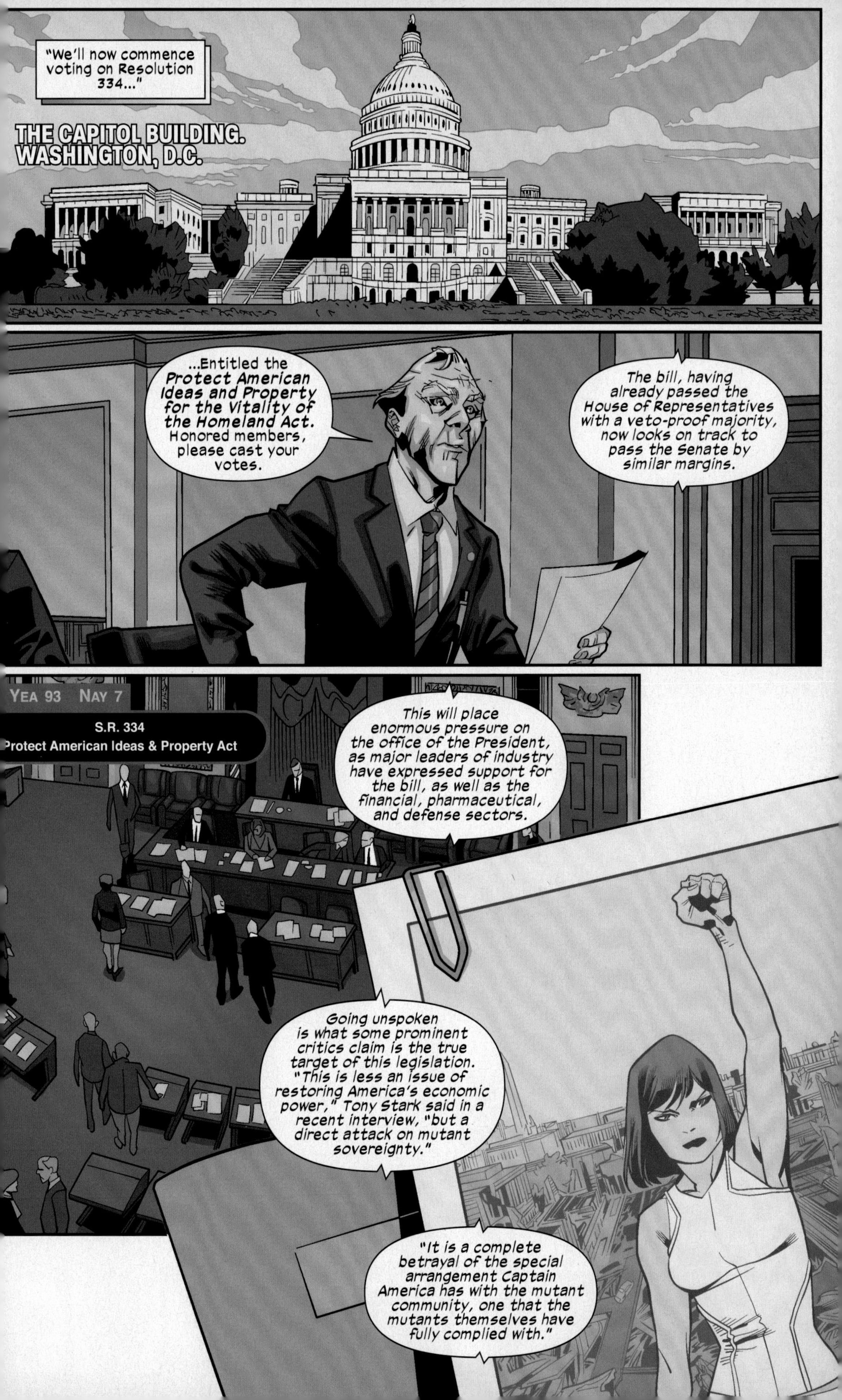

"We'll now commence voting on Resolution 334..."
THE CAPITOL BUILDING. WASHINGTON, D.C.
...Entitled the ***Protect American Ideas and Property for the Vitality of the Homeland Act.*** Honored members, please cast your votes.
The bill, having already passed the House of Representatives with a veto-proof majority, now looks on track to pass the Senate by similar margins.
YEA 93 NAY 7
S.R. 334
Protect American Ideas & Property Act
This will place enormous pressure on the office of the President, as major leaders of industry have expressed support for the bill, as well as the financial, pharmaceutical, and defense sectors.
Going unspoken is what some prominent critics claim is the true target of this legislation. "This is less an issue of restoring America's economic power," Tony Stark said in a recent interview, "but a direct attack on mutant sovereignty."
"It is a complete betrayal of the special arrangement Captain America has with the mutant community, one that the mutants themselves have fully complied with."

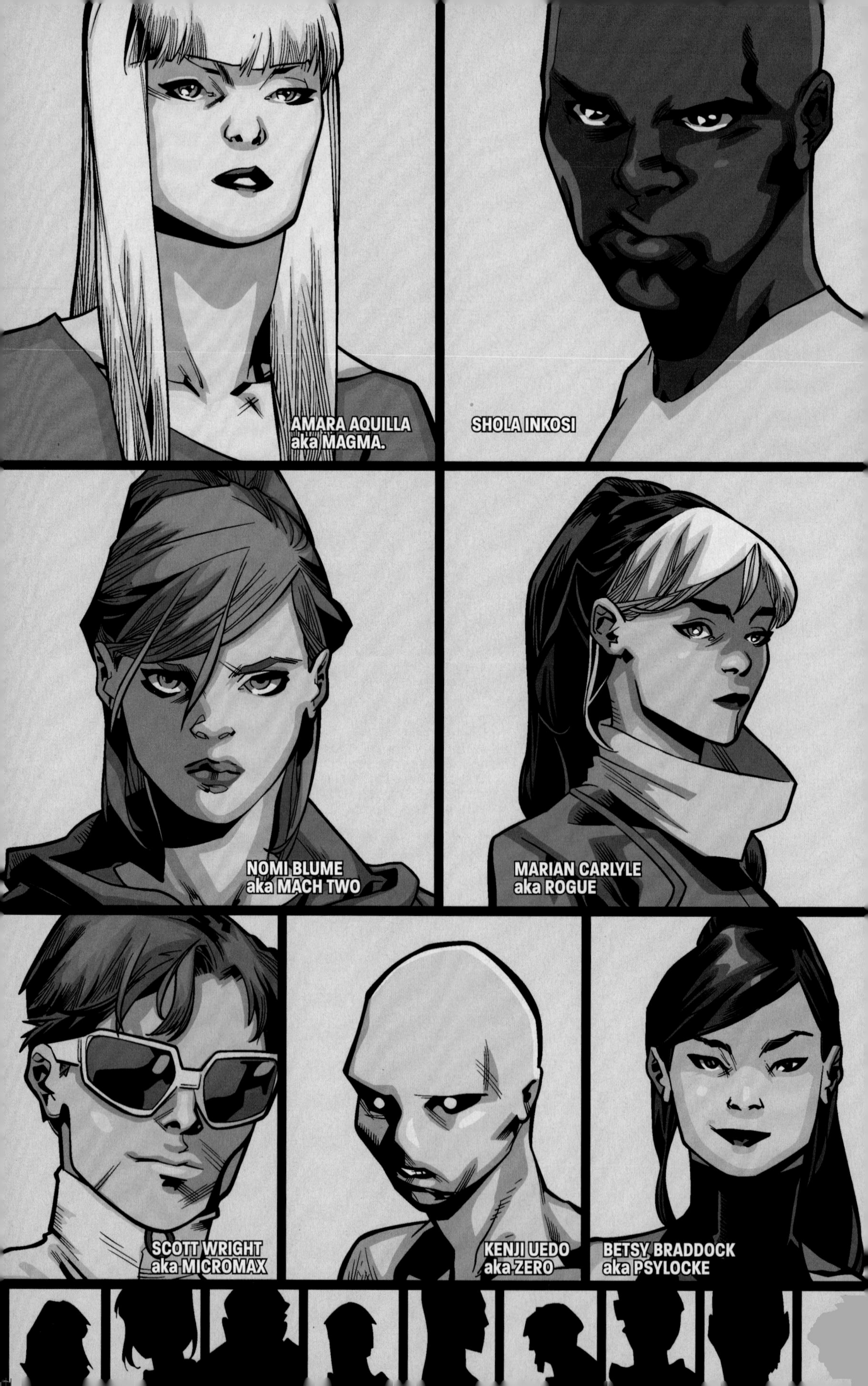
AMARA AQUILLA
aka MAGMA.
SHOLA INKOSI
NOMI BLUME
aka MACH TWO
MARIAN CARLYLE
aka ROGUE
SCOTT WRIGHT
aka MICROMAX
KENJI UEDO
aka ZERO
BETSY BRADDOCK
aka PSYLOCKE

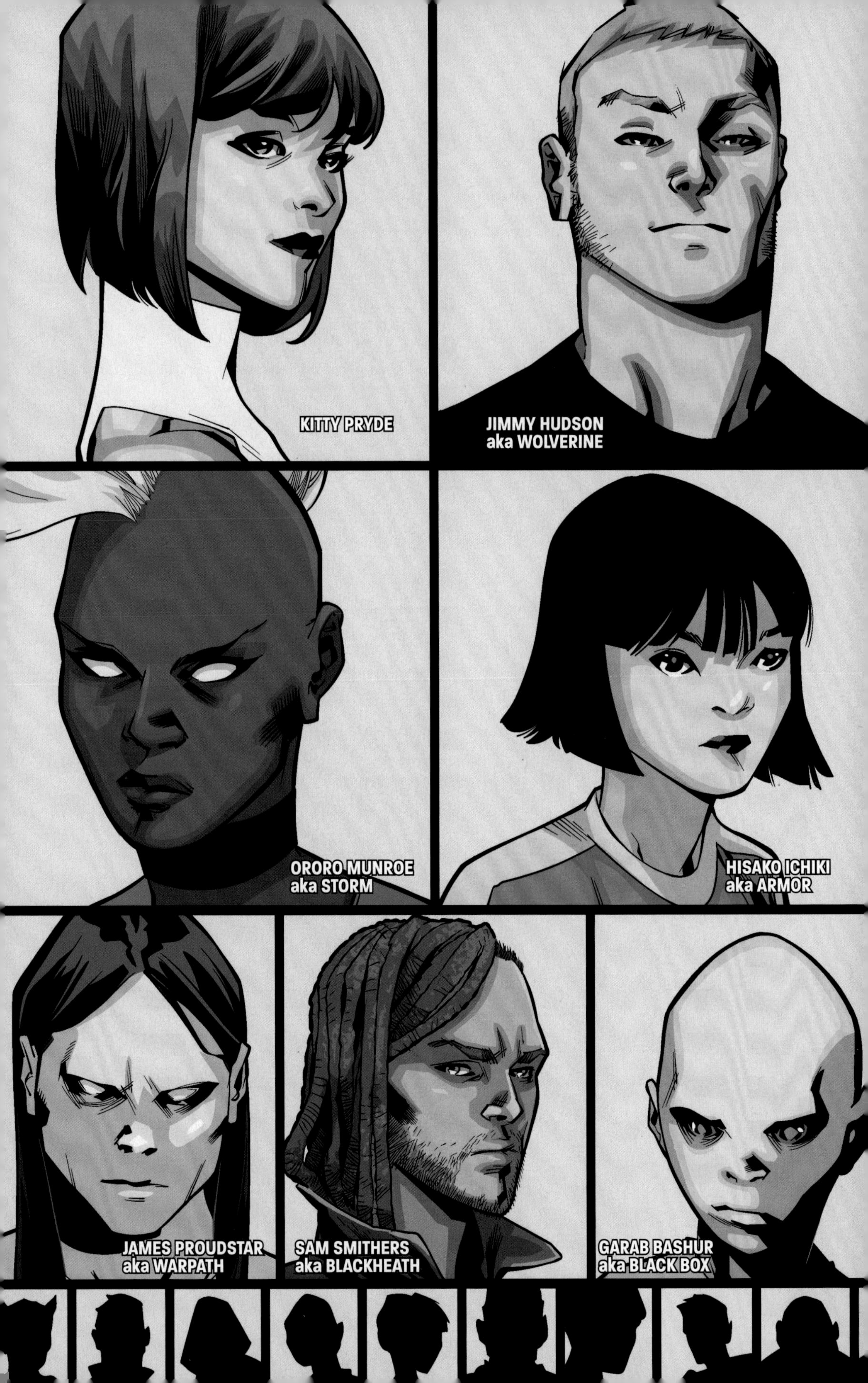
KITTY PRYDE
JIMMY HUDSON aka WOLVERINE
ORORO MUNROE aka STORM
HISAKO ICHIKI aka ARMOR
JAMES PROUDSTAR aka WARPATH
SAM SMITHERS aka BLACKHEATH
GARAB BASHUR aka BLACK BOX

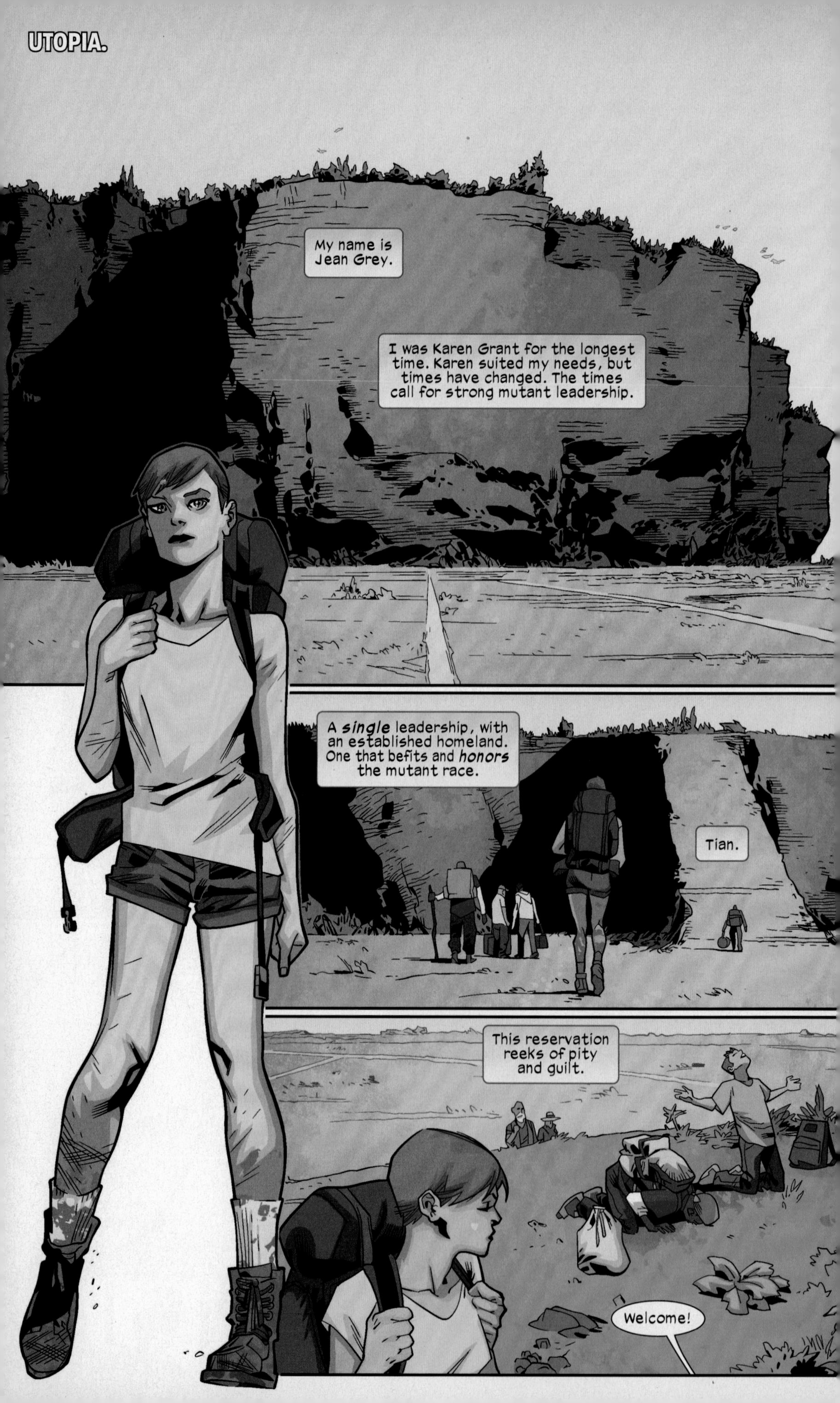
UTOPIA.
My name is Jean Grey.
I was Karen Grant for the longest time. Karen suited my needs, but times have changed. The times call for strong mutant leadership.
A single leadership, with an established homeland. One that befits and honors the mutant race.
Tian.
This reservation reeks of pity and guilt.
Welcome!

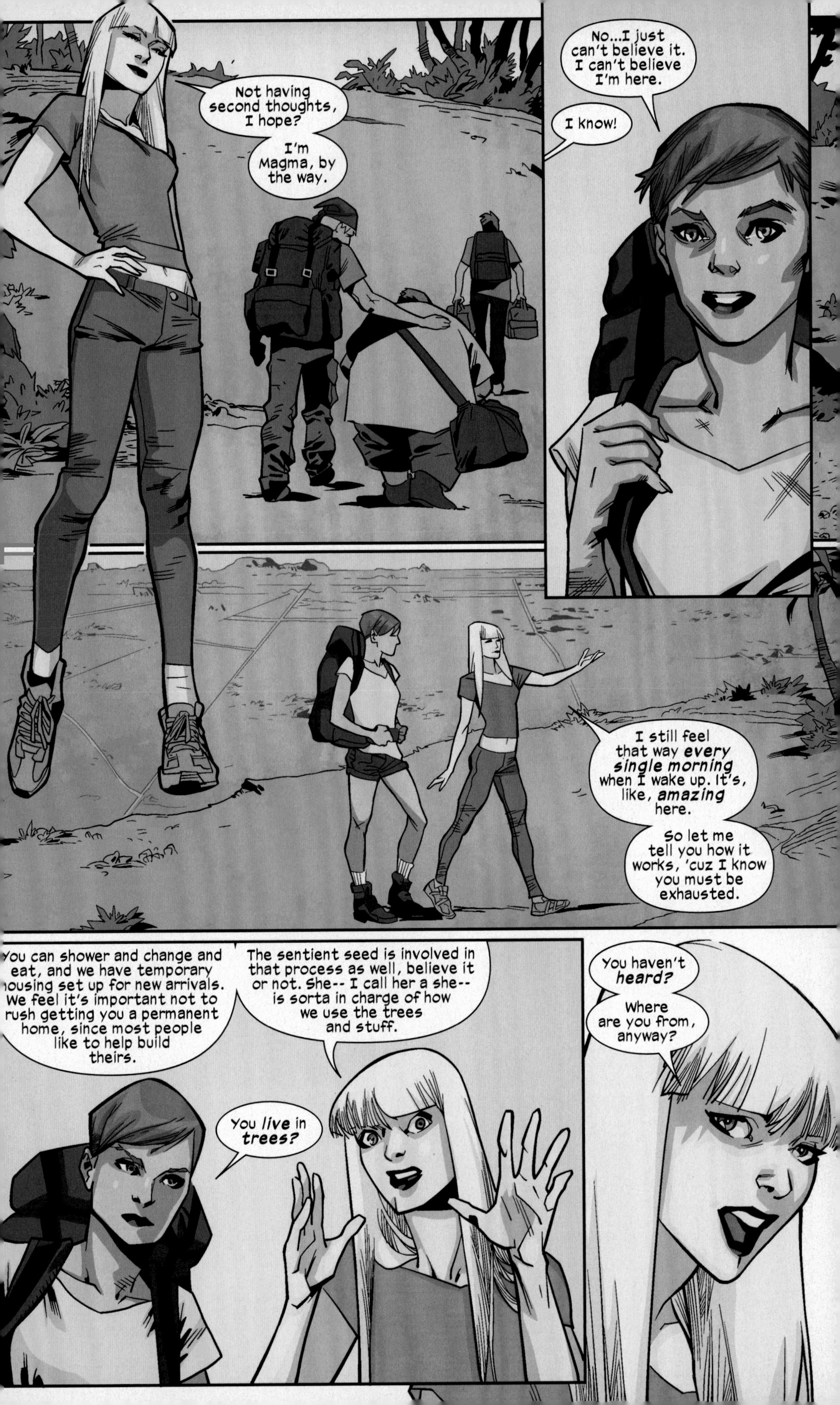
Not having second thoughts, I hope?
I'm Magma, by the way.
No...I just can't believe it. I can't believe I'm here.
I know!
I still feel that way *every single morning* when I wake up. It's, like, *amazing* here.
So let me tell you how it works, 'cuz I know you must be exhausted.
You can shower and change and eat, and we have temporary housing set up for new arrivals. We feel it's important not to rush getting you a permanent home, since most people like to help build theirs.
The sentient seed is involved in that process as well, believe it or not. She-- I call her a she-- is sorta in charge of how we use the trees and stuff.
You *live* in *trees?*
You haven't *heard?*
Where are you from, anyway?

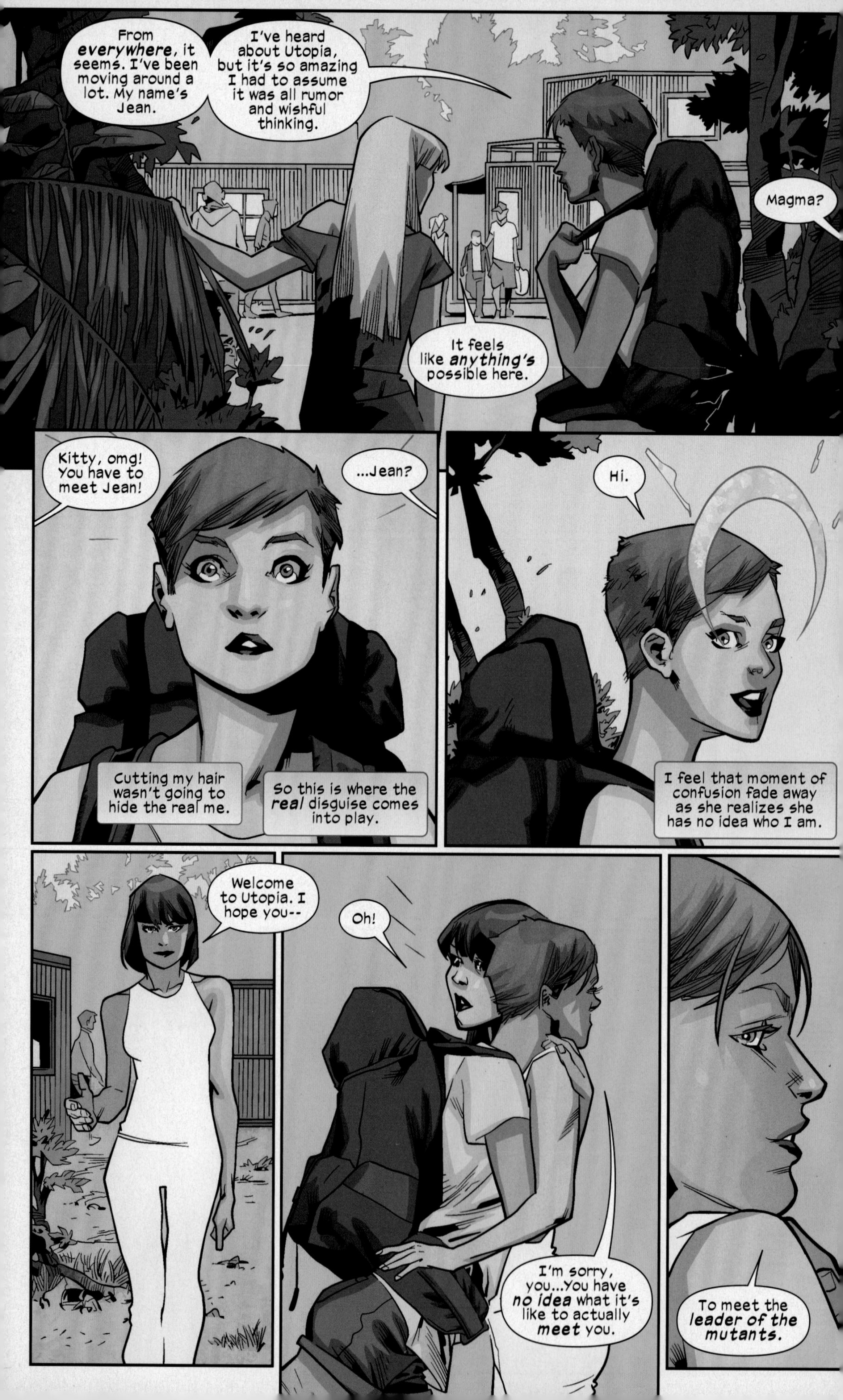
From everywhere, it seems. I've been moving around a lot. My name's Jean.
I've heard about Utopia, but it's so amazing I had to assume it was all rumor and wishful thinking.
It feels like anything's possible here.
Magma?
Kitty, omg! You have to meet Jean!
...Jean?
Cutting my hair wasn't going to hide the real me.
So this is where the real disguise comes into play.
Hi.
I feel that moment of confusion fade away as she realizes she has no idea who I am.
Welcome to Utopia. I hope you--
Oh!
I'm sorry, you...You have no idea what it's like to actually meet you.
To meet the leader of the mutants.

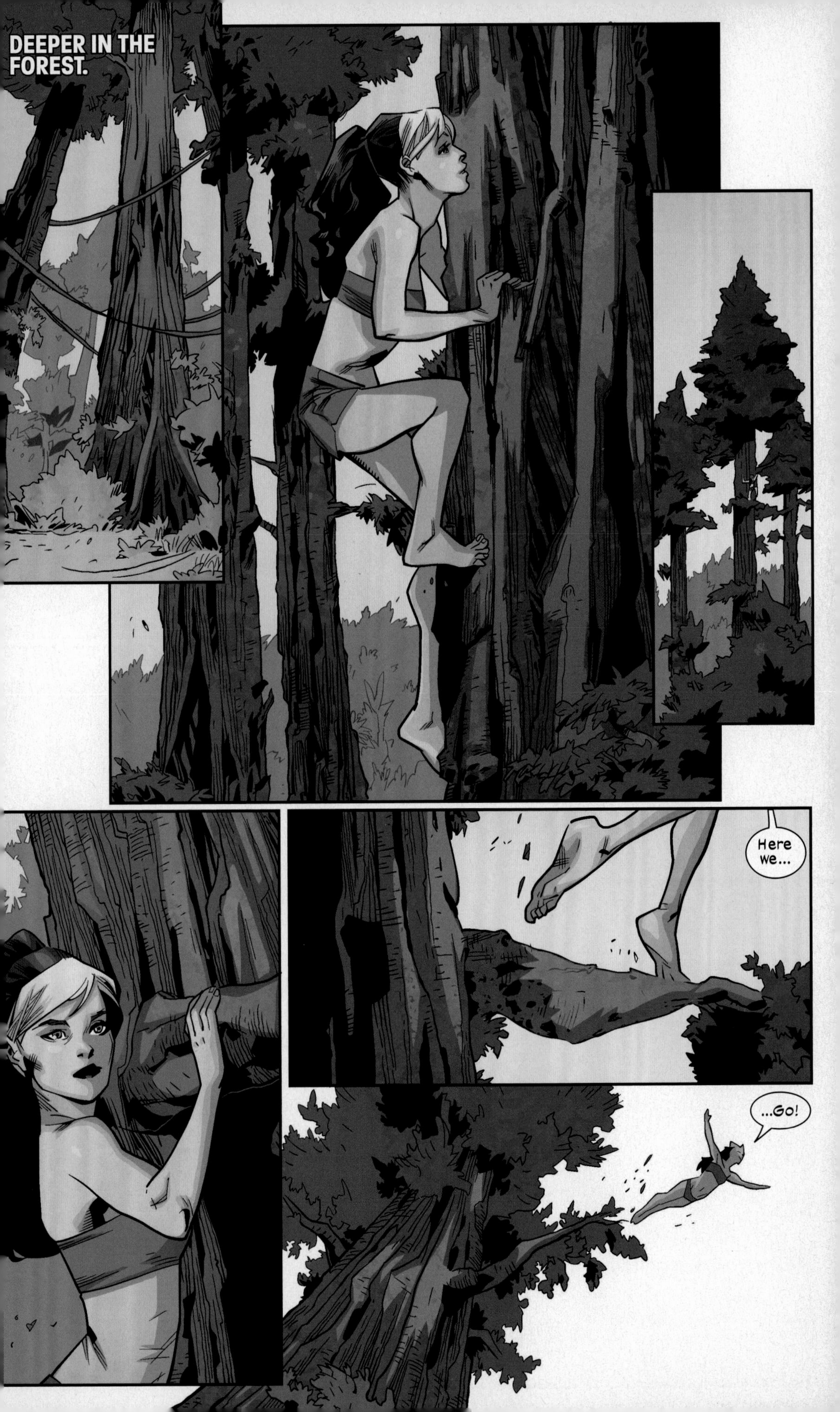
DEEPER IN THE FOREST.
Here we...
...Go!

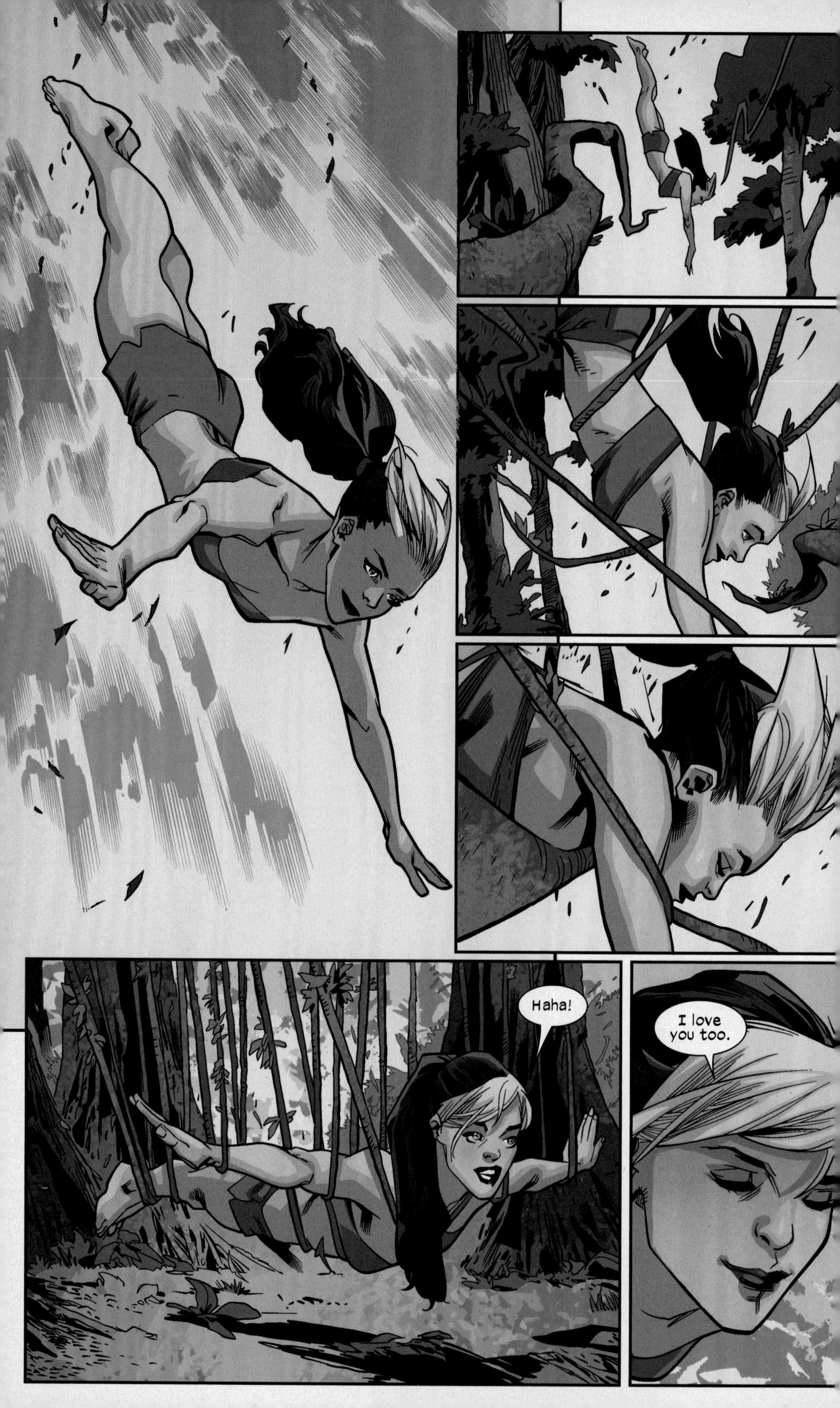
Haha!
I love you too.

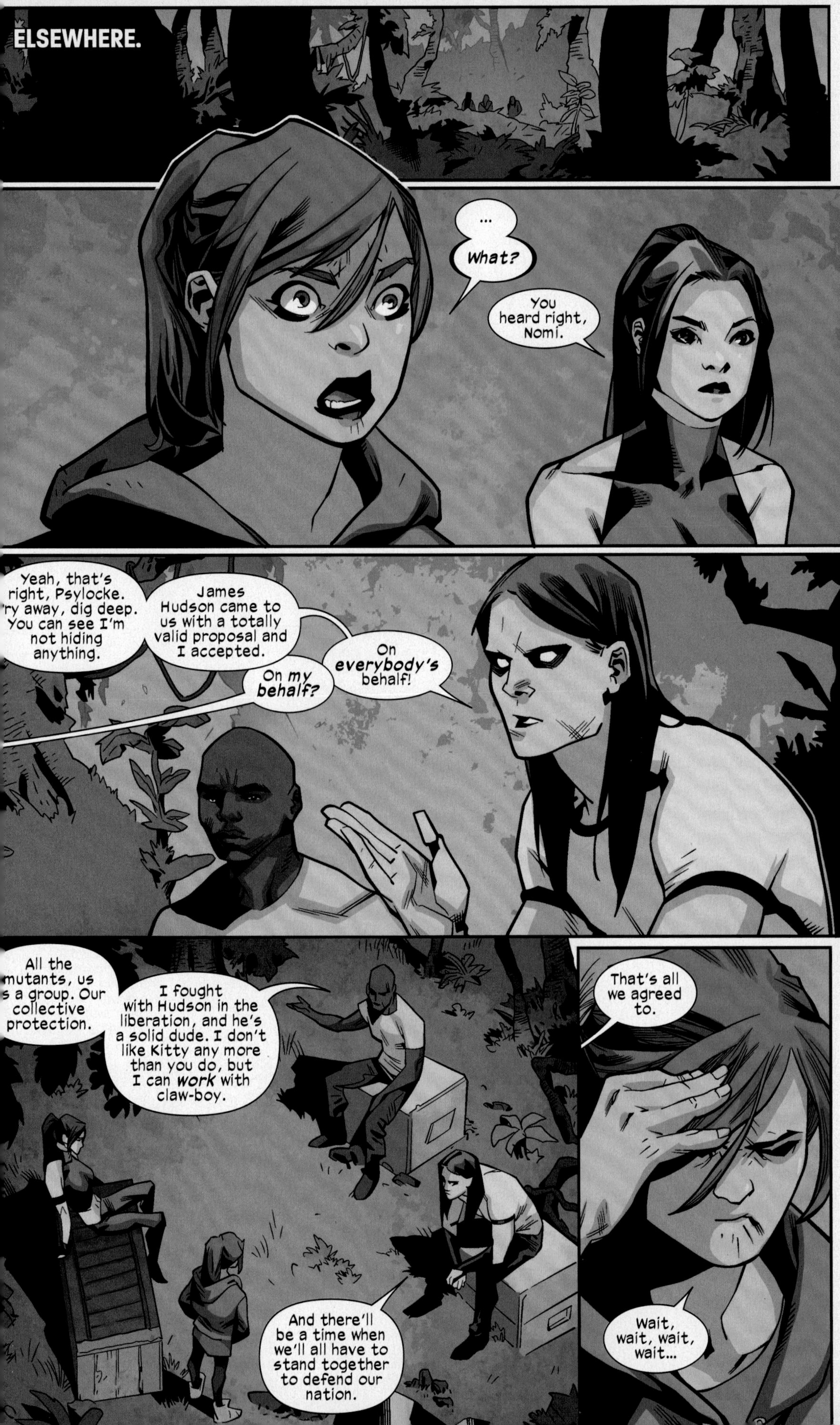
ELSEWHERE.
...
What?
You heard right, Nomi.
Yeah, that's right, Psylocke. ry away, dig deep. You can see I'm not hiding anything.
James Hudson came to us with a totally valid proposal and I accepted.
On my behalf?
On everybody's behalf!
All the mutants, us s a group. Our collective protection.
I fought with Hudson in the liberation, and he's a solid dude. I don't like Kitty any more than you do, but I can work with claw-boy.
That's all we agreed to.
And there'll be a time when we'll all have to stand together to defend our nation.
Wait, wait, wait, wait...

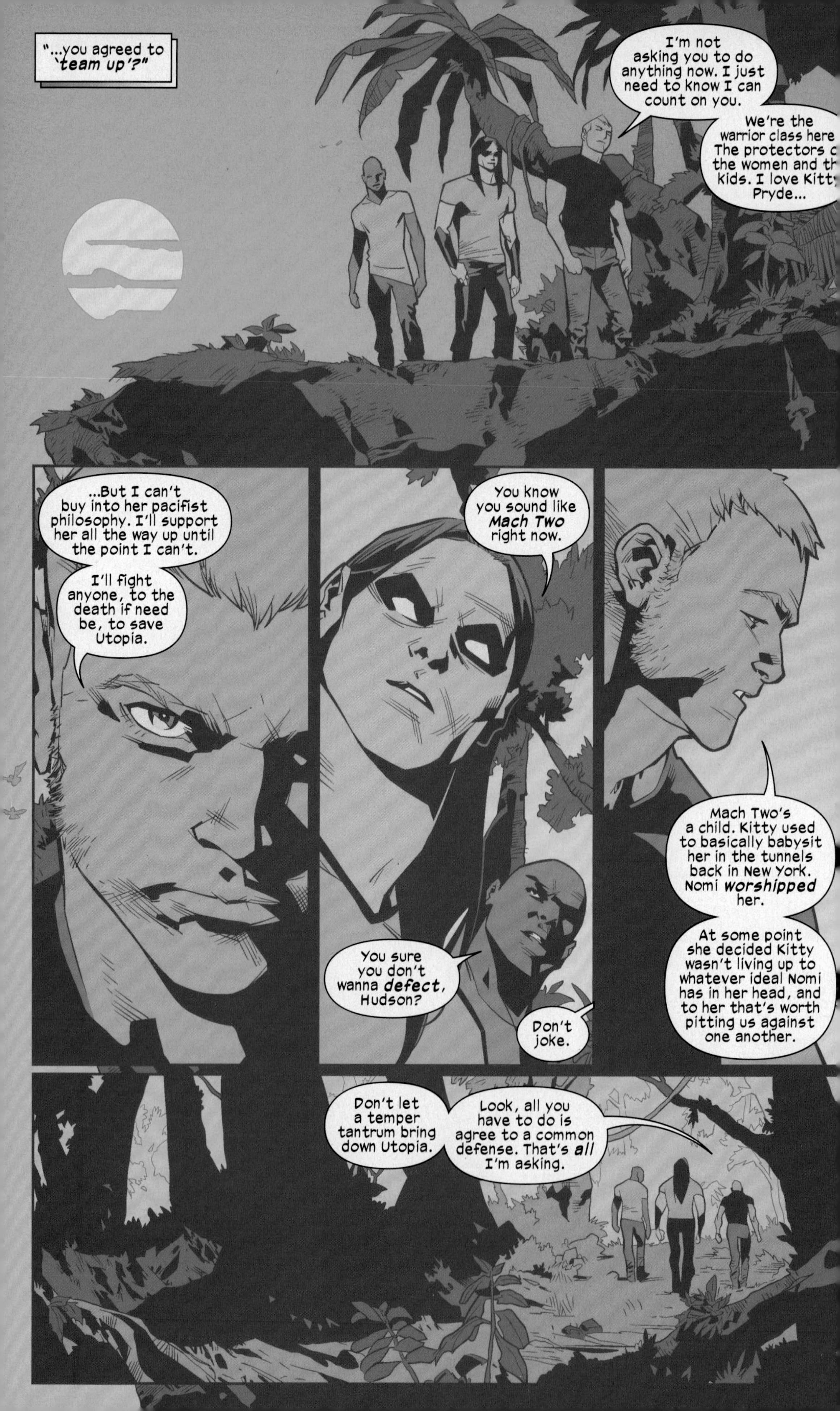
"...you agreed to 'team up'?"
I'm not asking you to do anything now. I just need to know I can count on you.
We're the warrior class here. The protectors of the women and the kids. I love Kitty Pryde...
...But I can't buy into her pacifist philosophy. I'll support her all the way up until the point I can't.
I'll fight anyone, to the death if need be, to save Utopia.
You know you sound like Mach Two right now.
You sure you don't wanna defect, Hudson?
Don't joke.
Mach Two's a child. Kitty used to basically babysit her in the tunnels back in New York. Nomi worshipped her.
At some point she decided Kitty wasn't living up to whatever ideal Nomi has in her head, and to her that's worth pitting us against one another.
Don't let a temper tantrum bring down Utopia.
Look, all you have to do is agree to a common defense. That's all I'm asking.

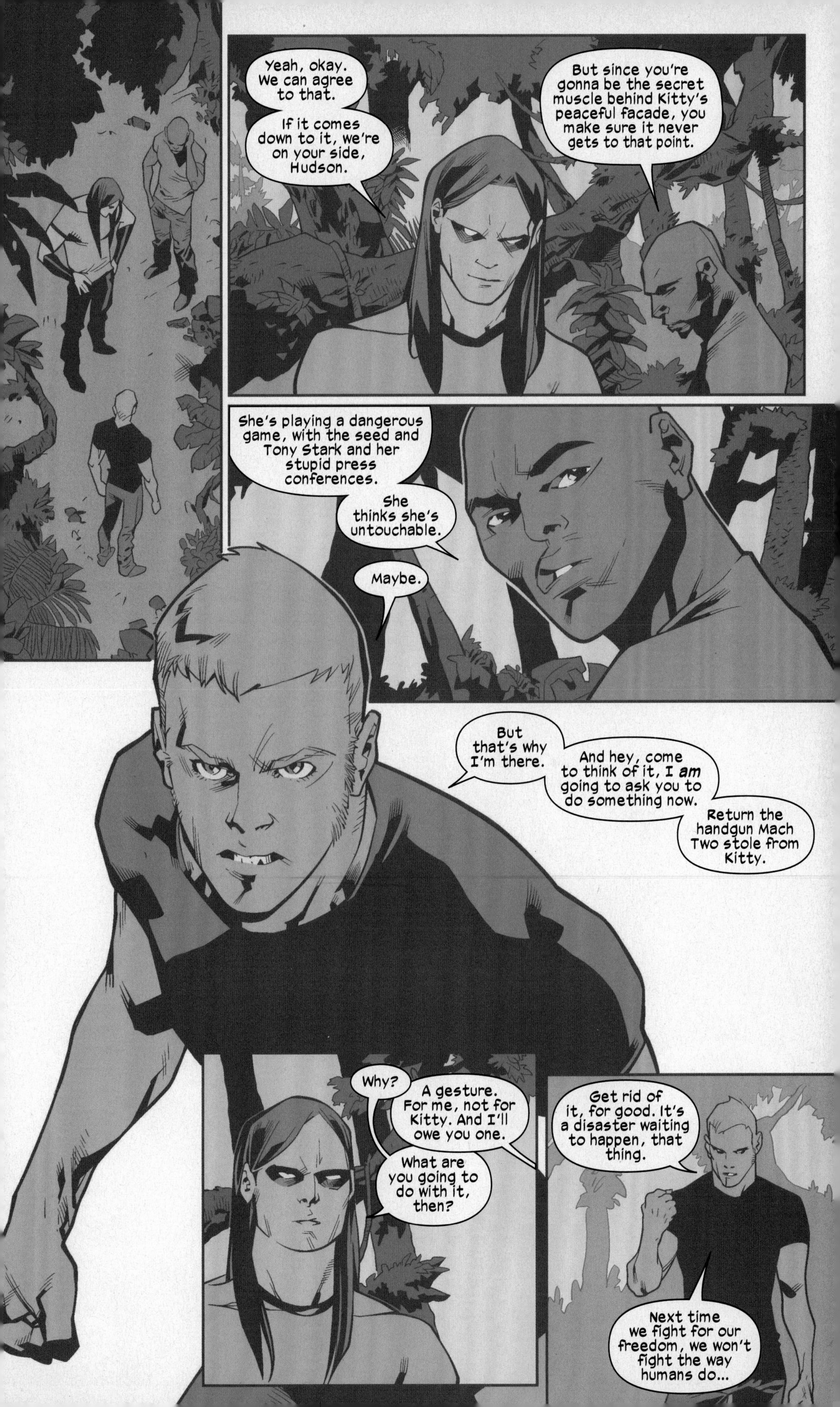
Yeah, okay. We can agree to that.
If it comes down to it, we're on your side, Hudson.
But since you're gonna be the secret muscle behind Kitty's peaceful facade, you make sure it never gets to that point.
She's playing a dangerous game, with the seed and Tony Stark and her stupid press conferences.
She thinks she's untouchable.
Maybe.
But that's why I'm there.
And hey, come to think of it, I *am* going to ask you to do something now.
Return the handgun Mach Two stole from Kitty.
Why?
A gesture. For me, not for Kitty. And I'll owe you one.
What are you going to do with it, then?
Get rid of it, for good. It's a disaster waiting to happen, that thing.
Next time we fight for our freedom, we won't fight the way humans do...

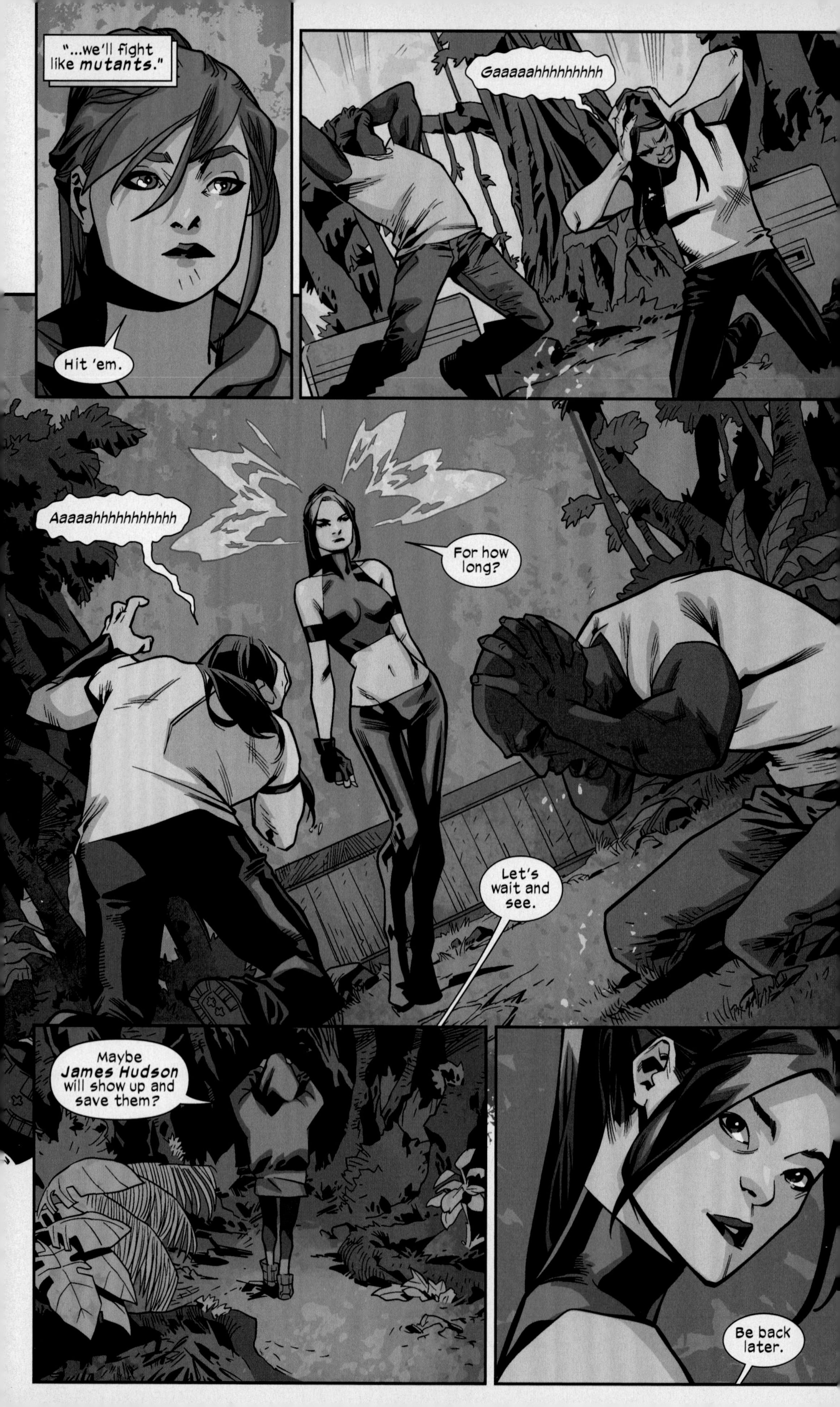
"...we'll fight like mutants."
Hit 'em.
Gaaaaahhhhhhhhh
Aaaaahhhhhhhhhh
For how long?
Let's wait and see.
Maybe James Hudson will show up and save them?
Be back later.

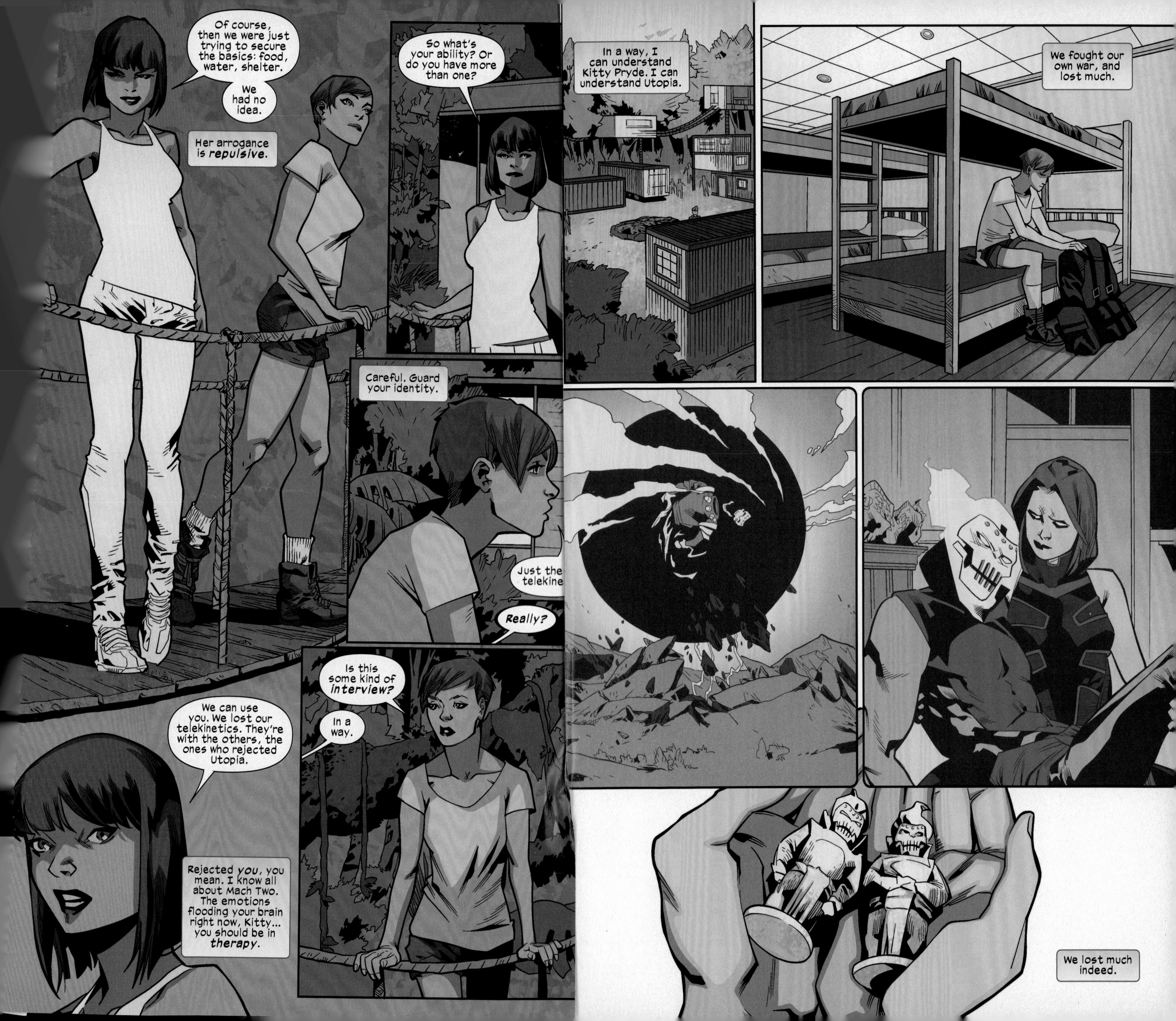
Of course, then we were just trying to secure the basics: food, water, shelter.
We had no idea.
Her arrogance is *repulsive*.
So what's your ability? Or do you have more than one?
Careful. Guard your identity.
Just the telekine
Really?
Is this some kind of *interview?*
In a way.
We can use you. We lost our telekinetics. They're with the others, the ones who rejected Utopia.
Rejected *you*, you mean. I know all about Mach Two. The emotions flooding your brain right now, Kitty... you should be in *therapy*.
In a way, I can understand Kitty Pryde. I can understand Utopia.
We fought our own war, and lost much.
We lost much indeed.

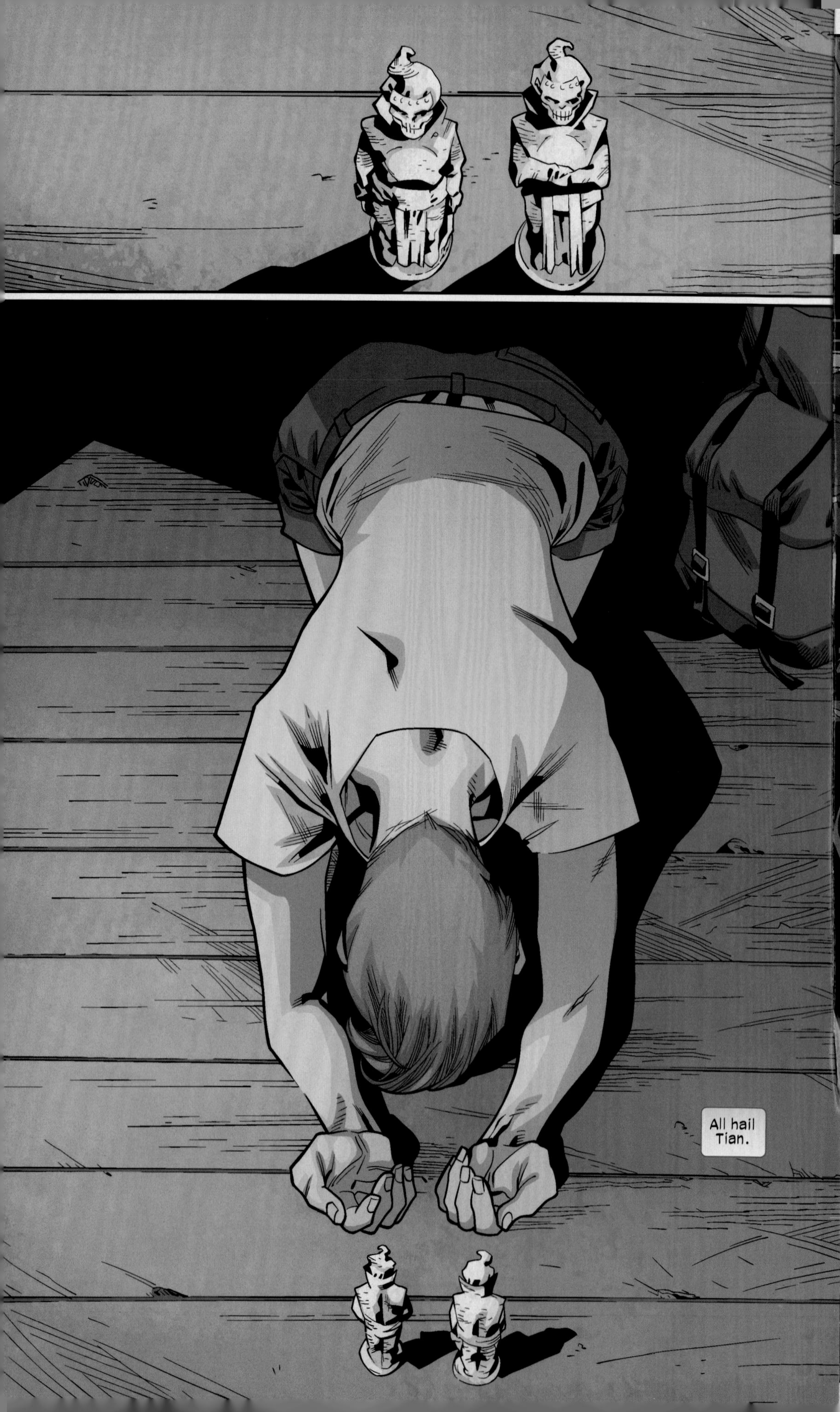
All hail Tian.

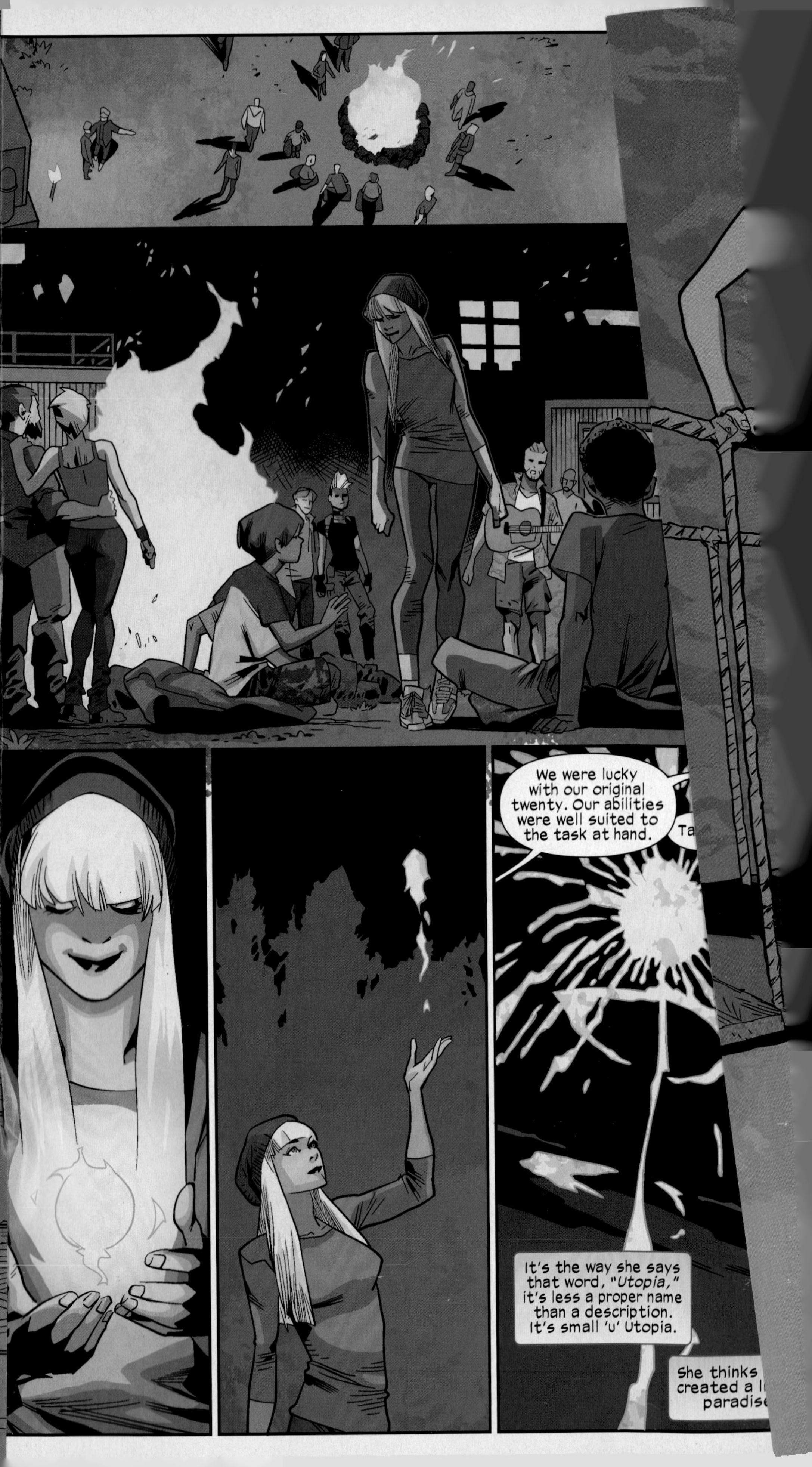
We were lucky with our original twenty. Our abilities were well suited to the task at hand.
It's the way she says that word, "*Utopia*," it's less a proper name than a description. It's small 'u' Utopia.
She thinks
created a

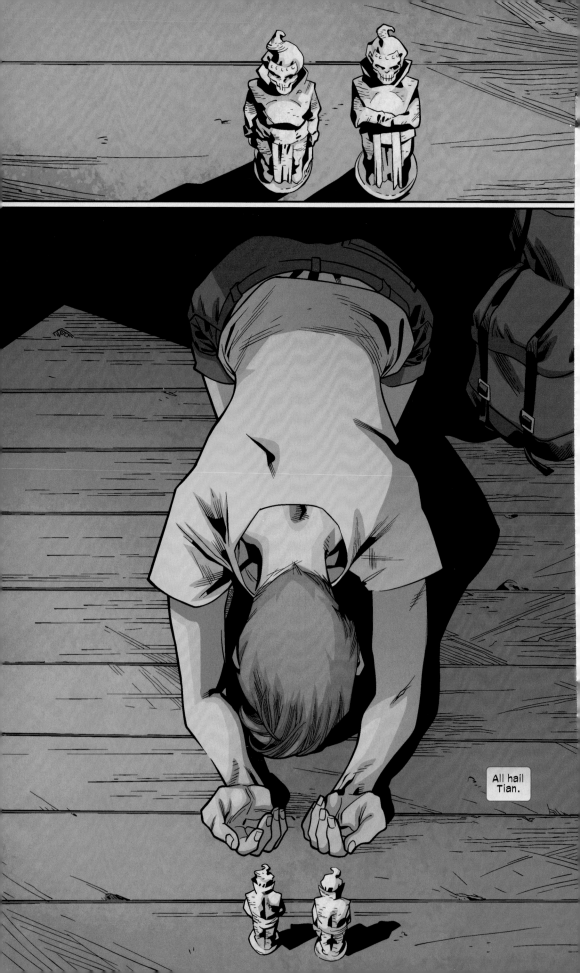

All hail
Tian.

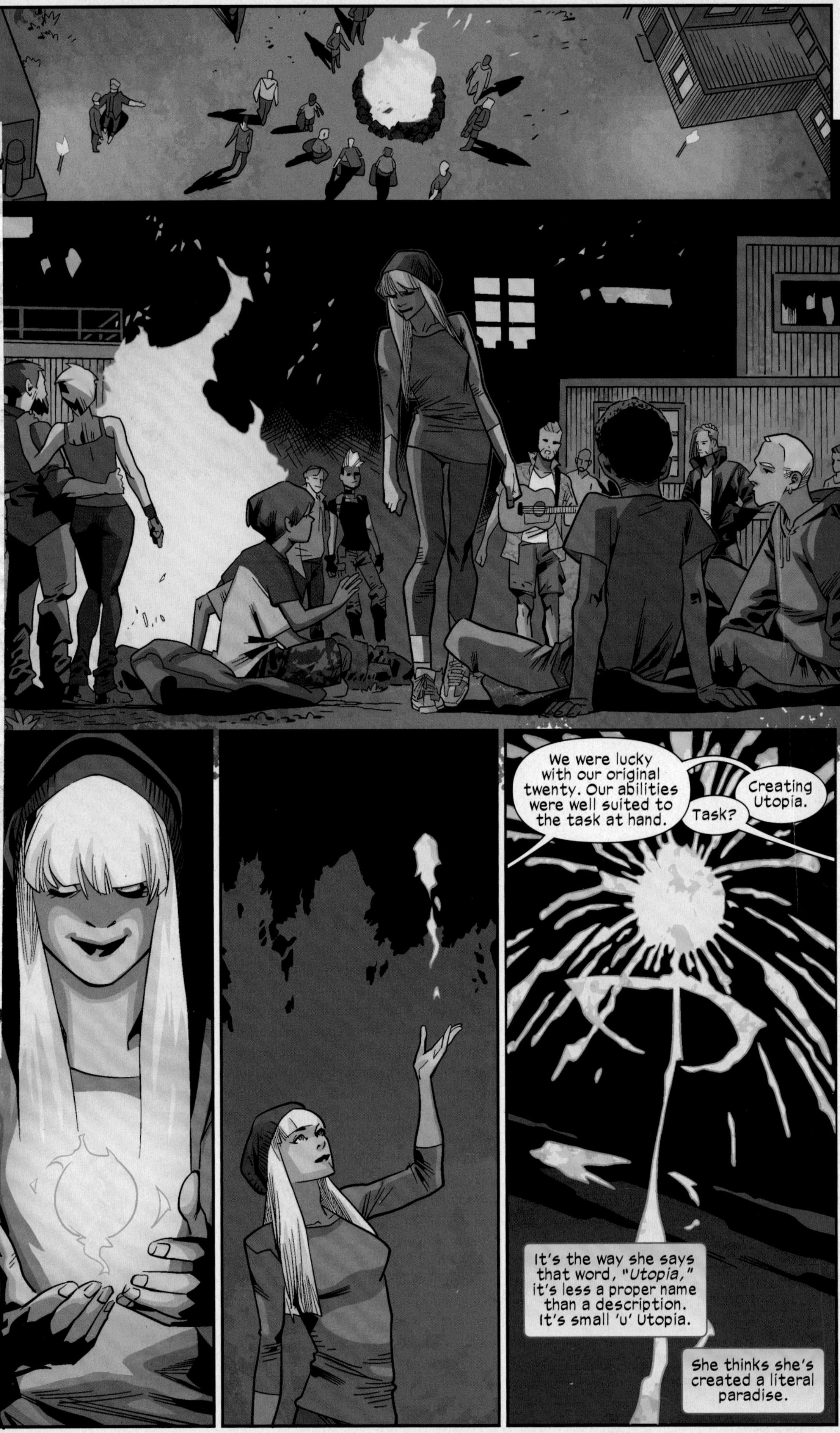
We were lucky with our original twenty. Our abilities were well suited to the task at hand.
Task?
Creating Utopia.
It's the way she says that word, "*Utopia,*" it's less a proper name than a description. It's small 'u' Utopia.
She thinks she's created a literal paradise.

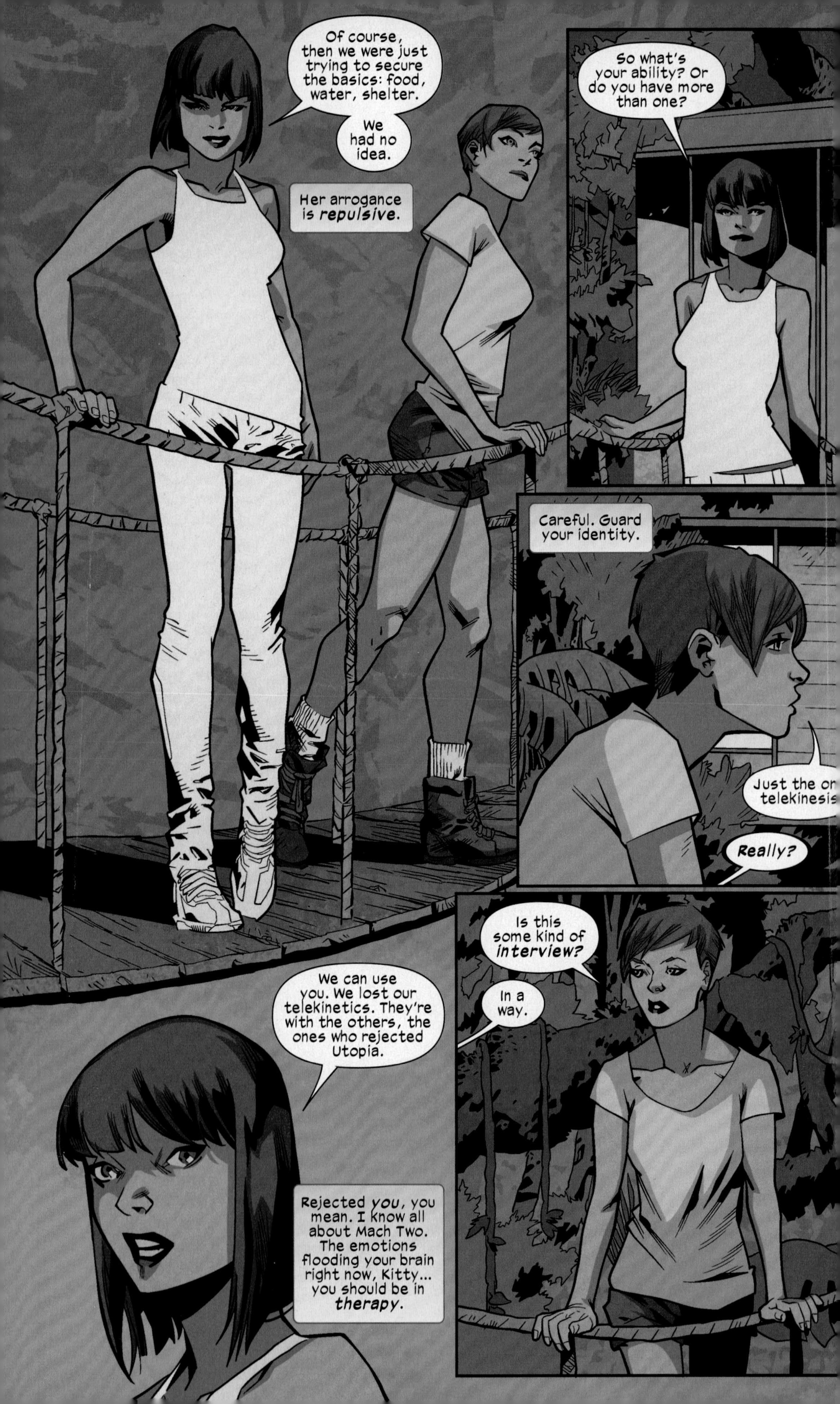

Of course, then we were just trying to secure the basics: food, water, shelter.
We had no idea.
Her arrogance is *repulsive*.
So what's your ability? Or do you have more than one?
Careful. Guard your identity.
Just the or telekinesis
Really?
We can use you. We lost our telekinetics. They're with the others, the ones who rejected Utopia.
Rejected *you*, you mean. I know all about Mach Two. The emotions flooding your brain right now, Kitty... you should be in *therapy*.
Is this some kind of *interview?*
In a way.

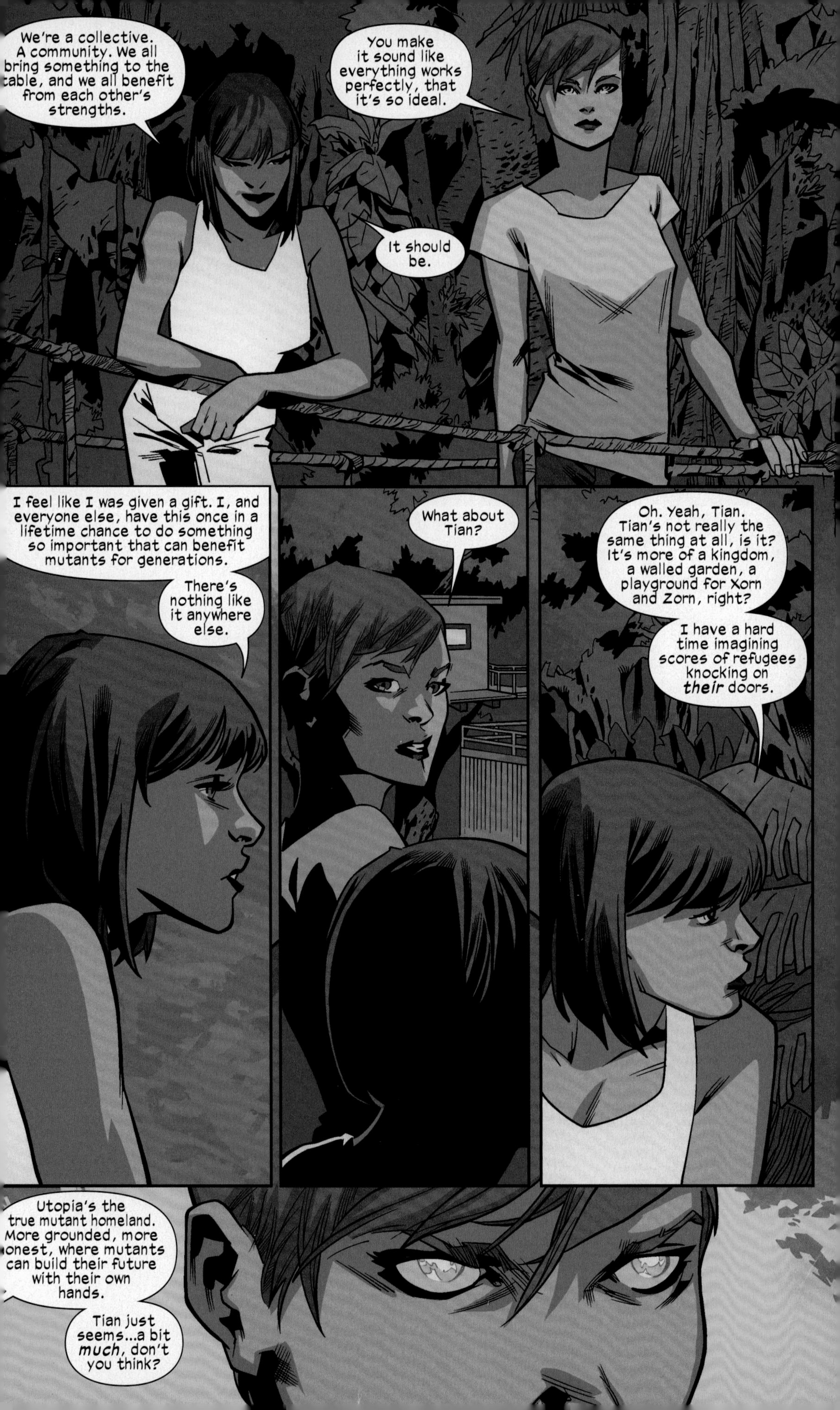
We're a collective. A community. We all bring something to the table, and we all benefit from each other's strengths.
You make it sound like everything works perfectly, that it's so ideal.
It should be.
I feel like I was given a gift. I, and everyone else, have this once in a lifetime chance to do something so important that can benefit mutants for generations.
There's nothing like it anywhere else.
What about Tian?
Oh. Yeah, Tian. Tian's not really the same thing at all, is it? It's more of a kingdom, a walled garden, a playground for Xorn and Zorn, right?
I have a hard time imagining scores of refugees knocking on *their* doors.
Utopia's the true mutant homeland. More grounded, more honest, where mutants can build their future with their own hands.
Tian just seems...a bit *much*, don't you think?

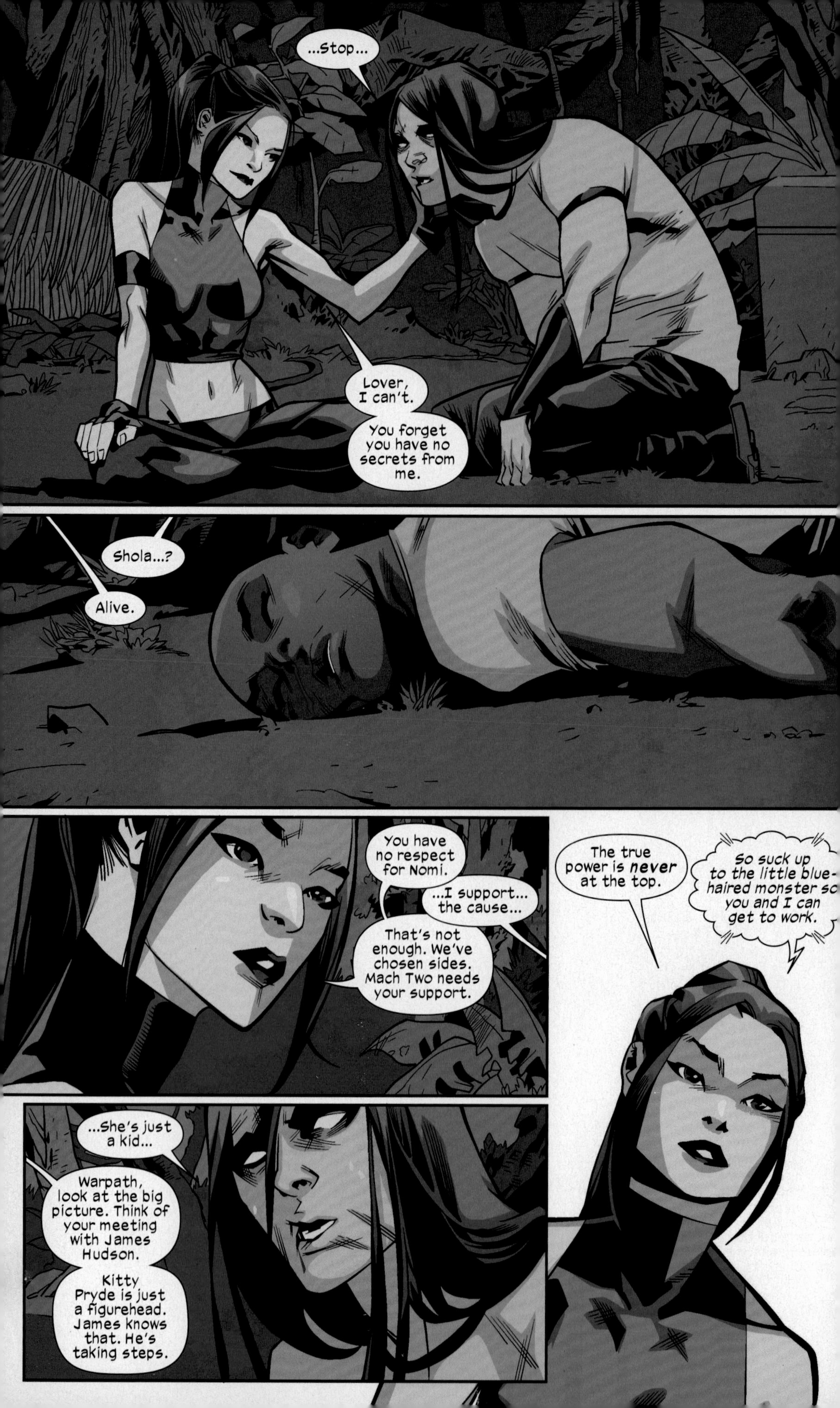
...Stop...
Lover, I can't.
You forget you have no secrets from me.
Shola...?
Alive.
You have no respect for Nomi.
...I support... the cause...
That's not enough. We've chosen sides. Mach Two needs your support.
The true power is *never* at the top.
So suck up to the little blue-haired monster so you and I can get to work.
...She's just a kid...
Warpath, look at the big picture. Think of your meeting with James Hudson.
Kitty Pryde is just a figurehead. James knows that. He's taking steps.

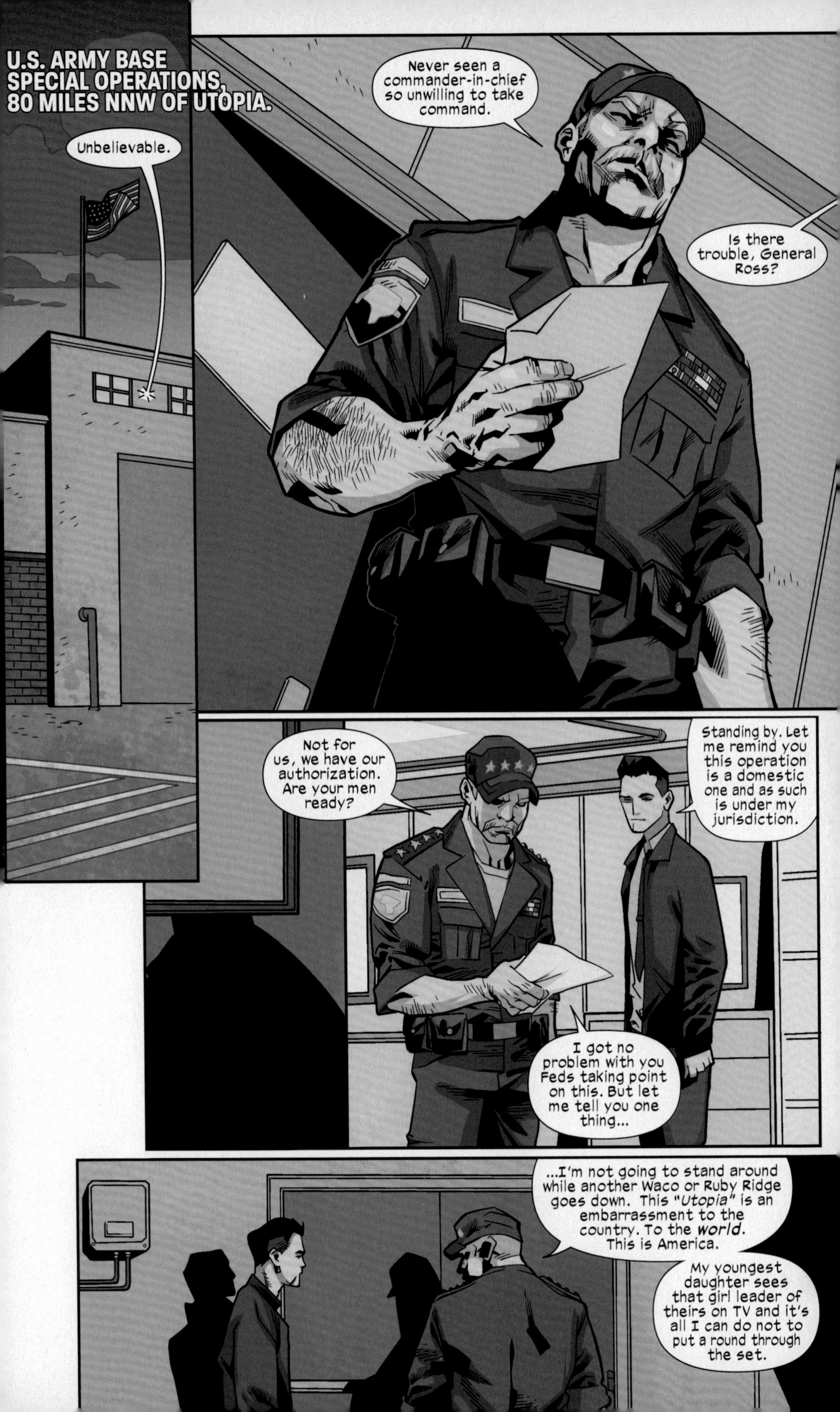
U.S. ARMY BASE SPECIAL OPERATIONS, 80 MILES NNW OF UTOPIA.
Unbelievable.
Never seen a commander-in-chief so unwilling to take command.
Is there trouble, General Ross?
Not for us, we have our authorization. Are your men ready?
Standing by. Let me remind you this operation is a domestic one and as such is under my jurisdiction.
I got no problem with you Feds taking point on this. But let me tell you one thing...
...I'm not going to stand around while another Waco or Ruby Ridge goes down. This "Utopia" is an embarrassment to the country. To the world. This is America.
My youngest daughter sees that girl leader of theirs on TV and it's all I can do not to put a round through the set.

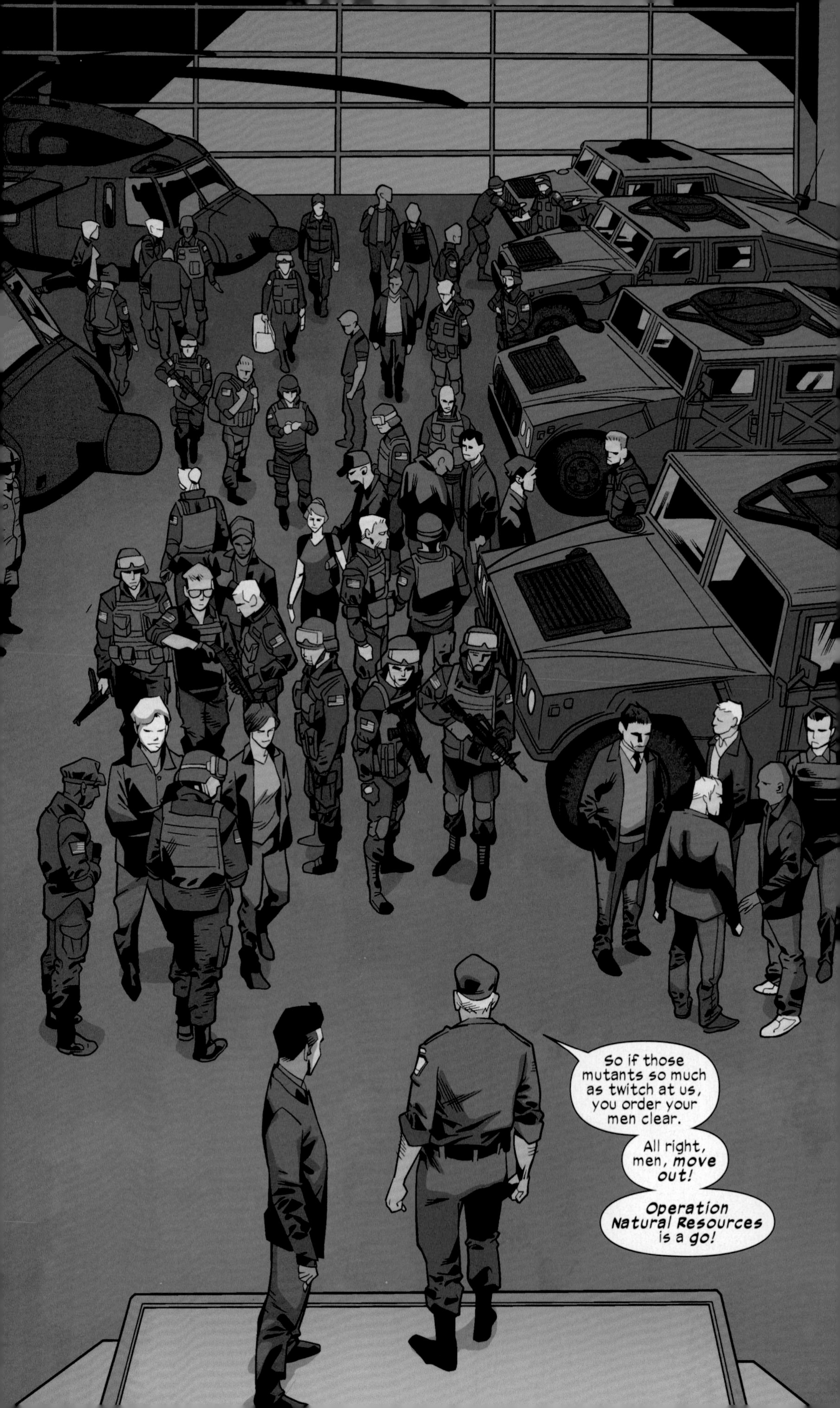

So if those mutants so much as twitch at us, you order your men clear.
All right, men, *move out!*
Operation Natural Resources is a *go!*

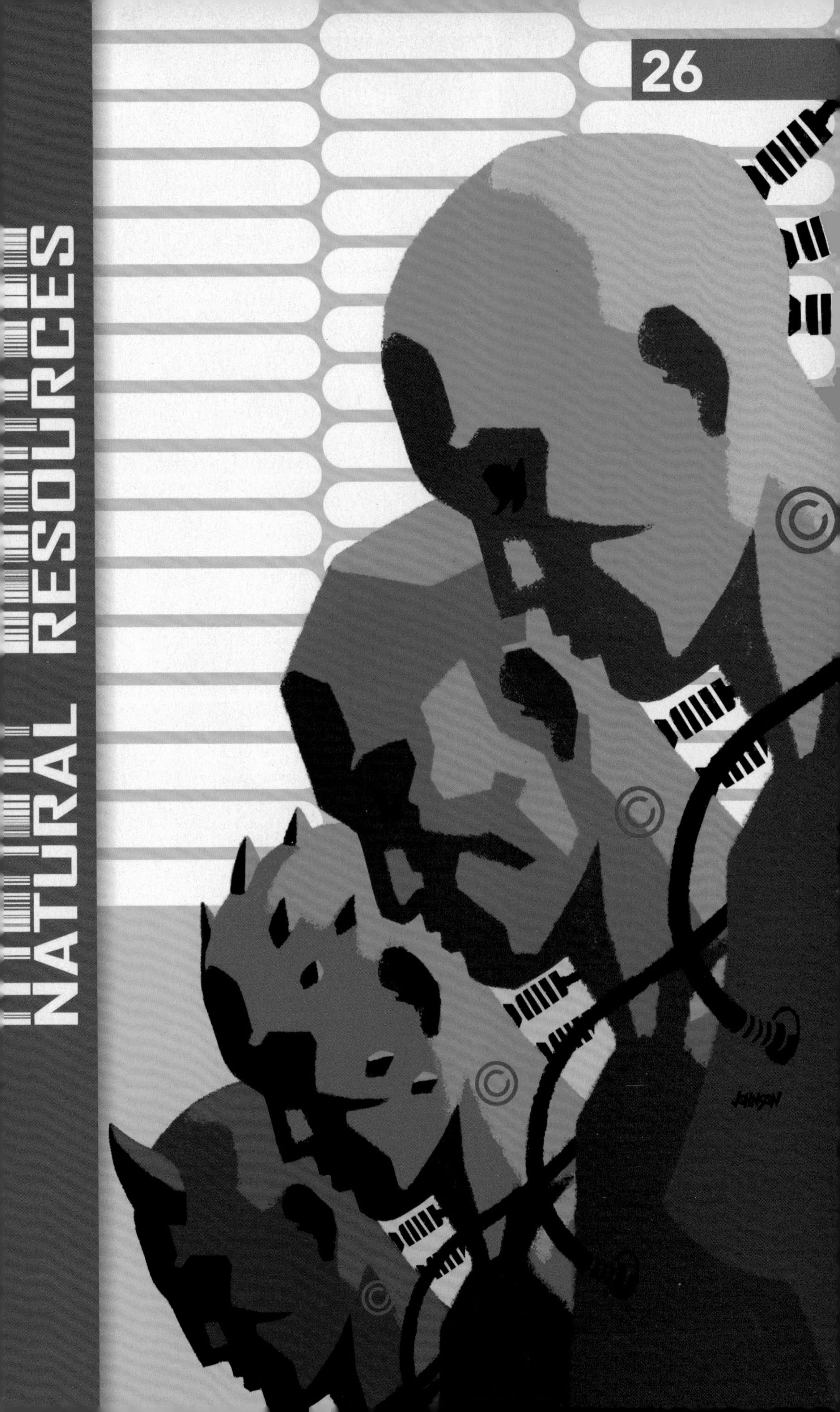
NATURAL RESOURCES
26
JOHNSON

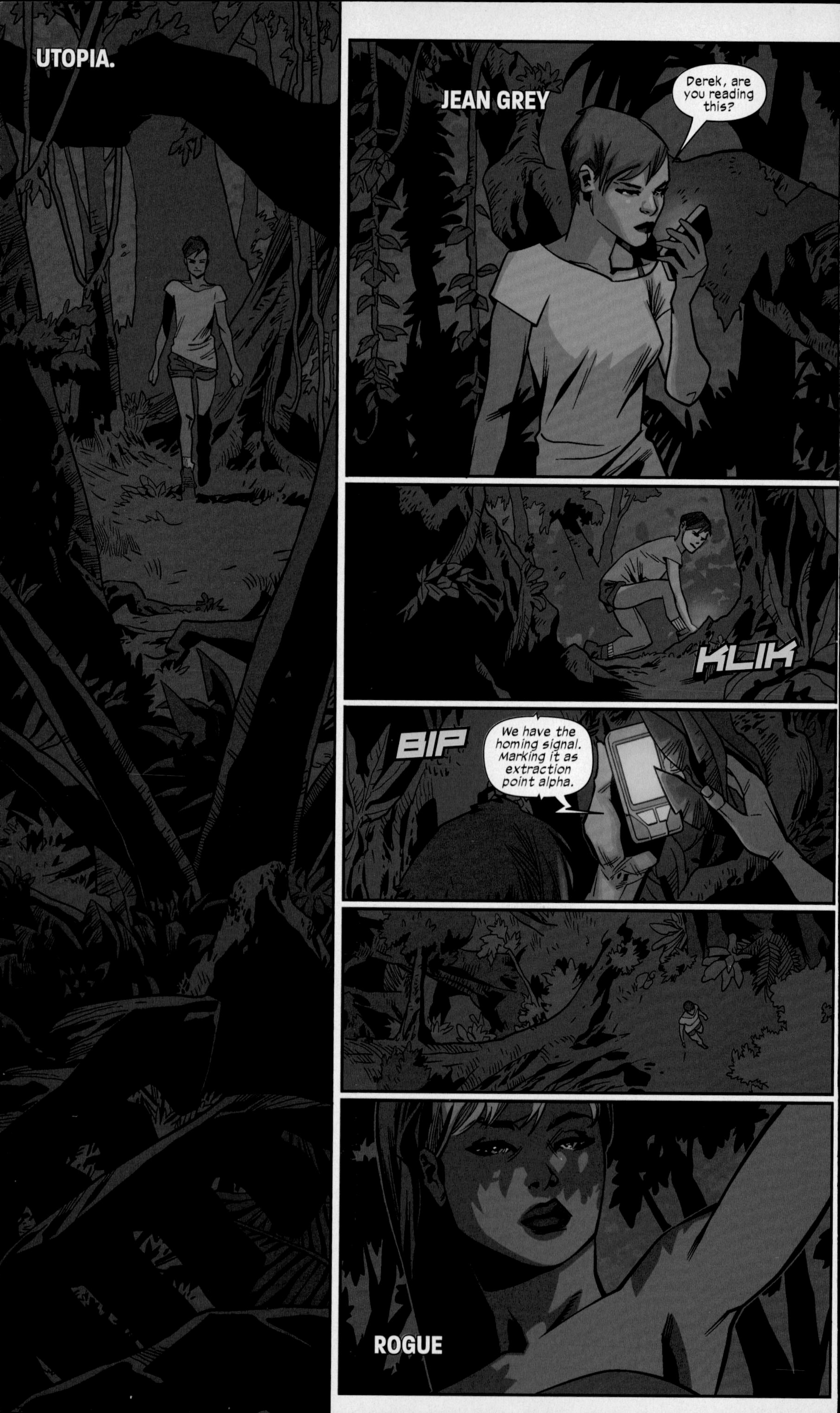
UTOPIA.
JEAN GREY
Derek, are you reading this?
KLIK
BIP
We have the homing signal. Marking it as extraction point alpha.
ROGUE

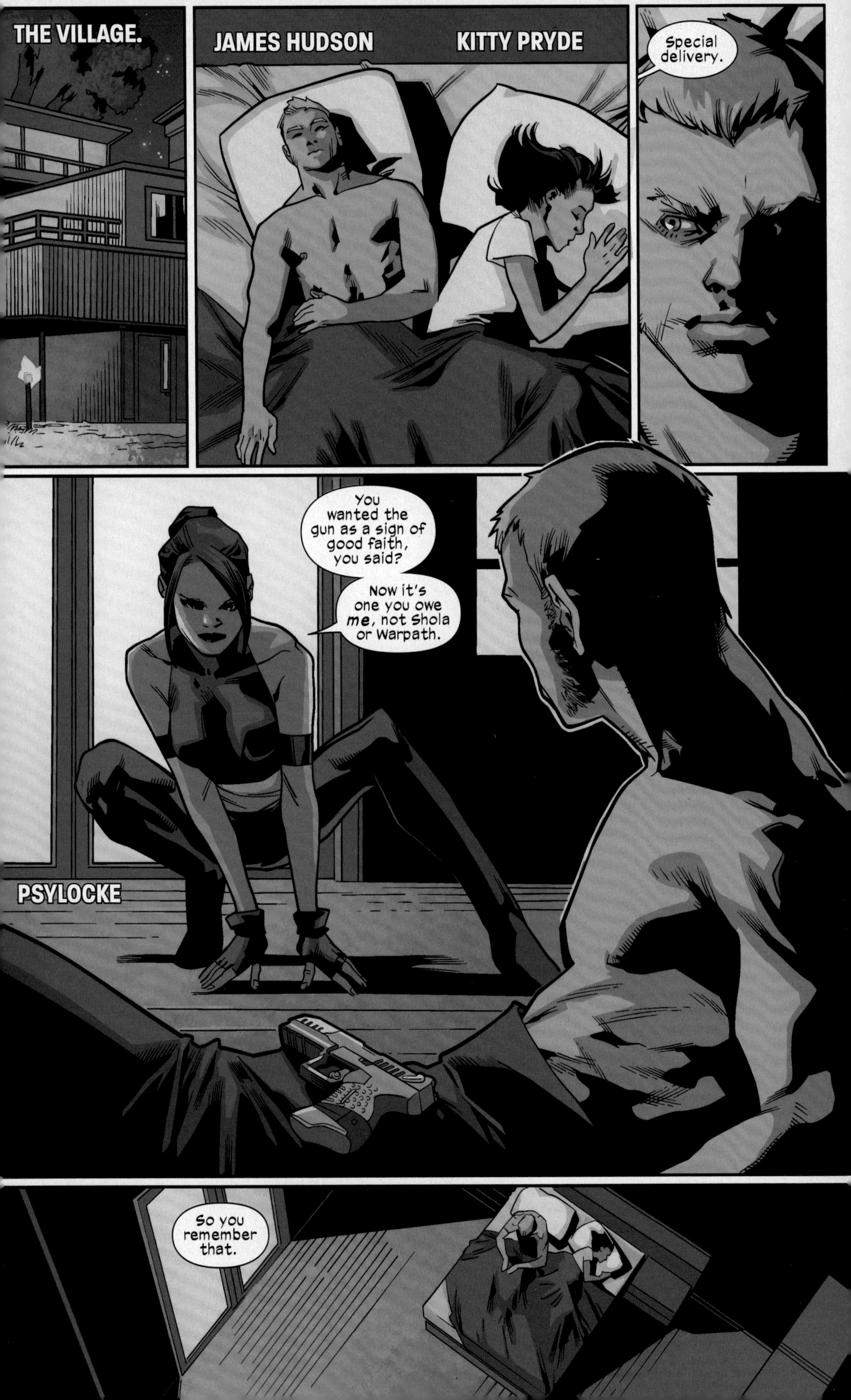
THE VILLAGE.
JAMES HUDSON
KITTY PRYDE
Special delivery.
You wanted the gun as a sign of good faith, you said?
Now it's one you owe *me*, not Shola or Warpath.
PSYLOCKE
So you remember that.

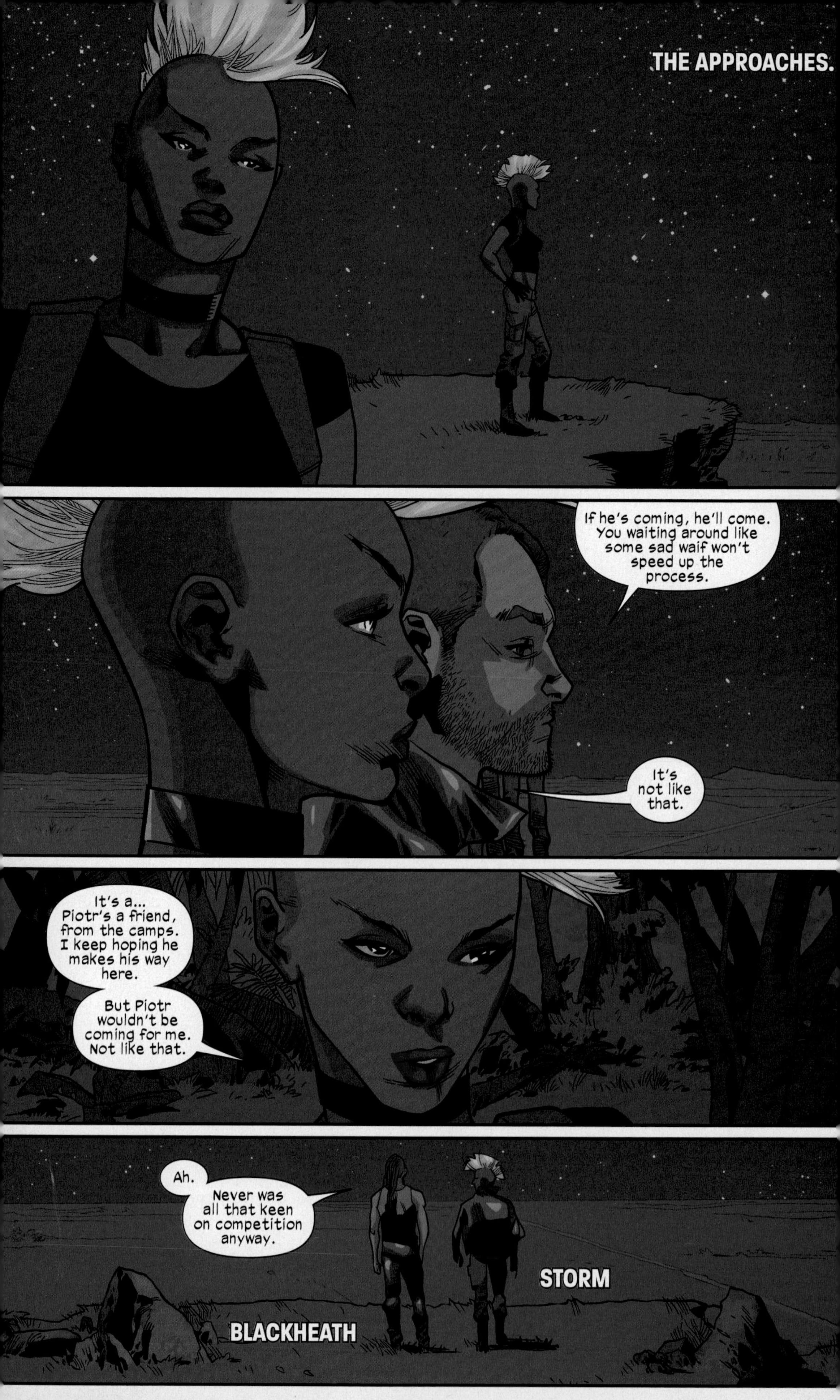
THE APPROACHES.
If he's coming, he'll come. You waiting around like some sad waif won't speed up the process.
It's not like that.
It's a... Piotr's a friend, from the camps. I keep hoping he makes his way here.
But Piotr wouldn't be coming for me. Not like that.
Ah.
Never was all that keen on competition anyway.
STORM
BLACKHEATH

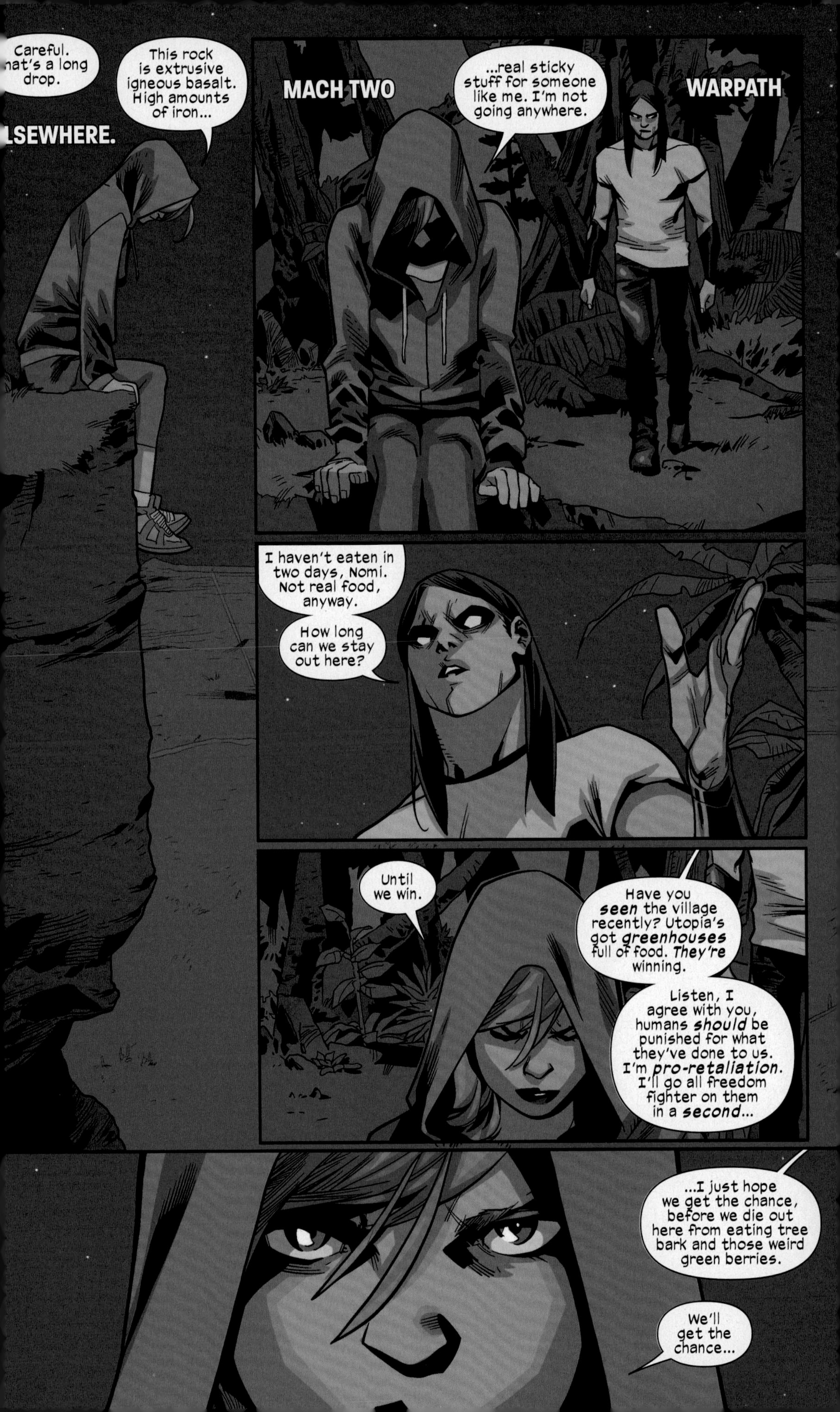
Careful.
nat's a long drop.
LSEWHERE.
This rock is extrusive igneous basalt. High amounts of iron...
MACH TWO
WARPATH
...real sticky stuff for someone like me. I'm not going anywhere.
I haven't eaten in two days, Nomi. Not real food, anyway.
How long can we stay out here?
Until we win.
Have you *seen* the village recently? Utopia's got *greenhouses* full of food. *They're* winning.
Listen, I agree with you, humans *should* be punished for what they've done to us. I'm *pro-retaliation*. I'll go all freedom fighter on them in a *second*...
...I just hope we get the chance, before we die out here from eating tree bark and those weird green berries.
We'll get the chance...

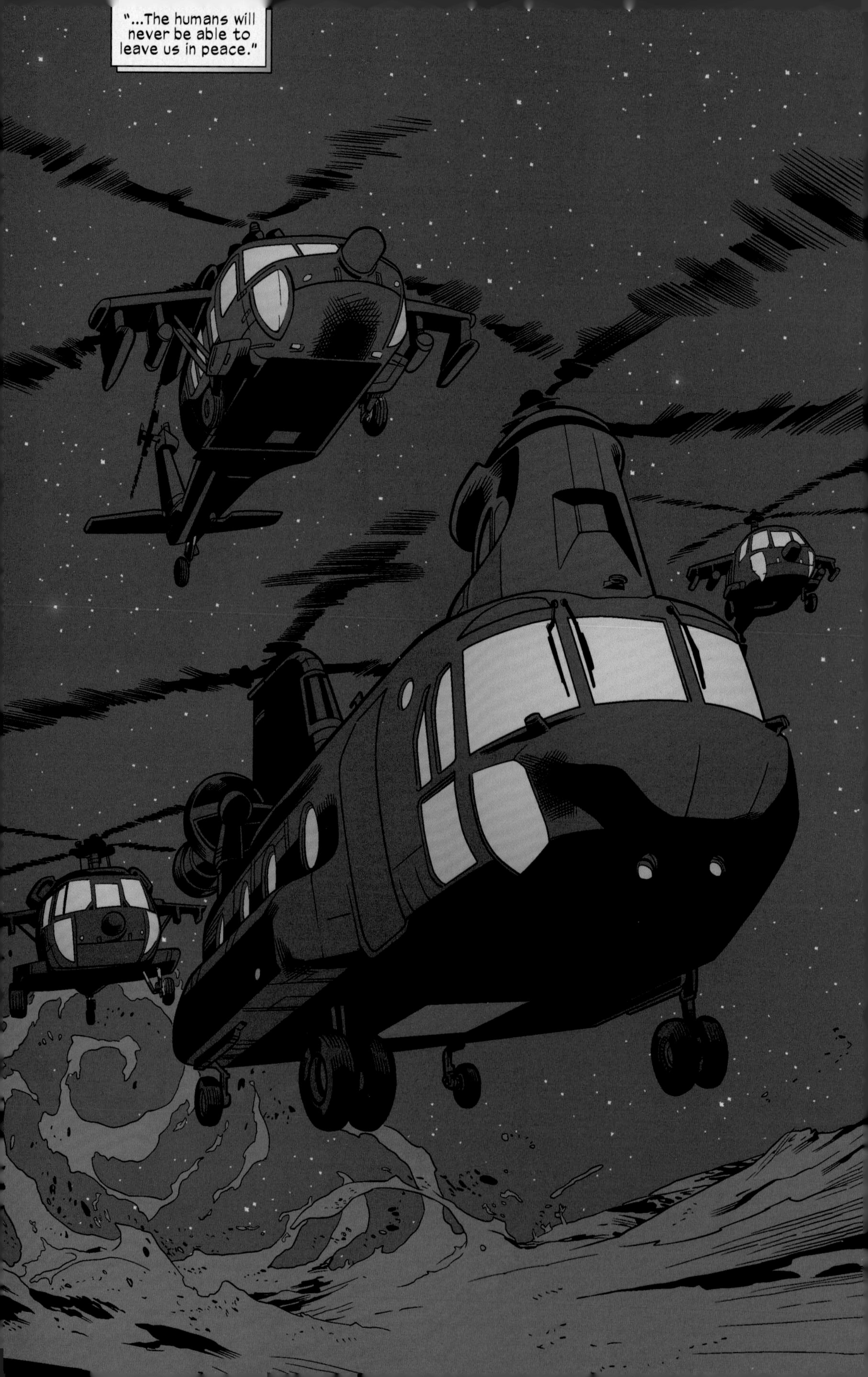
"...The humans will never be able to leave us in peace."

We have comms up. Countermeasures coming online now. Drones nearly in position to provide us full visual surveillance over the whole reservation.

But...these *are* mutants, General Ross...

If they want a way around our systems, they'll probably find one.

Kitty Pryde's been shown again and again that the power of the media moves her cause forward. I'm going to deny her that.

We're restricting the airspace, scrambling satellite coverage and cell communications...

...road-blocking this whole area fifty miles out...

...we can't afford any witnesses.

Or martyrs.

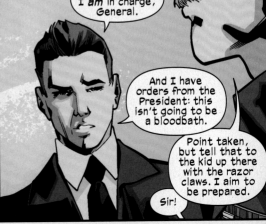

I am in charge, General.

And I have orders from the President: this isn't going to be a bloodbath.

Point taken, but tell that to the kid up there with the razor claws. I aim to be prepared.

Sir!

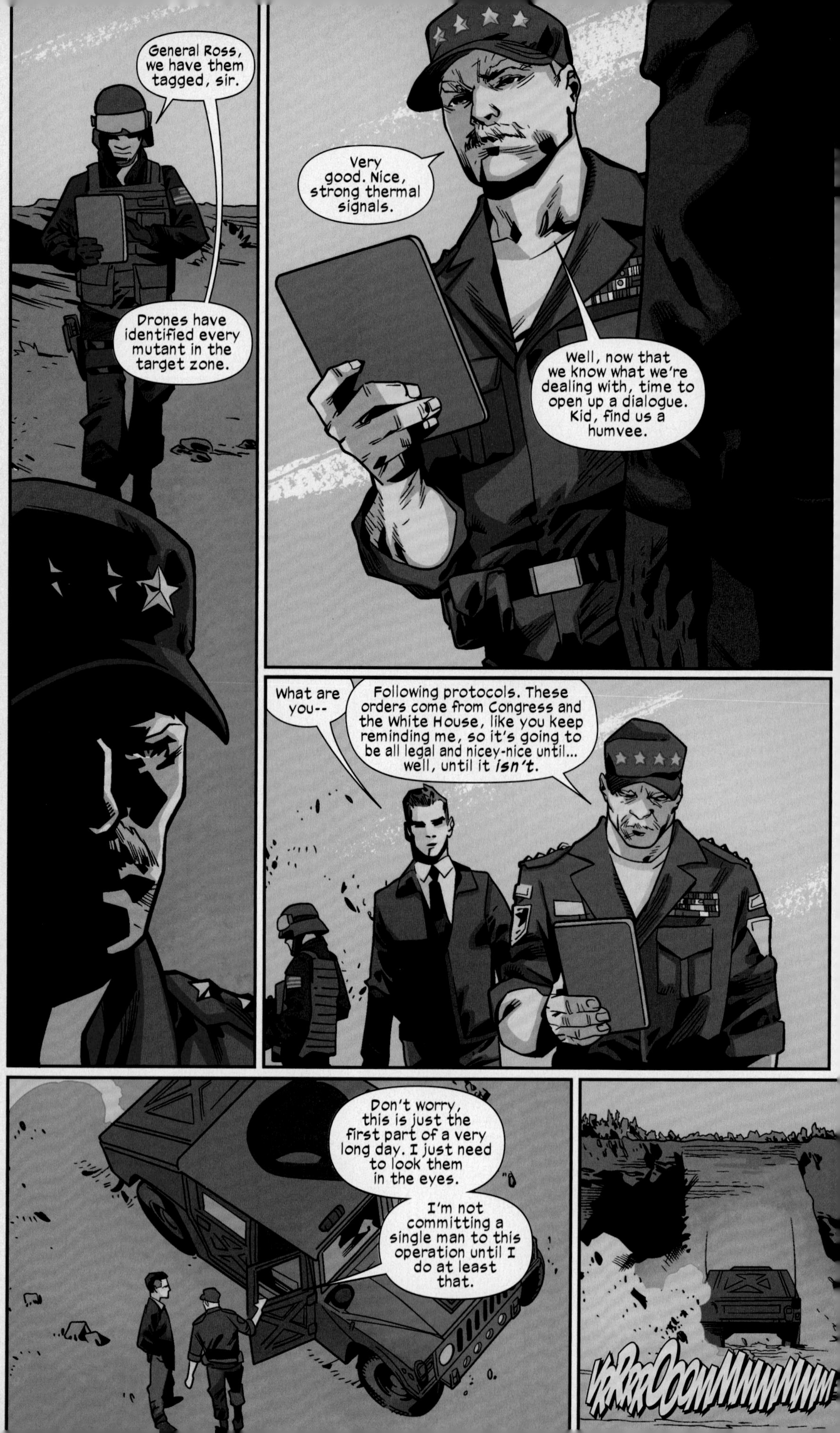
General Ross, we have them tagged, sir.
Drones have identified every mutant in the target zone.
Very good. Nice, strong thermal signals.
Well, now that we know what we're dealing with, time to open up a dialogue. Kid, find us a humvee.
What are you--
Following protocols. These orders come from Congress and the White House, like you keep reminding me, so it's going to be all legal and nicey-nice until... well, until it isn't.
Don't worry, this is just the first part of a very long day. I just need to look them in the eyes.
I'm not committing a single man to this operation until I do at least that.
VRRRROOOMMMMMMM

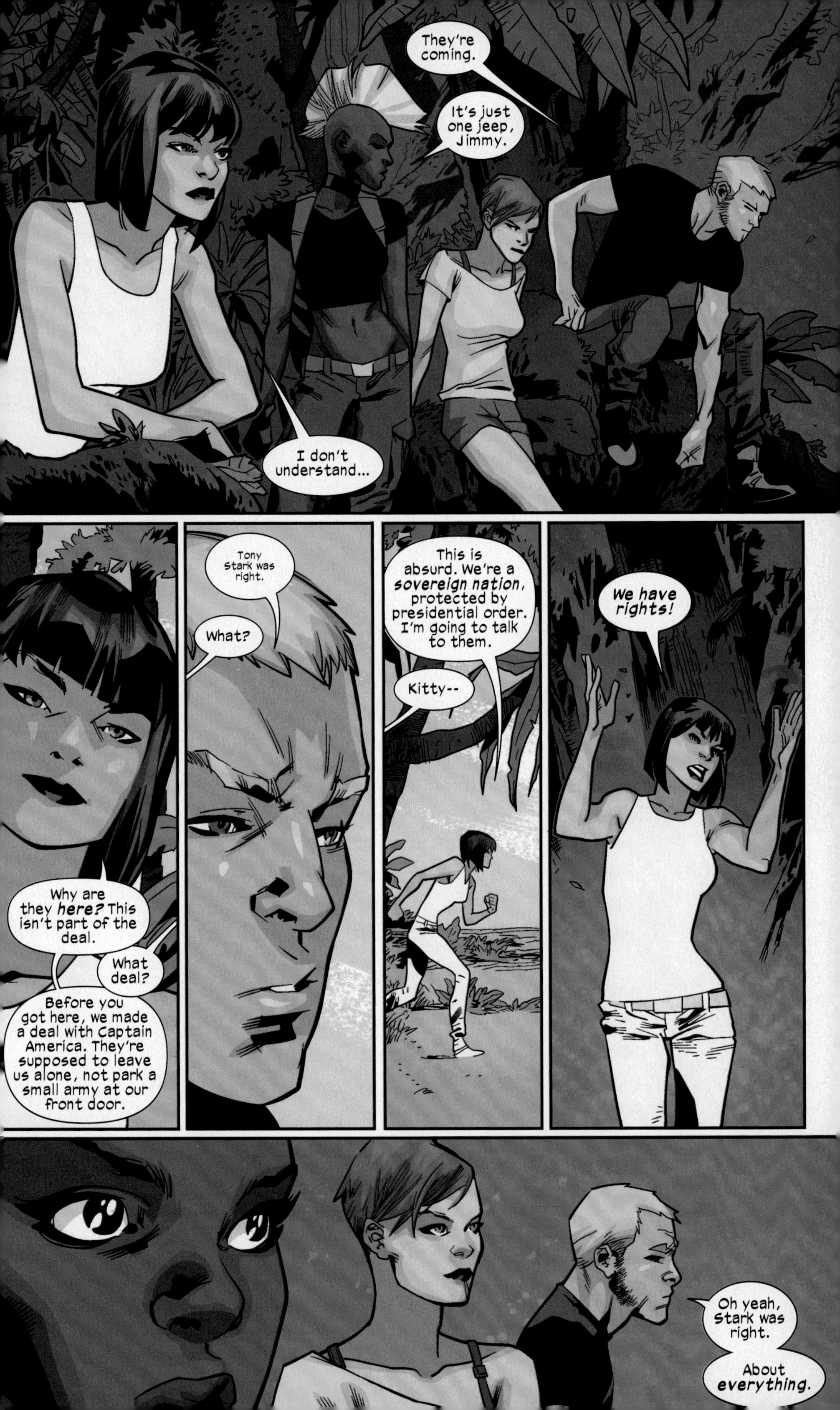
They're coming.
It's just one jeep, Jimmy.
I don't understand...
Why are they here? This isn't part of the deal.
What deal?
Before you got here, we made a deal with Captain America. They're supposed to leave us alone, not park a small army at our front door.
Tony Stark was right.
What?
This is absurd. We're a sovereign nation, protected by presidential order. I'm going to talk to them.
Kitty--
We have rights!
Oh yeah, Stark was right.
About everything.

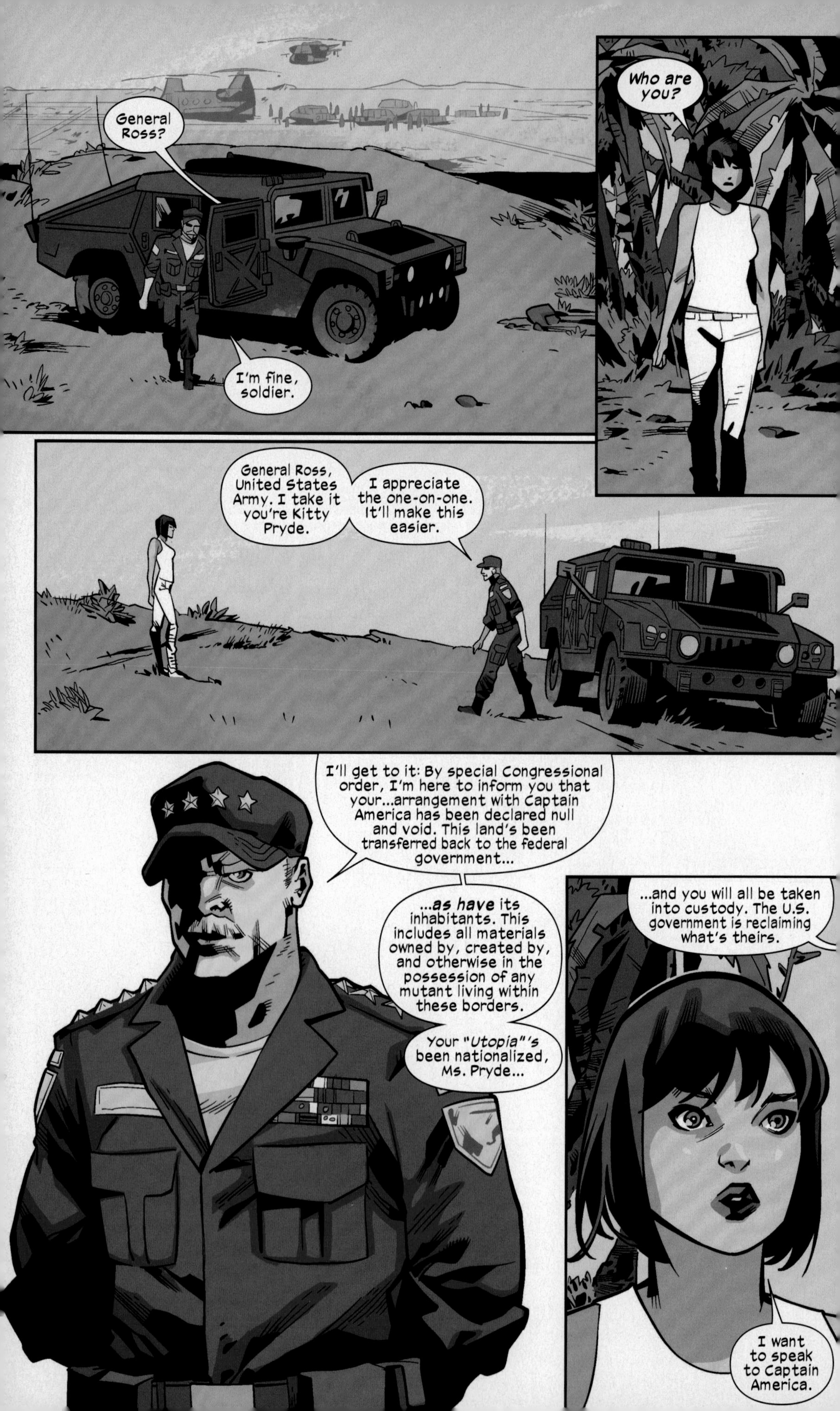
General Ross?
I'm fine, soldier.
Who are you?
General Ross, United States Army. I take it you're Kitty Pryde.
I appreciate the one-on-one. It'll make this easier.
I'll get to it: By special Congressional order, I'm here to inform you that your...arrangement with Captain America has been declared null and void. This land's been transferred back to the federal government...
...as have its inhabitants. This includes all materials owned by, created by, and otherwise in the possession of any mutant living within these borders.
Your "Utopia"'s been nationalized, Ms. Pryde...
...and you will all be taken into custody. The U.S. government is reclaiming what's theirs.
I want to speak to Captain America.

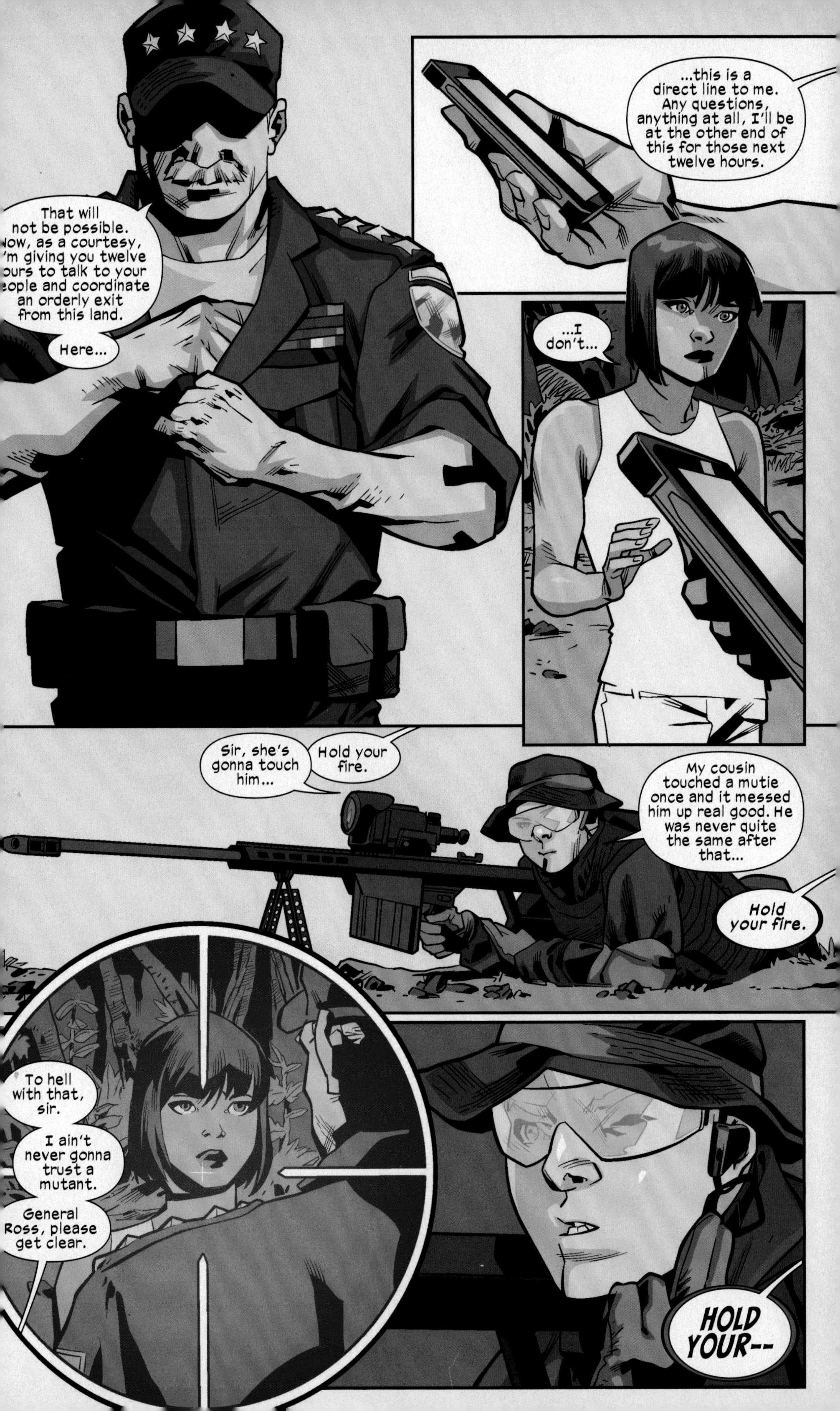
That will not be possible. Now, as a courtesy, I'm giving you twelve hours to talk to your people and coordinate an orderly exit from this land.
Here...
...this is a direct line to me. Any questions, anything at all, I'll be at the other end of this for those next twelve hours.
...I don't...
Sir, she's gonna touch him...
Hold your fire.
My cousin touched a mutie once and it messed him up real good. He was never quite the same after that...
Hold your fire.
To hell with that, sir.
I ain't never gonna trust a mutant.
General Ross, please get clear.
HOLD YOUR--

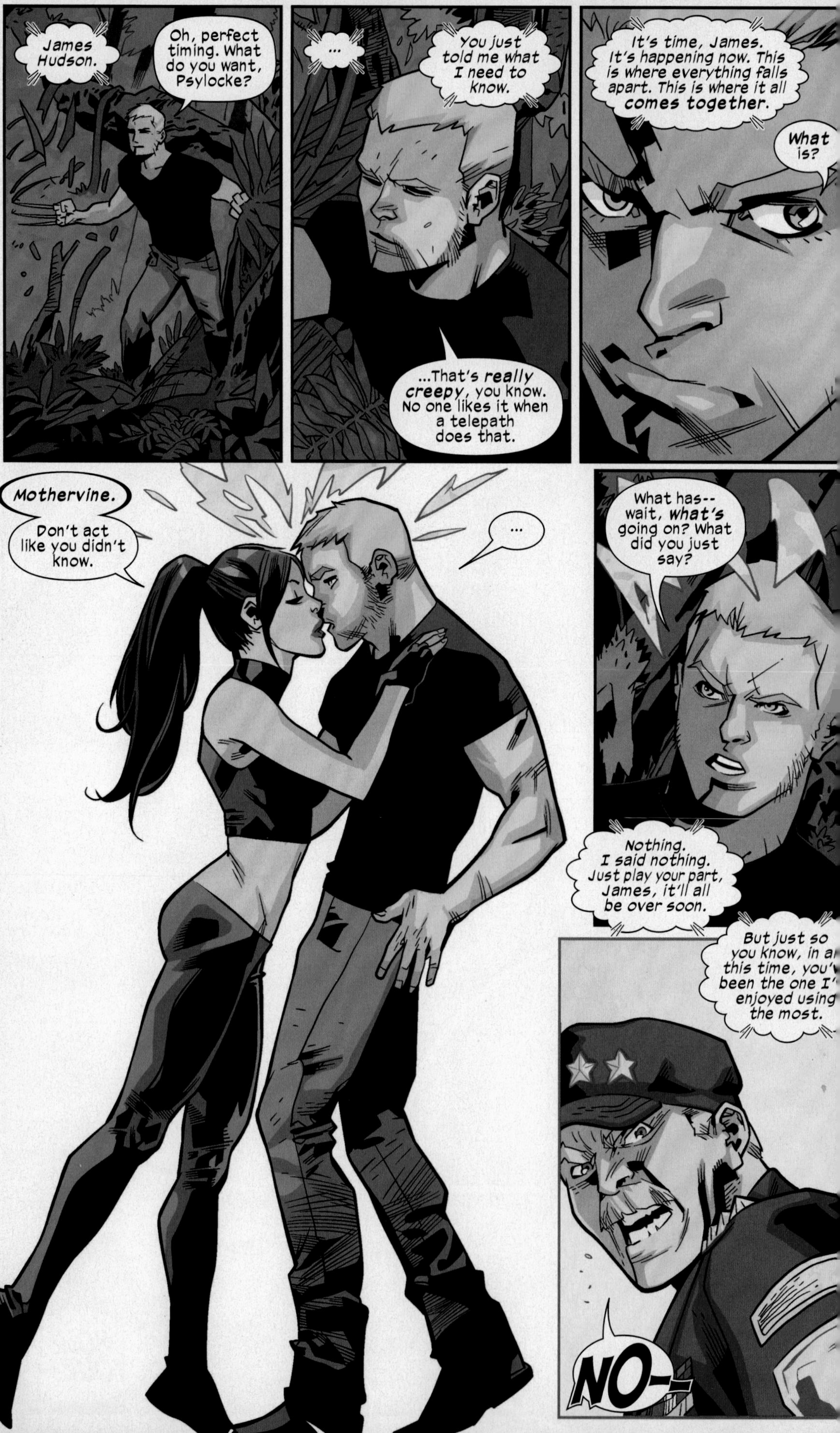
James Hudson.
Oh, perfect timing. What do you want, Psylocke?
...
You just told me what I need to know.
...That's *really creepy*, you know. No one likes it when a telepath does that.
It's time, James. It's happening now. This is where everything falls apart. This is where it all **comes together**.
What is?
Mothervine.
Don't act like you didn't know.
...
What has--wait, *what's* going on? What did you just say?
Nothing. I said nothing. Just play your part, James, it'll all be over soon.
But just so you know, in al this time, you'\ been the one I' enjoyed using the most.
NO--

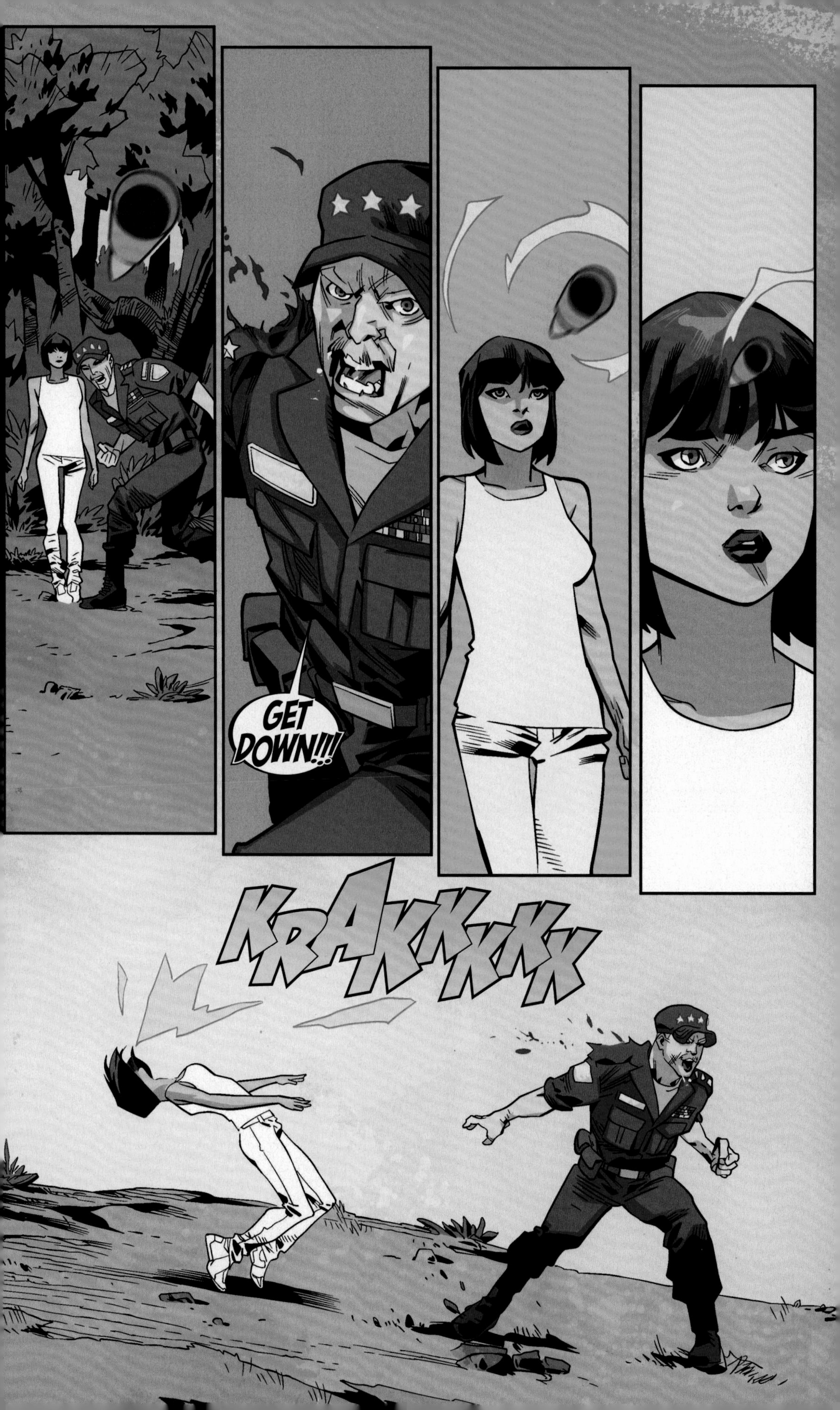
GET DOWN!!!
KRAKKKKK

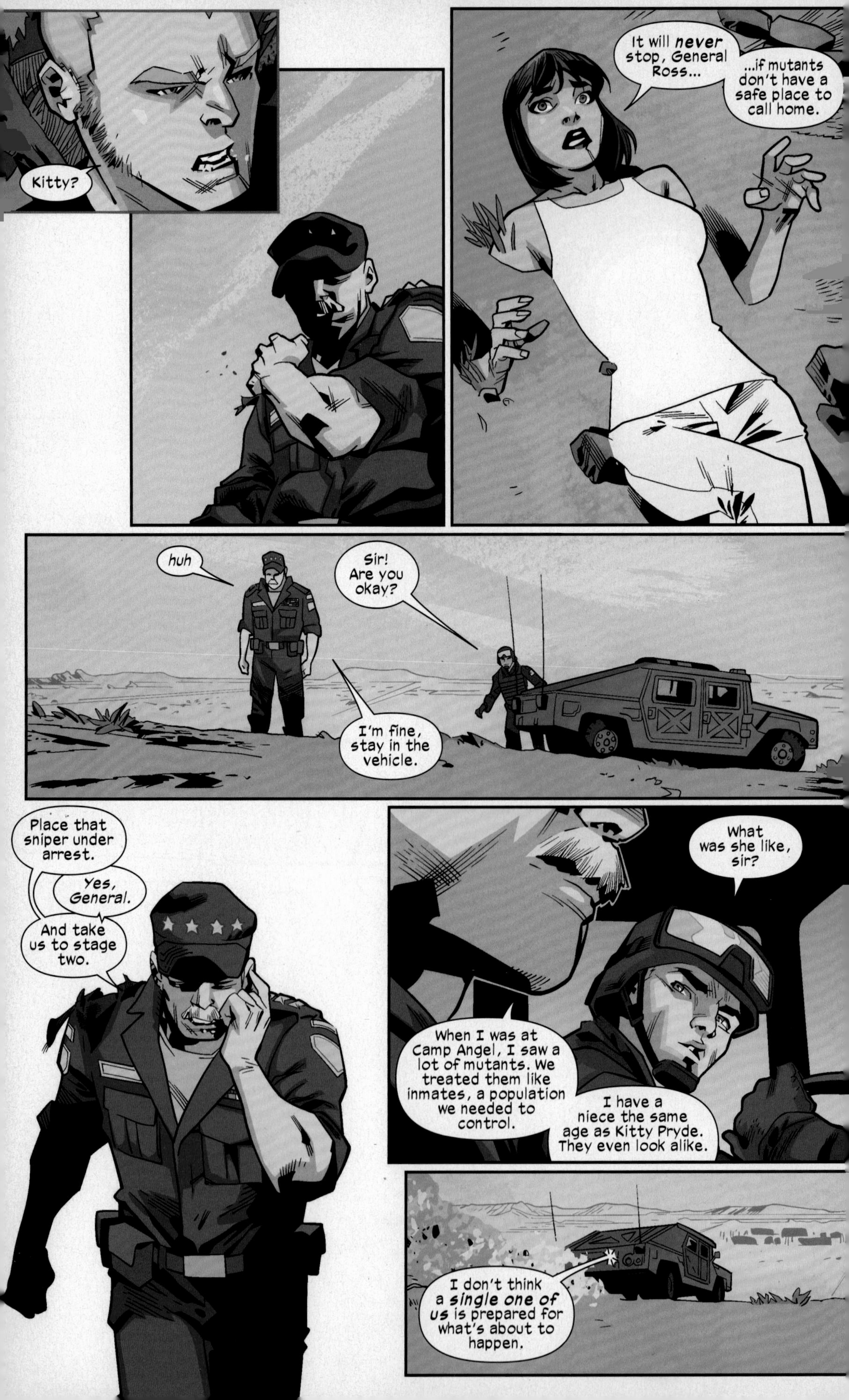

Kitty?
It will never stop, General Ross...
...if mutants don't have a safe place to call home.
huh
Sir! Are you okay?
I'm fine, stay in the vehicle.
Place that sniper under arrest.
Yes, General.
And take us to stage two.
What was she like, sir?
When I was at Camp Angel, I saw a lot of mutants. We treated them like inmates, a population we needed to control.
I have a niece the same age as Kitty Pryde. They even look alike.
I don't think a single one of us is prepared for what's about to happen.

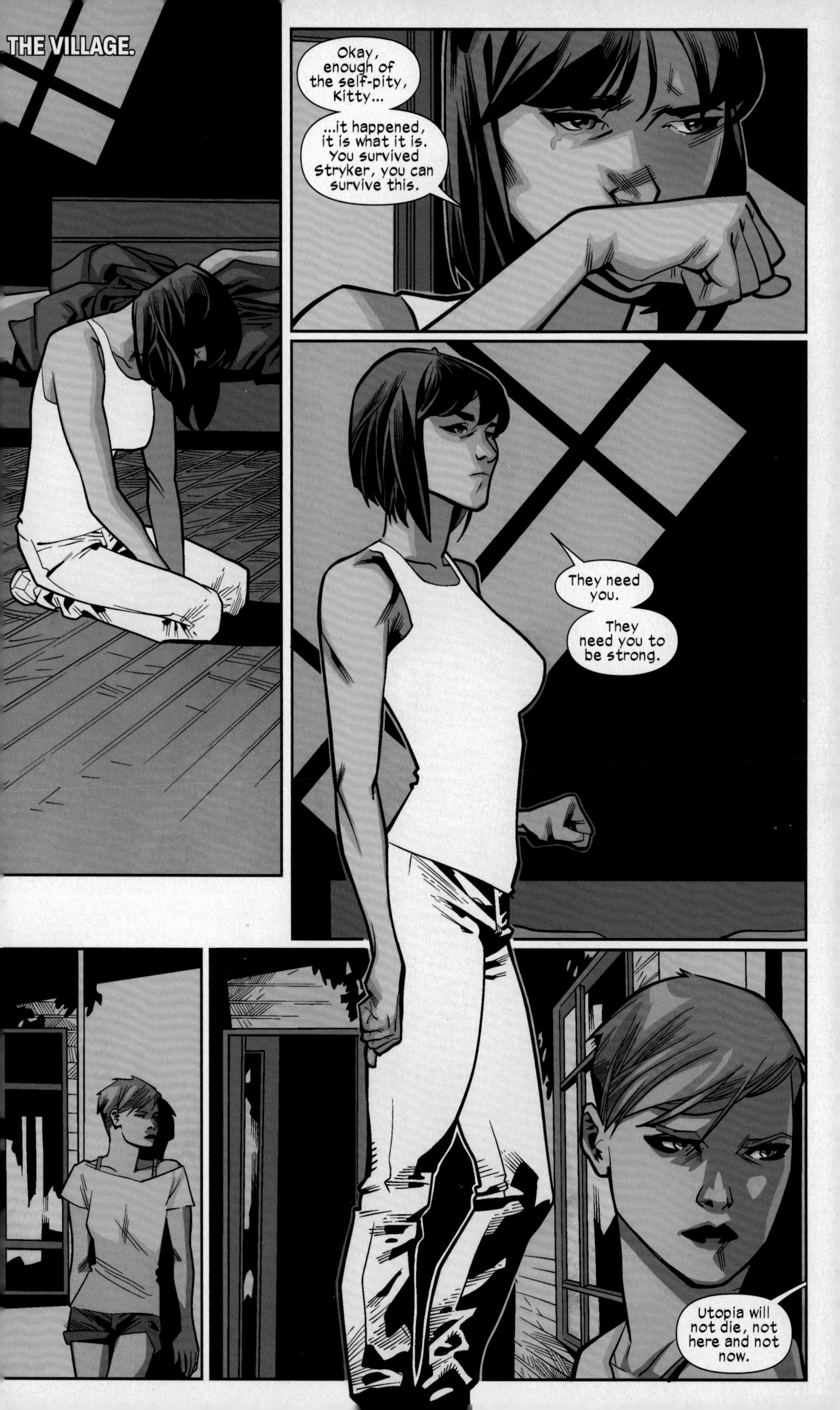
THE VILLAGE.
Okay, enough of the self-pity, Kitty...
...it happened, it is what it is. You survived Stryker, you can survive this.
They need you.
They need you to be strong.
Utopia will not die, not here and not now.

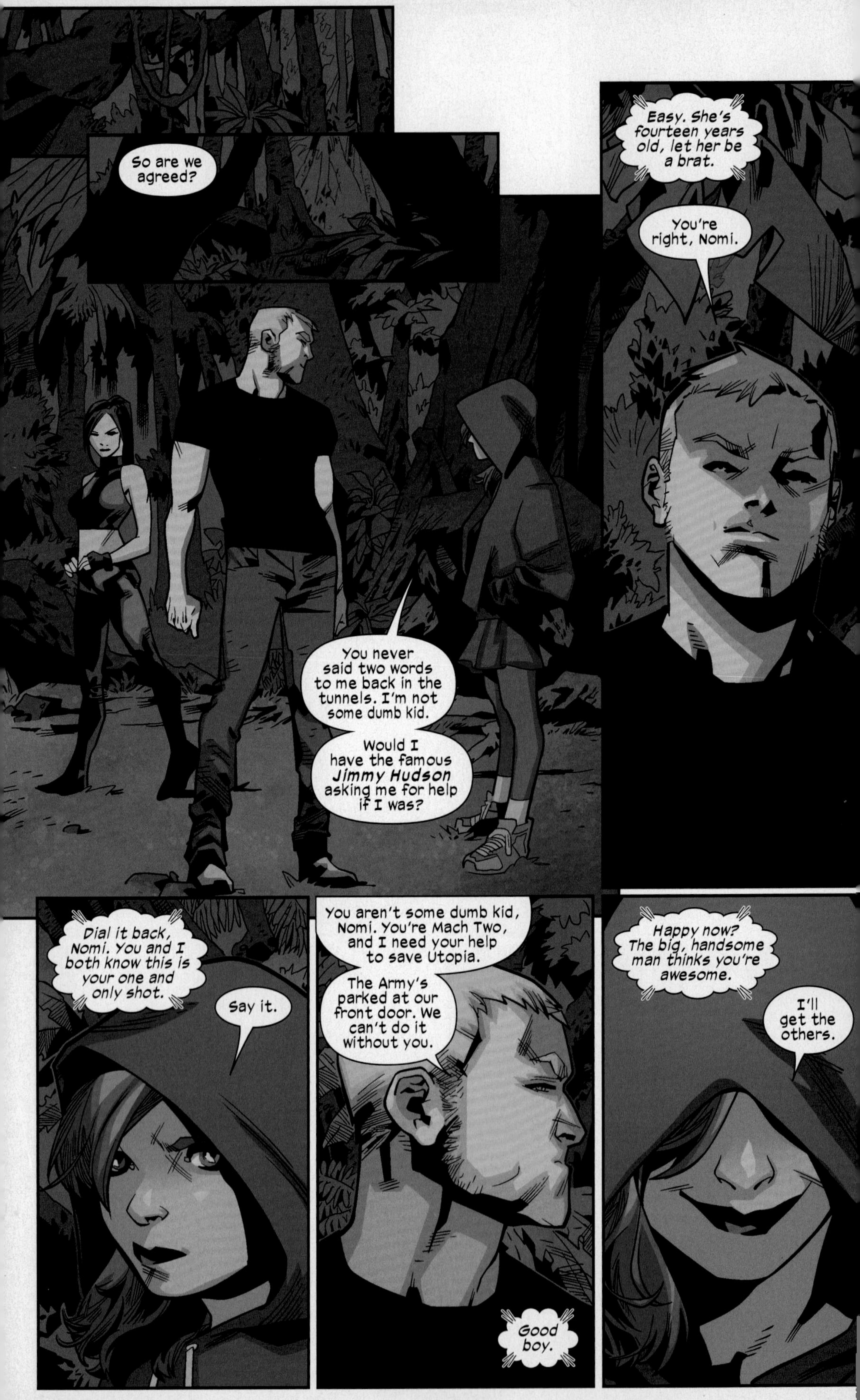
So are we agreed?
You never said two words to me back in the tunnels. I'm not some dumb kid.
Would I have the famous *Jimmy Hudson* asking me for help if I was?
Easy. She's fourteen years old, let her be a brat.
You're right, Nomi.
Dial it back, Nomi. You and I both know this is your one and only shot.
Say it.
You aren't some dumb kid, Nomi. You're Mach Two, and I need your help to save Utopia.
The Army's parked at our front door. We can't do it without you.
Good boy.
Happy now? The big, handsome man thinks you're awesome.
I'll get the others.

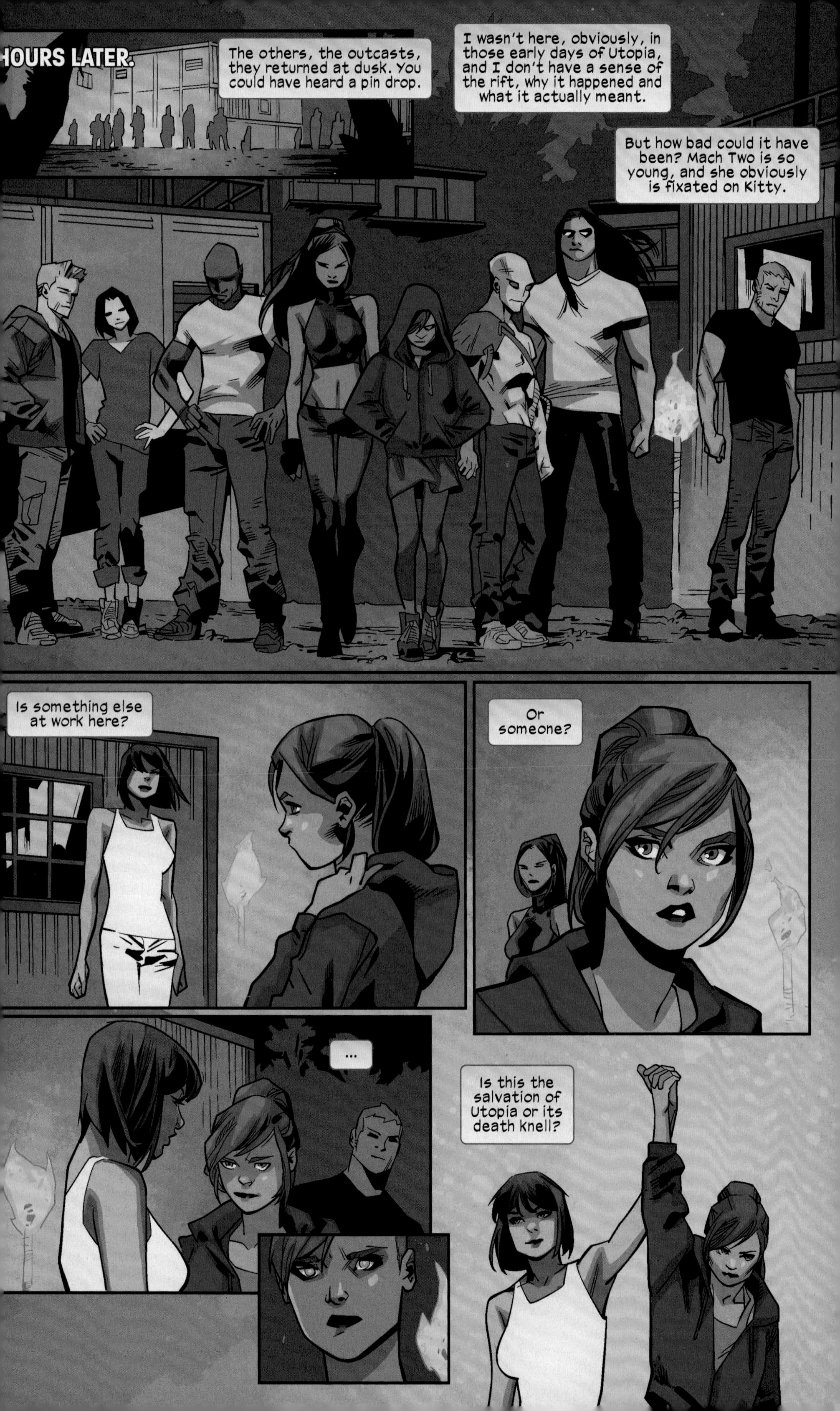
HOURS LATER.
The others, the outcasts, they returned at dusk. You could have heard a pin drop.
I wasn't here, obviously, in those early days of Utopia, and I don't have a sense of the rift, why it happened and what it actually meant.
But how bad could it have been? Mach Two is so young, and she obviously is fixated on Kitty.
Is something else at work here?
Or someone?
...
Is this the salvation of Utopia or its death knell?

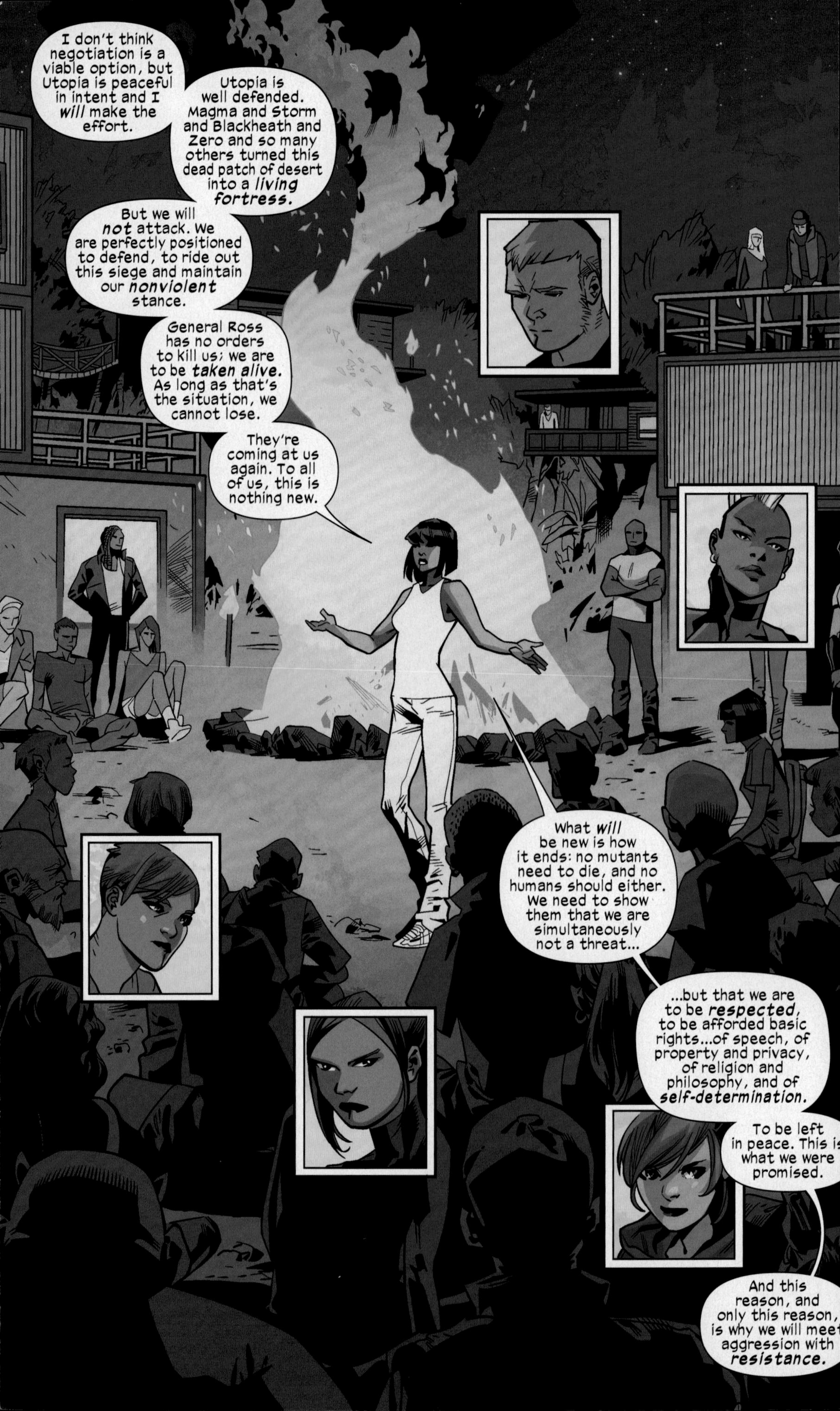

I don't think negotiation is a viable option, but Utopia is peaceful in intent and I *will* make the effort.
Utopia is well defended. Magma and Storm and Blackheath and Zero and so many others turned this dead patch of desert into a *living fortress.*
But we will *not* attack. We are perfectly positioned to defend, to ride out this siege and maintain our *nonviolent* stance.
General Ross has no orders to kill us; we are to be *taken alive.* As long as that's the situation, we cannot lose.
They're coming at us again. To all of us, this is nothing new.
What *will* be new is how it ends: no mutants need to die, and no humans should either. We need to show them that we are simultaneously not a threat...
...but that we are to be *respected*, to be afforded basic rights...of speech, of property and privacy, of religion and philosophy, and of *self-determination.*
To be left in peace. This is what we were promised.
And this reason, and only this reason, is why we will meet aggression with *resistance.*

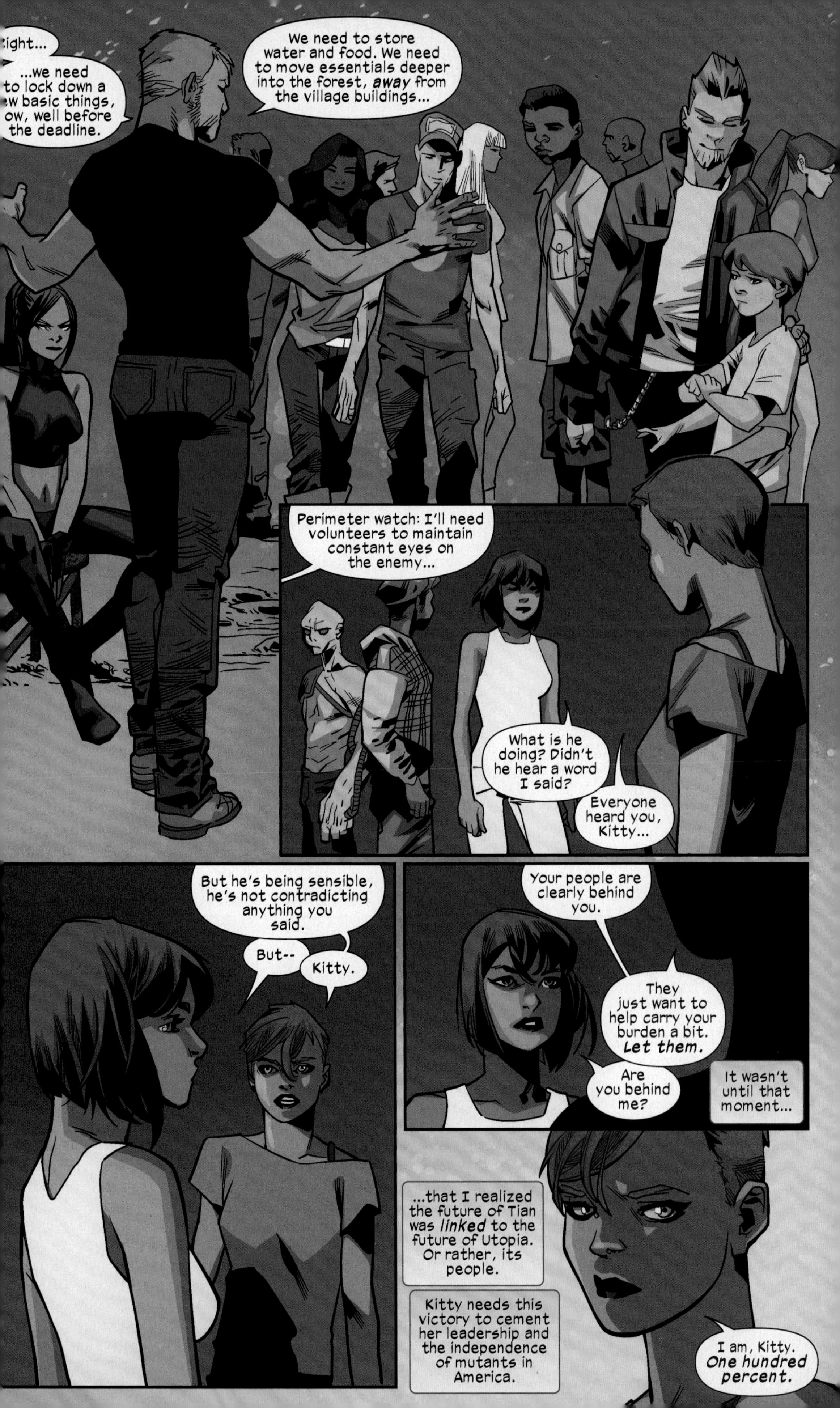

ight...
...we need to lock down a w basic things, ow, well before the deadline.
We need to store water and food. We need to move essentials deeper into the forest, *away* from the village buildings...
Perimeter watch: I'll need volunteers to maintain constant eyes on the enemy...
What is he doing? Didn't he hear a word I said?
Everyone heard you, Kitty...
But he's being sensible, he's not contradicting anything you said.
But--
Kitty.
Your people are clearly behind you.
They just want to help carry your burden a bit. **Let them.**
Are you behind me?
It wasn't until that moment...
...that I realized the future of Tian was *linked* to the future of Utopia. Or rather, its people.
Kitty needs this victory to cement her leadership and the independence of mutants in America.
I am, Kitty. ***One hundred percent.***

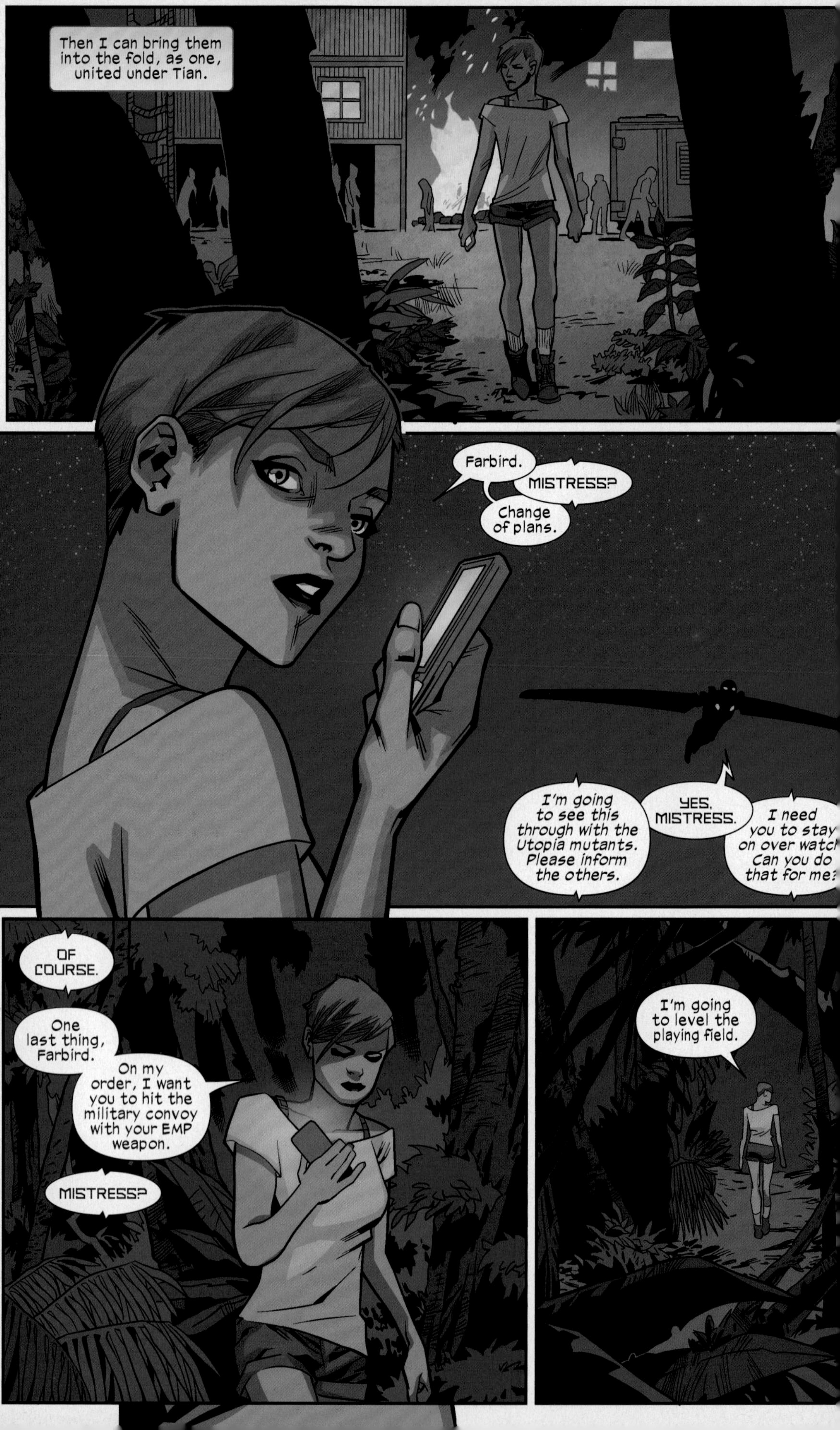
Then I can bring them into the fold, as one, united under Tian.
Farbird.
MISTRESS?
Change of plans.
I'm going to see this through with the Utopia mutants. Please inform the others.
YES, MISTRESS.
I need you to stay on over watc
Can you do that for me?
OF COURSE.
One last thing, Farbird.
On my order, I want you to hit the military convoy with your EMP weapon.
MISTRESS?
I'm going to level the playing field.

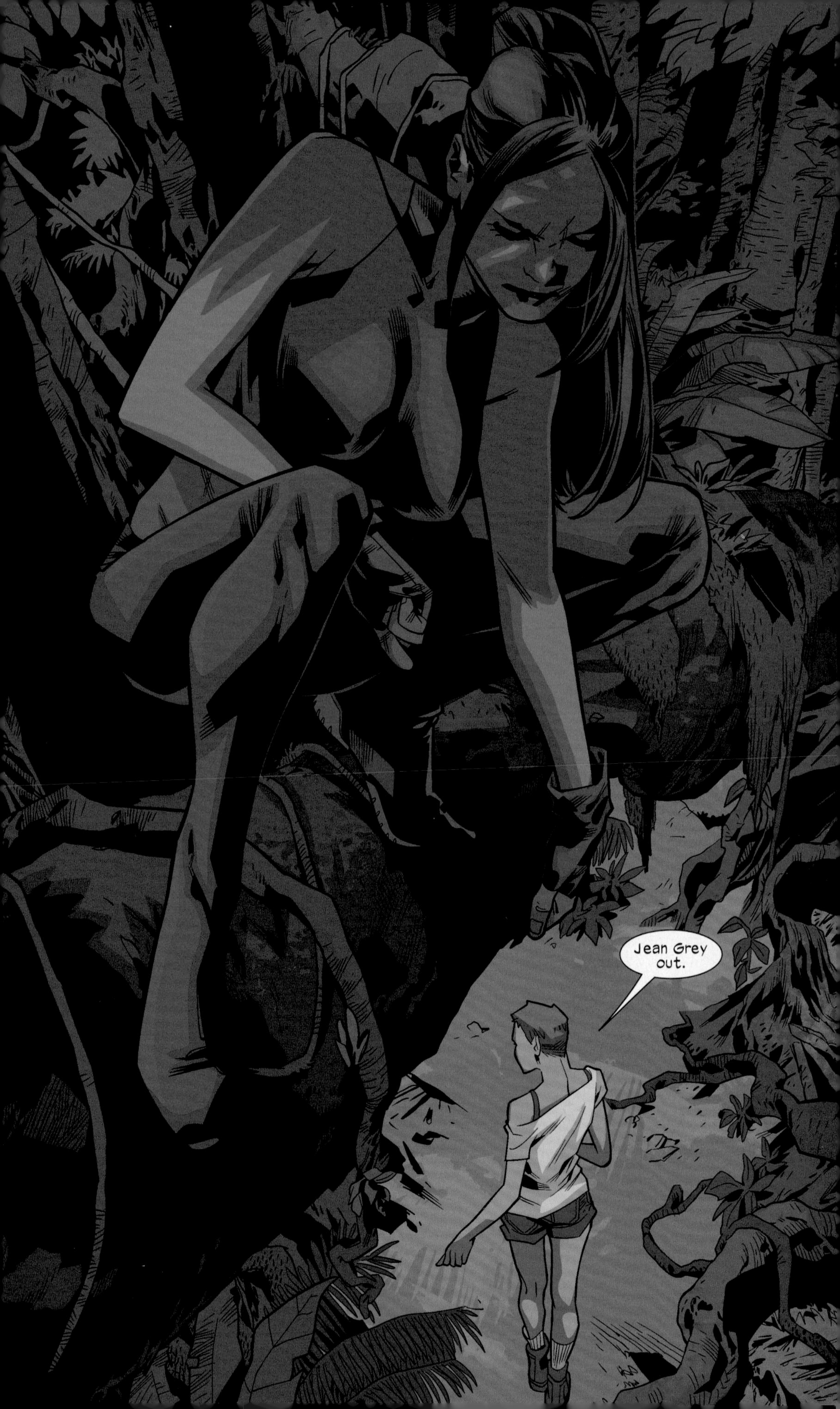
Jean Grey out.

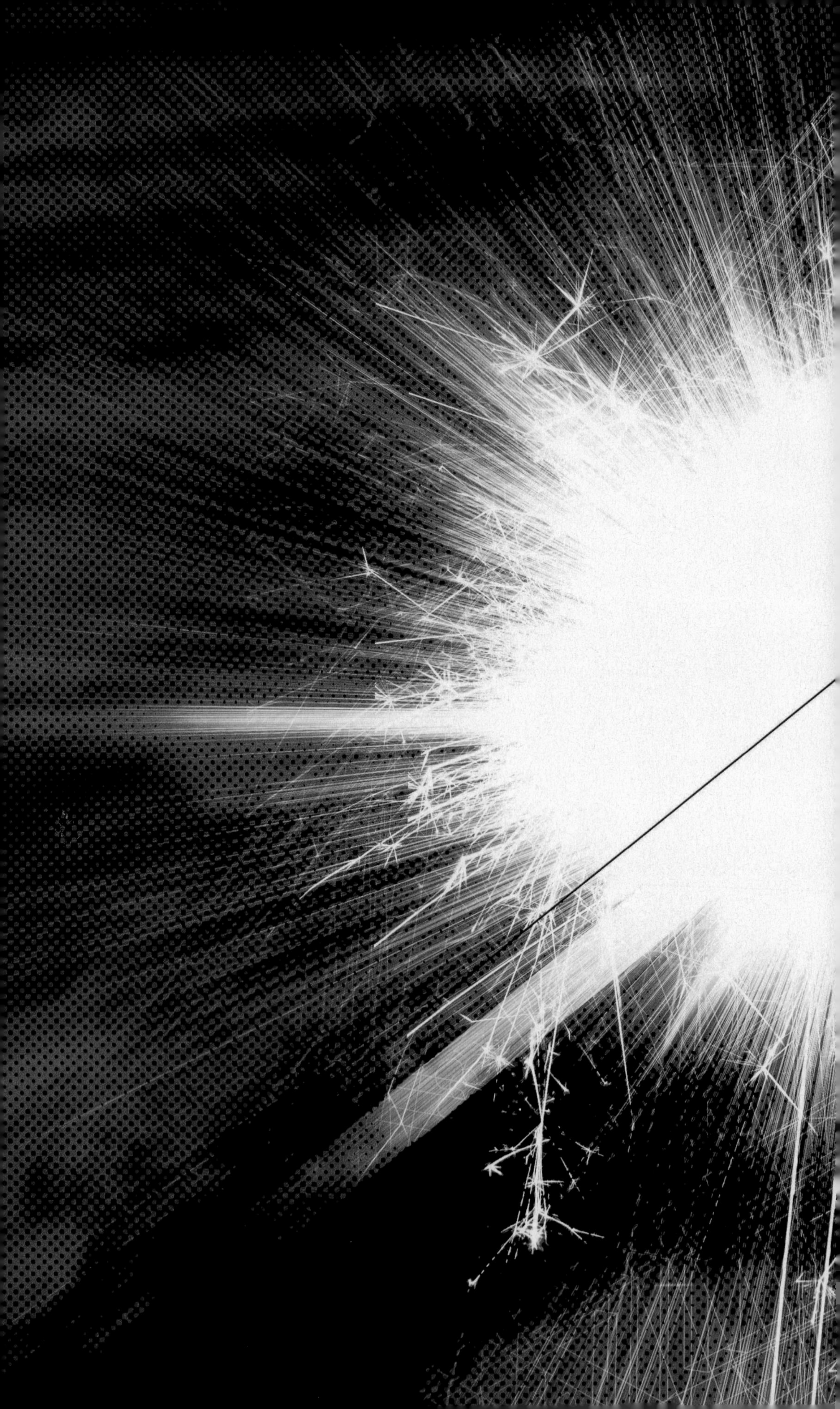

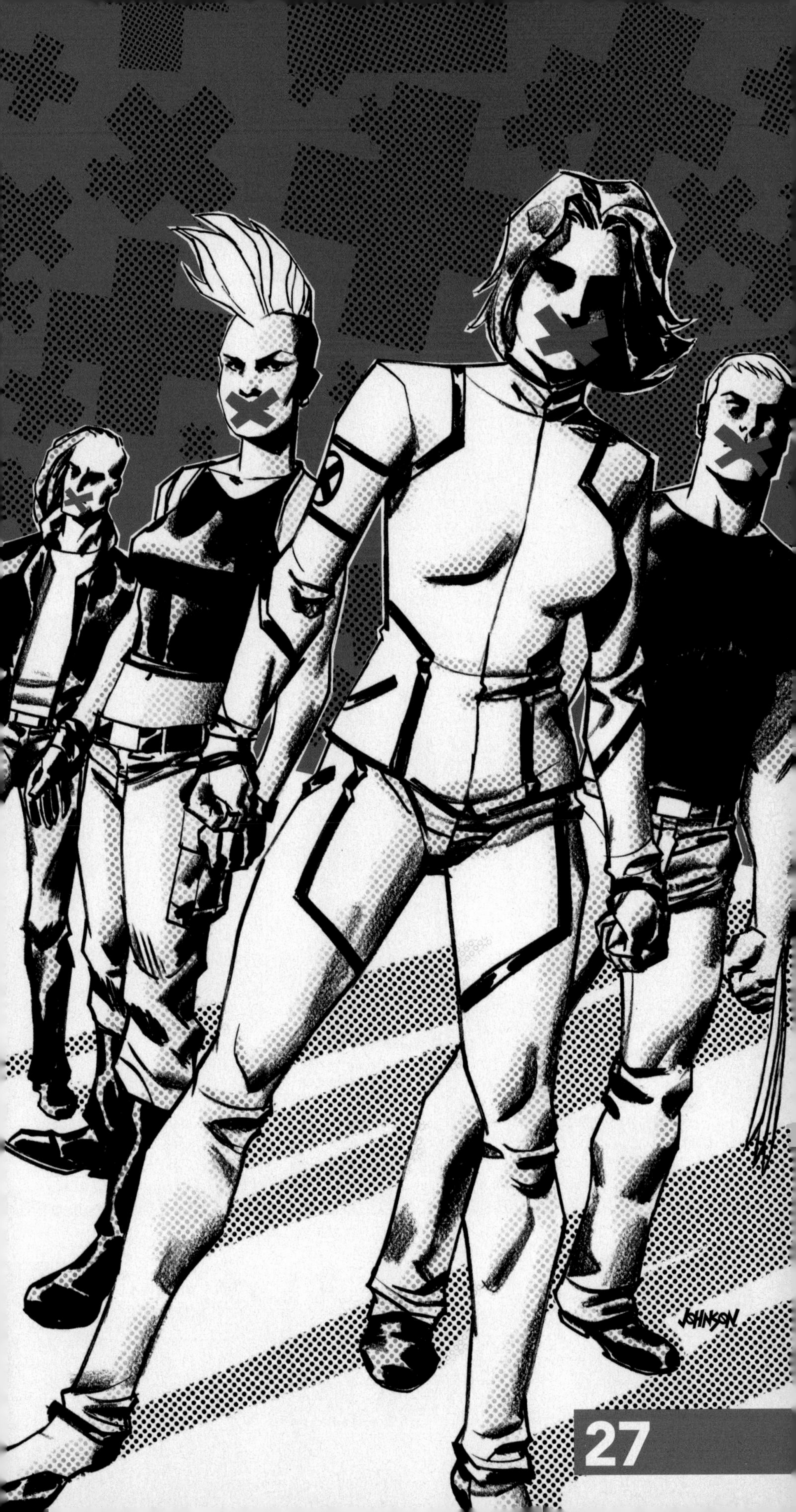
JOHNSON
27

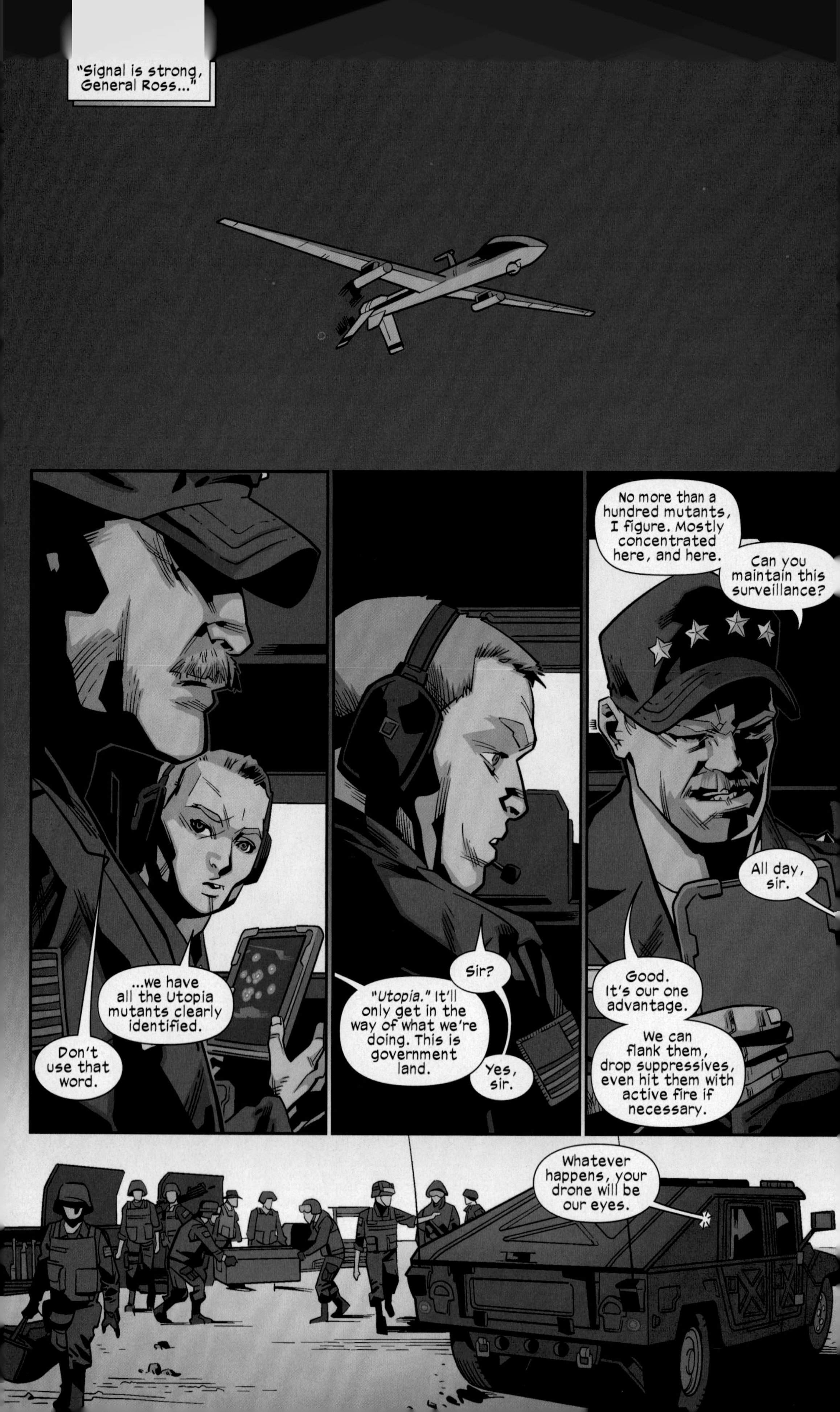
"Signal is strong, General Ross..."
...we have all the Utopia mutants clearly identified.
Don't use that word.
Sir?
"Utopia." It'll only get in the way of what we're doing. This is government land.
Yes, sir.
No more than a hundred mutants, I figure. Mostly concentrated here, and here.
Can you maintain this surveillance?
All day, sir.
Good. It's our one advantage.
We can flank them, drop suppressives, even hit them with active fire if necessary.
Whatever happens, your drone will be our eyes.

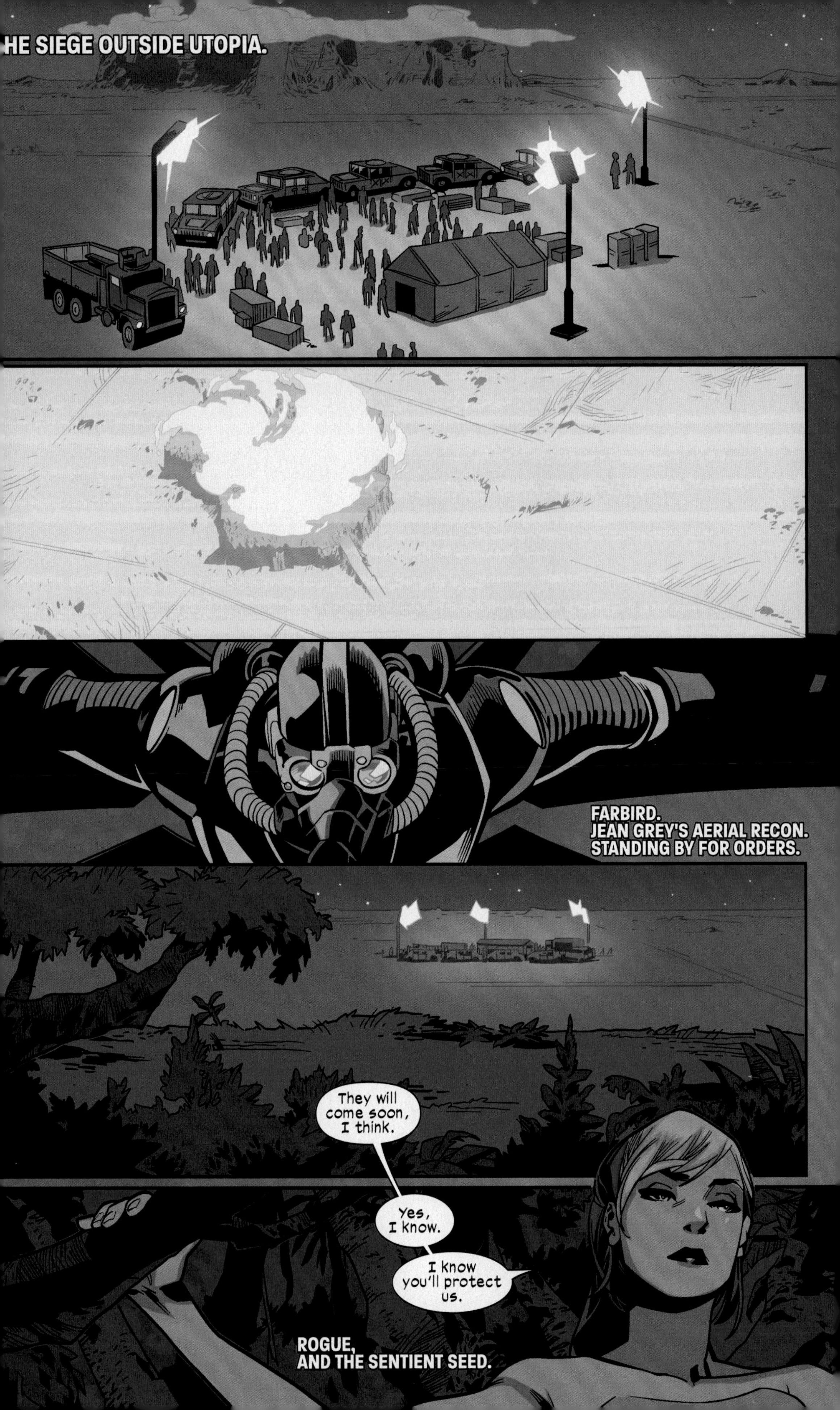
HE SIEGE OUTSIDE UTOPIA.
FARBIRD.
JEAN GREY'S AERIAL RECON.
STANDING BY FOR ORDERS.
They will come soon, I think.
Yes, I know.
I know you'll protect us.
ROGUE,
AND THE SENTIENT SEED.

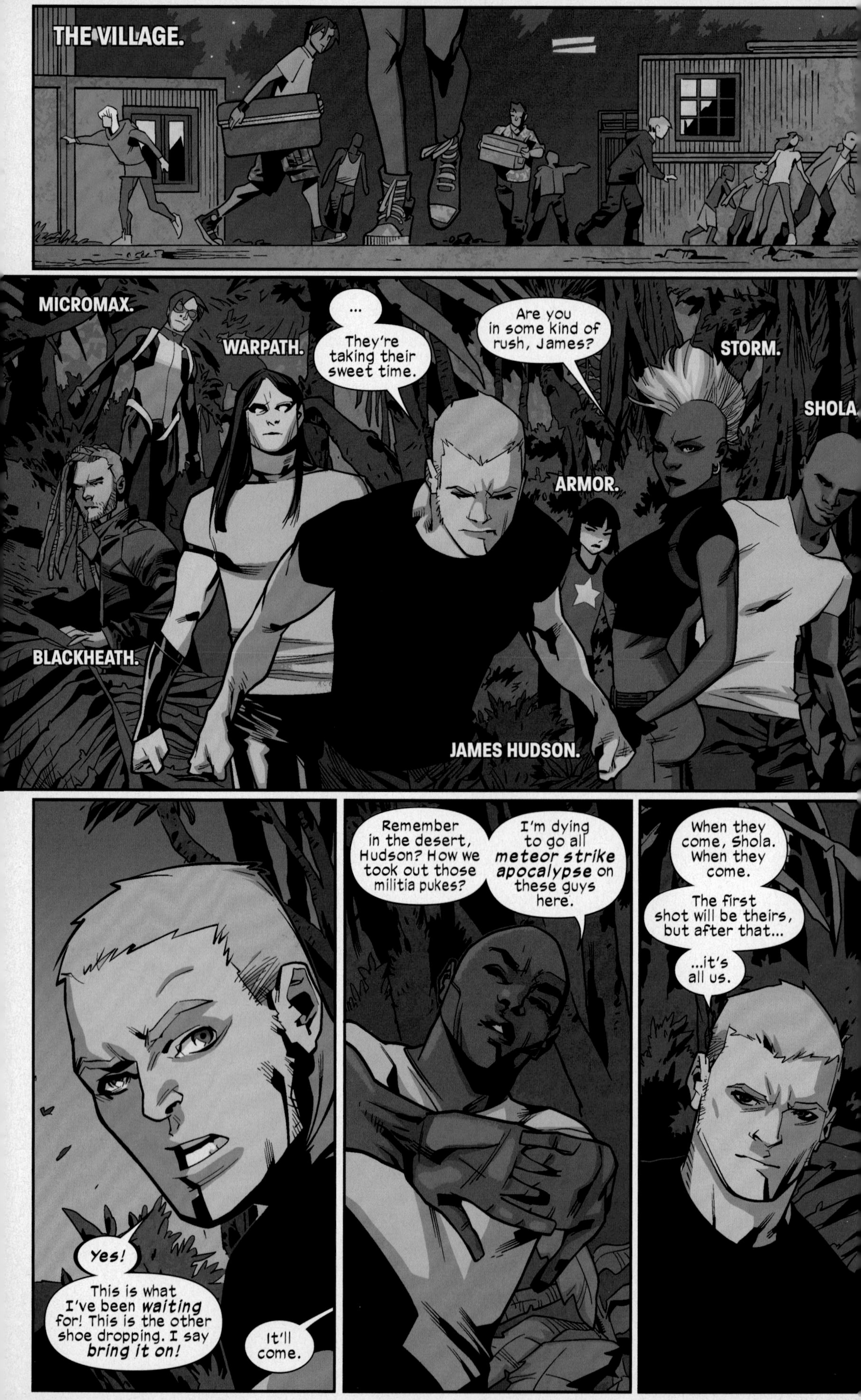
THE VILLAGE.
MICROMAX.
WARPATH.
...
They're taking their sweet time.
Are you in some kind of rush, James?
STORM.
SHOLA.
ARMOR.
BLACKHEATH.
JAMES HUDSON.
Yes!
This is what I've been waiting for! This is the other shoe dropping. I say bring it on!
It'll come.
Remember in the desert, Hudson? How we took out those militia pukes?
I'm dying to go all meteor strike apocalypse on these guys here.
When they come, Shola. When they come.
The first shot will be theirs, but after that...
...it's all us.

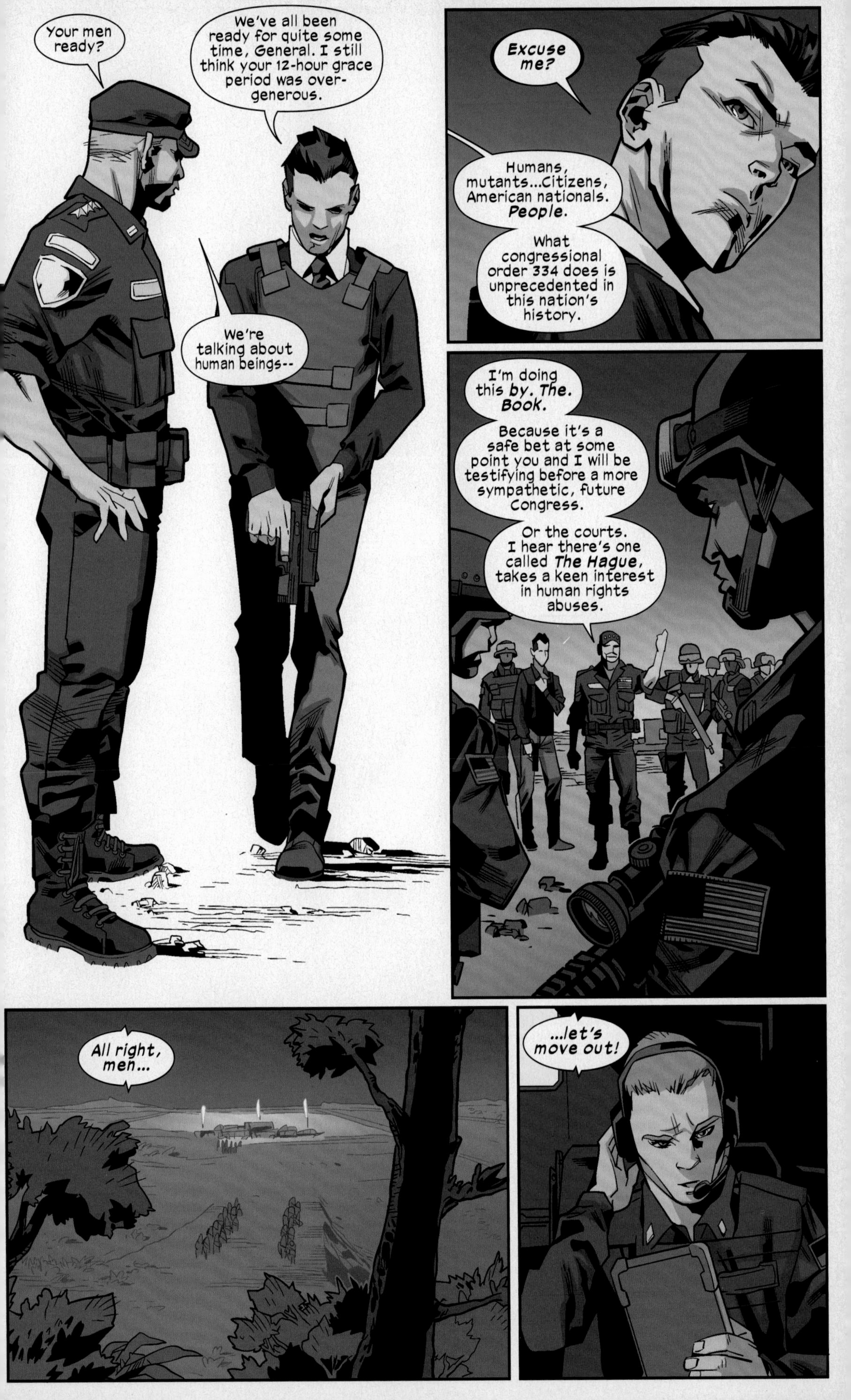

Your men ready?
We've all been ready for quite some time, General. I still think your 12-hour grace period was over-generous.
We're talking about human beings--
Excuse me?
Humans, mutants...Citizens, American nationals. People.
What congressional order 334 does is unprecedented in this nation's history.
I'm doing this by. The. Book.
Because it's a safe bet at some point you and I will be testifying before a more sympathetic, future Congress.
Or the courts. I hear there's one called The Hague, takes a keen interest in human rights abuses.
All right, men...
...let's move out!

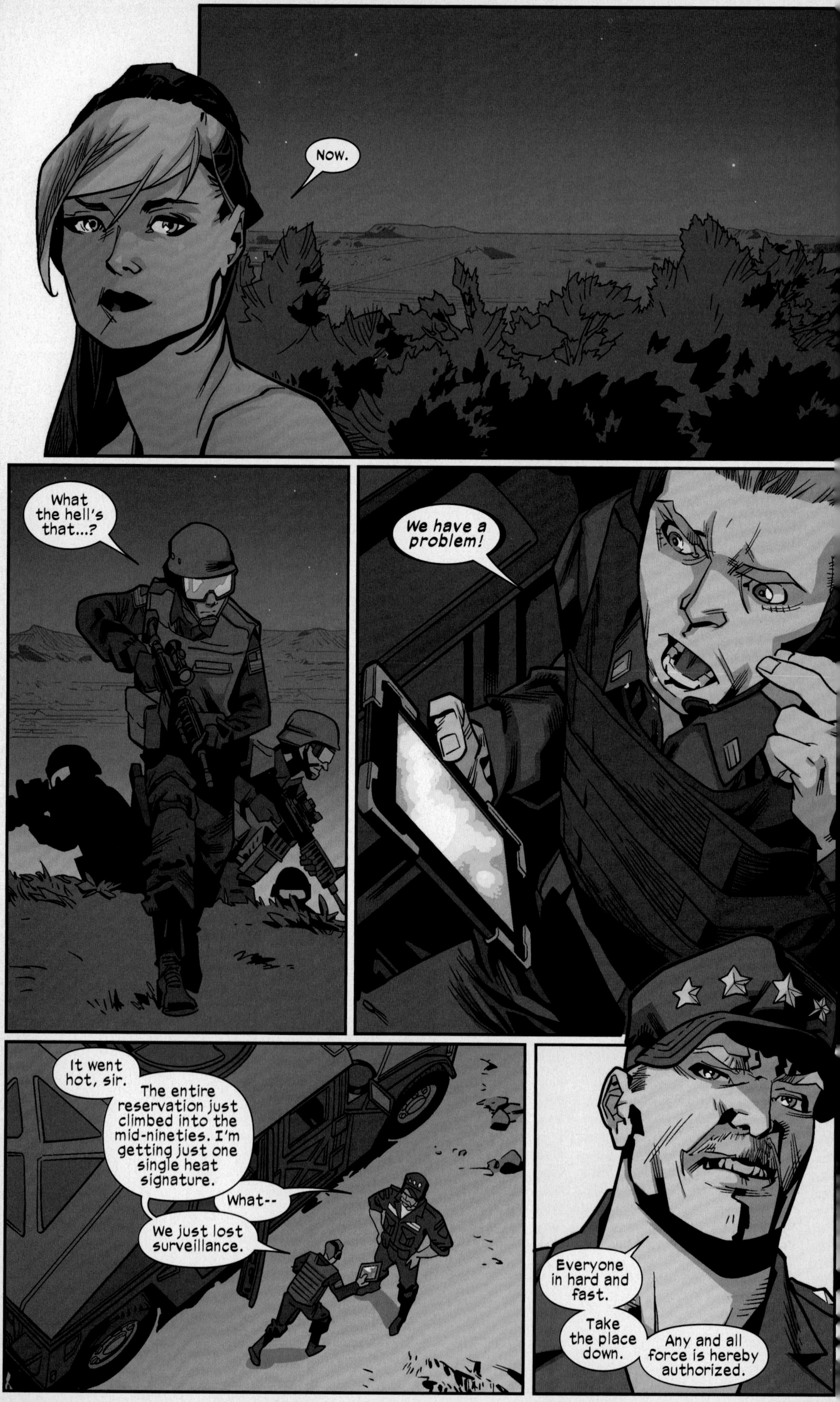
Now.
What the hell's that...?
We have a problem!
It went hot, sir.
The entire reservation just climbed into the mid-nineties. I'm getting just one single heat signature.
What--
We just lost surveillance.
Everyone in hard and fast.
Take the place down.
Any and all force is hereby authorized.

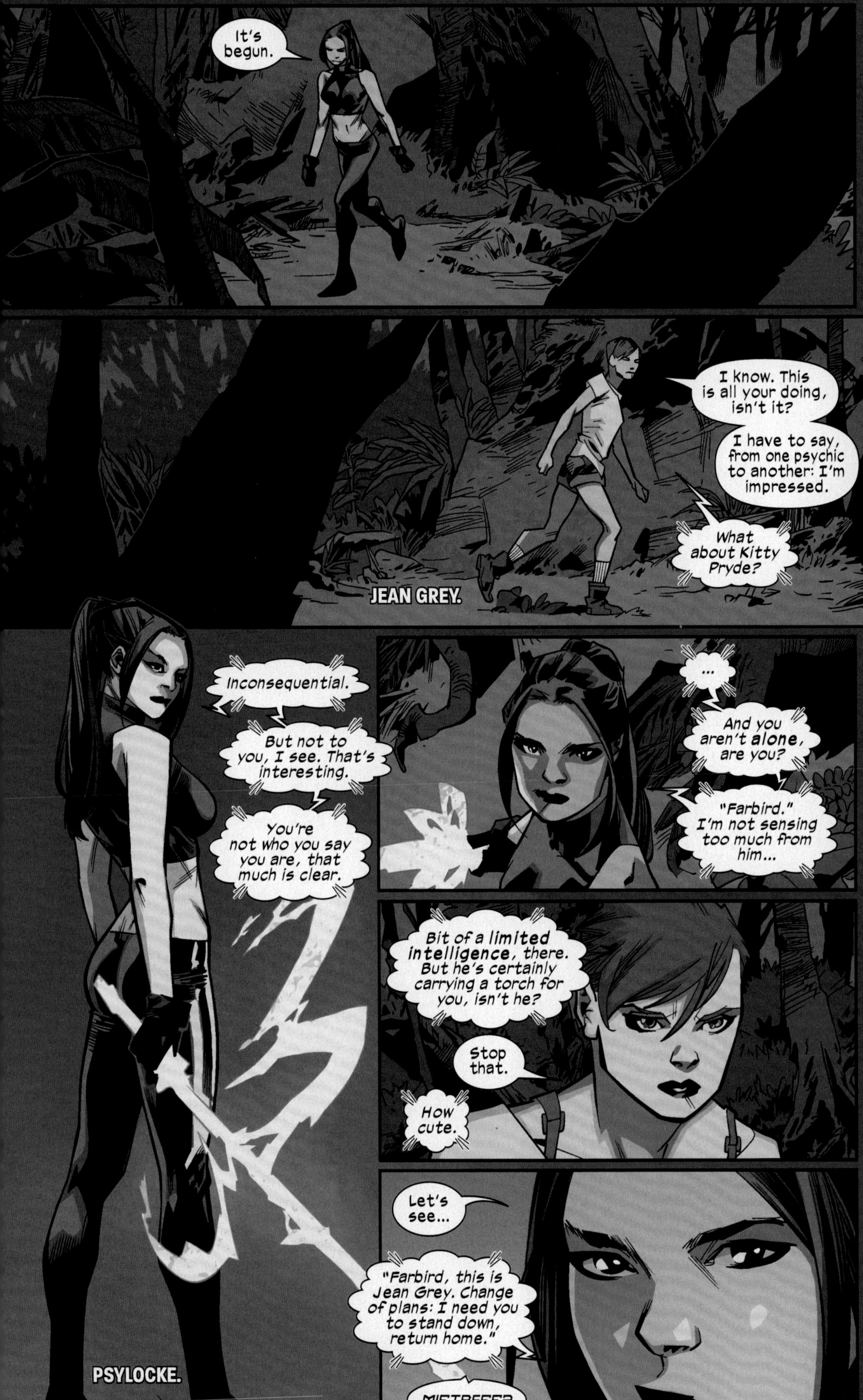

It's begun.
I know. This is all your doing, isn't it?
I have to say, from one psychic to another: I'm impressed.
What about Kitty Pryde?
JEAN GREY.
Inconsequential.
But not to you, I see. That's interesting.
You're not who you say you are, that much is clear.
...
And you aren't alone, are you?
"Farbird." I'm not sensing too much from him...
Bit of a limited intelligence, there. But he's certainly carrying a torch for you, isn't he?
Stop that.
How cute.
Let's see...
"Farbird, this is Jean Grey. Change of plans: I need you to stand down, return home."
MISTRESS?
PSYLOCKE.

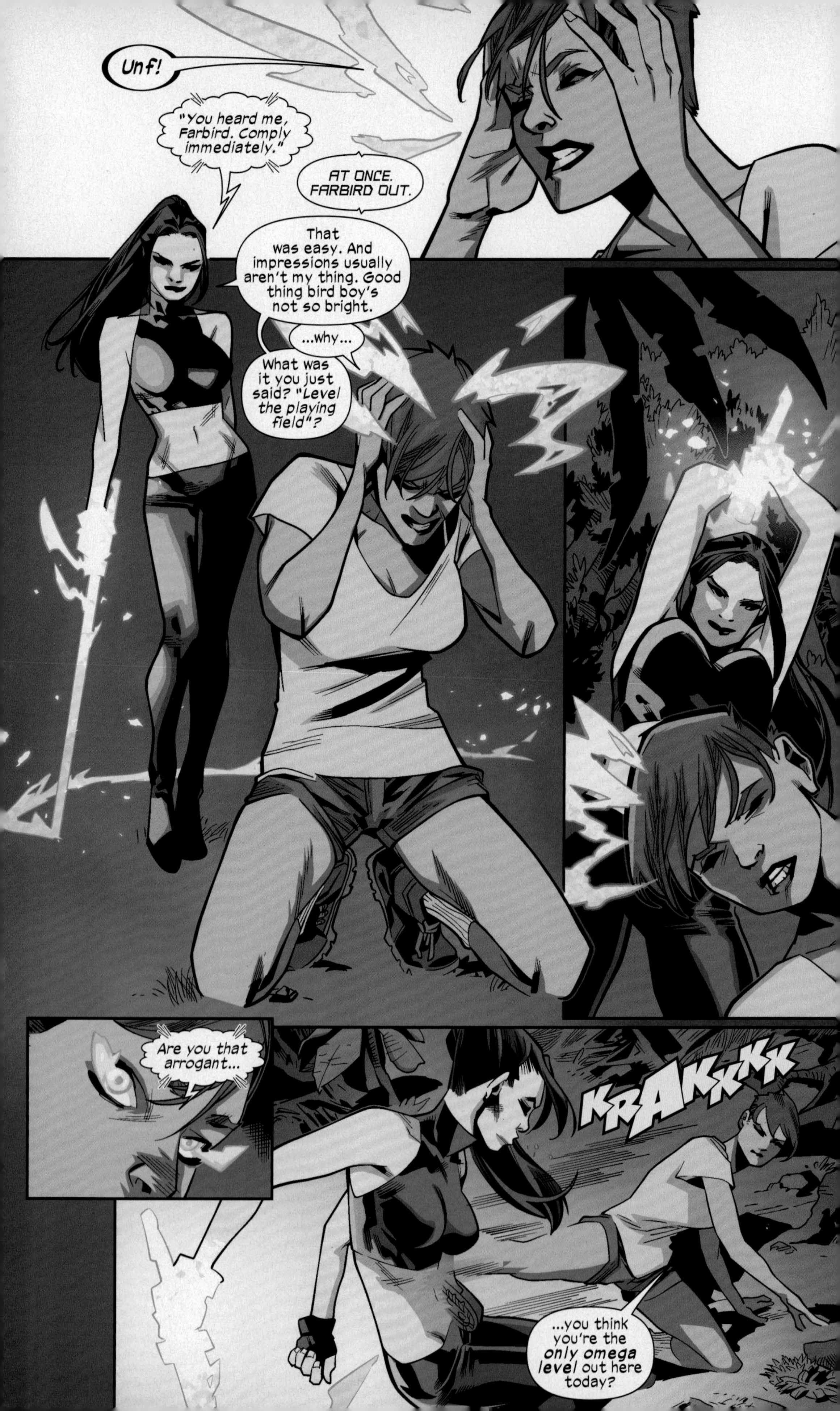

Unf!
"You heard me, Farbird. Comply immediately."
AT ONCE. FARBIRD OUT.
That was easy. And impressions usually aren't my thing. Good thing bird boy's not so bright.
...why...
What was it you just said? "Level the playing field"?
Are you that arrogant...
KRAKKKK
...you think you're the *only omega level* out here today?

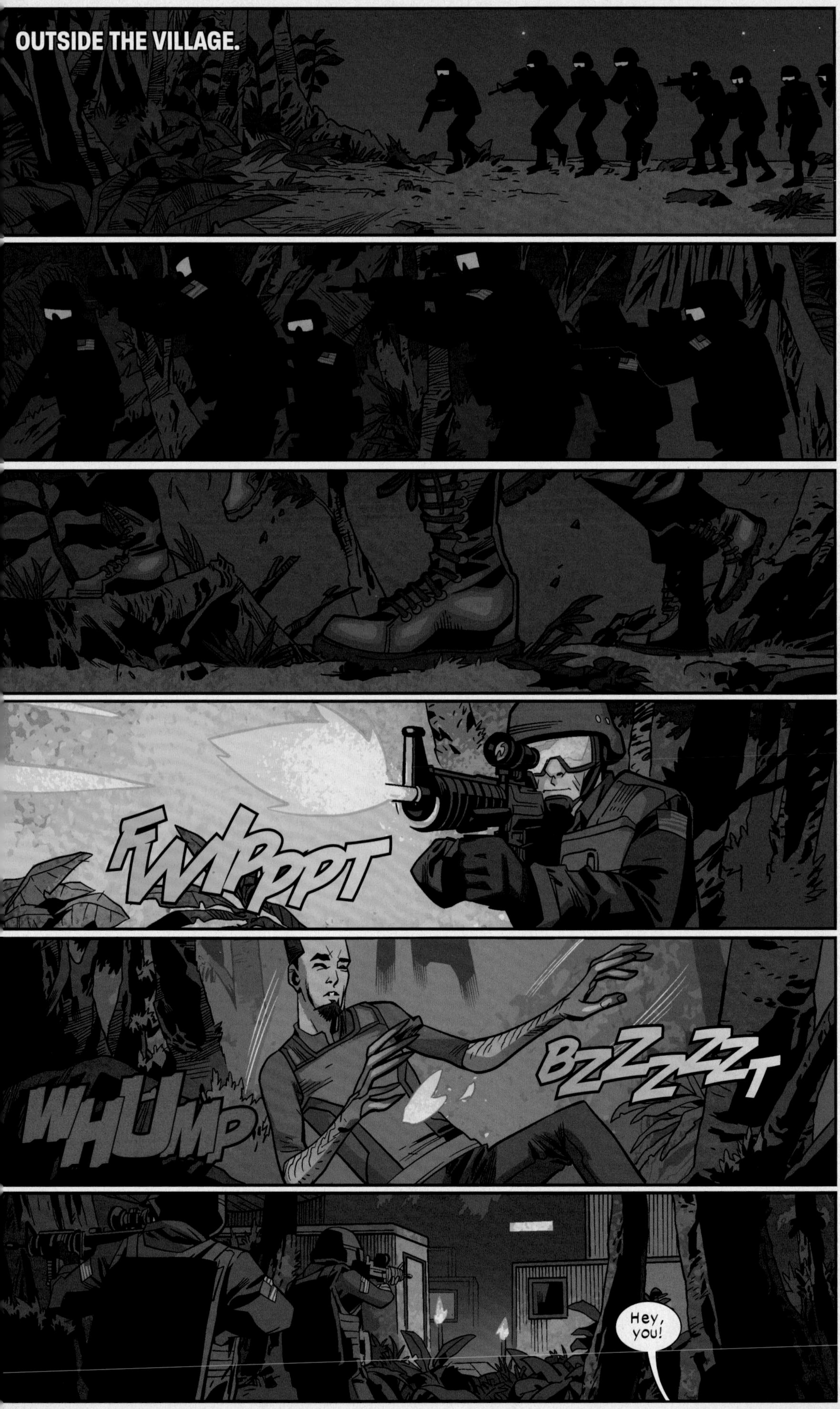
OUTSIDE THE VILLAGE.
FWAPPPT
WHUMP
BZZZZZT
Hey, you!

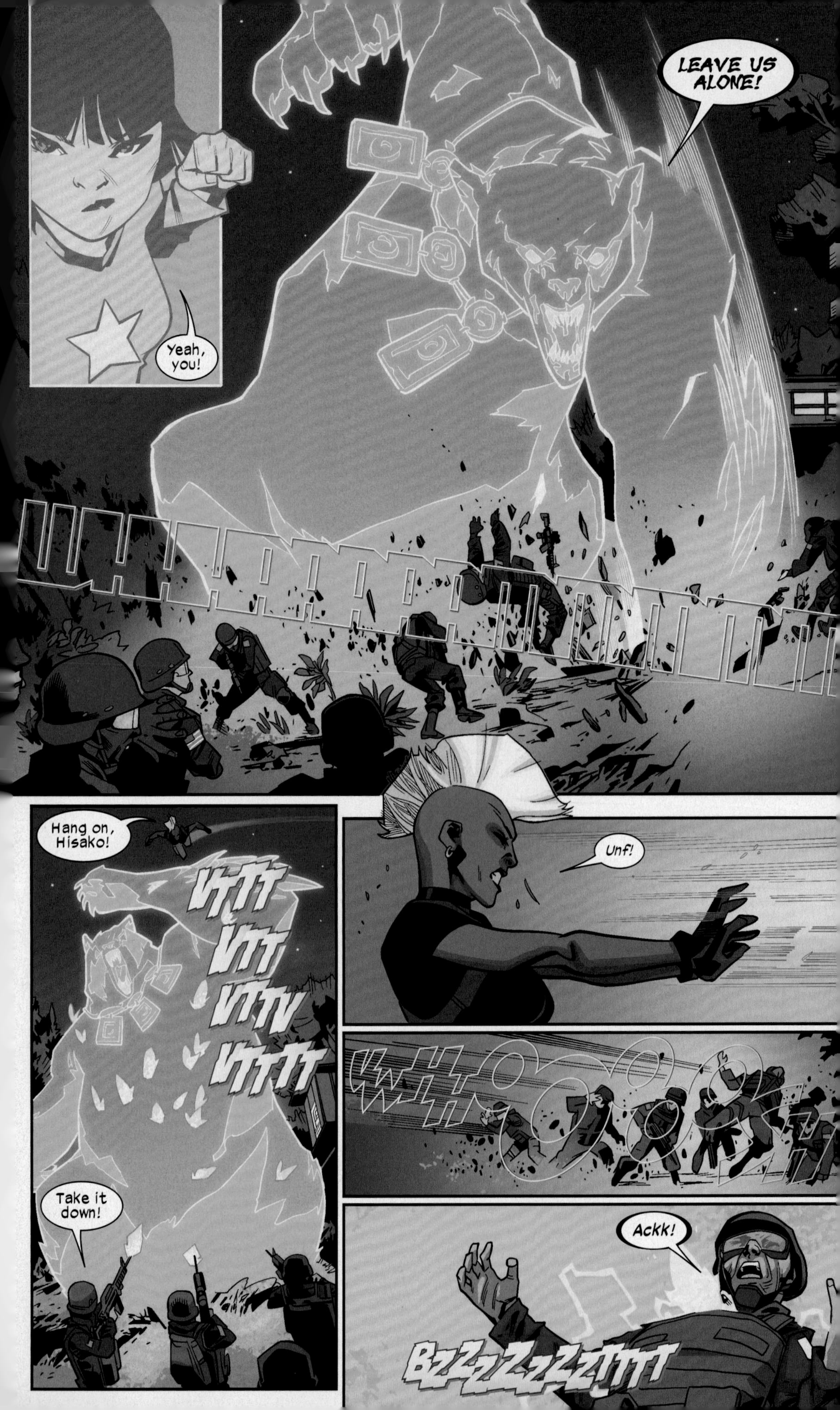

LEAVE US ALONE!
Yeah, you!
Hang on, Hisako!
Take it down!
Unf!
Ackk!
BZZZZZZZZTTTT

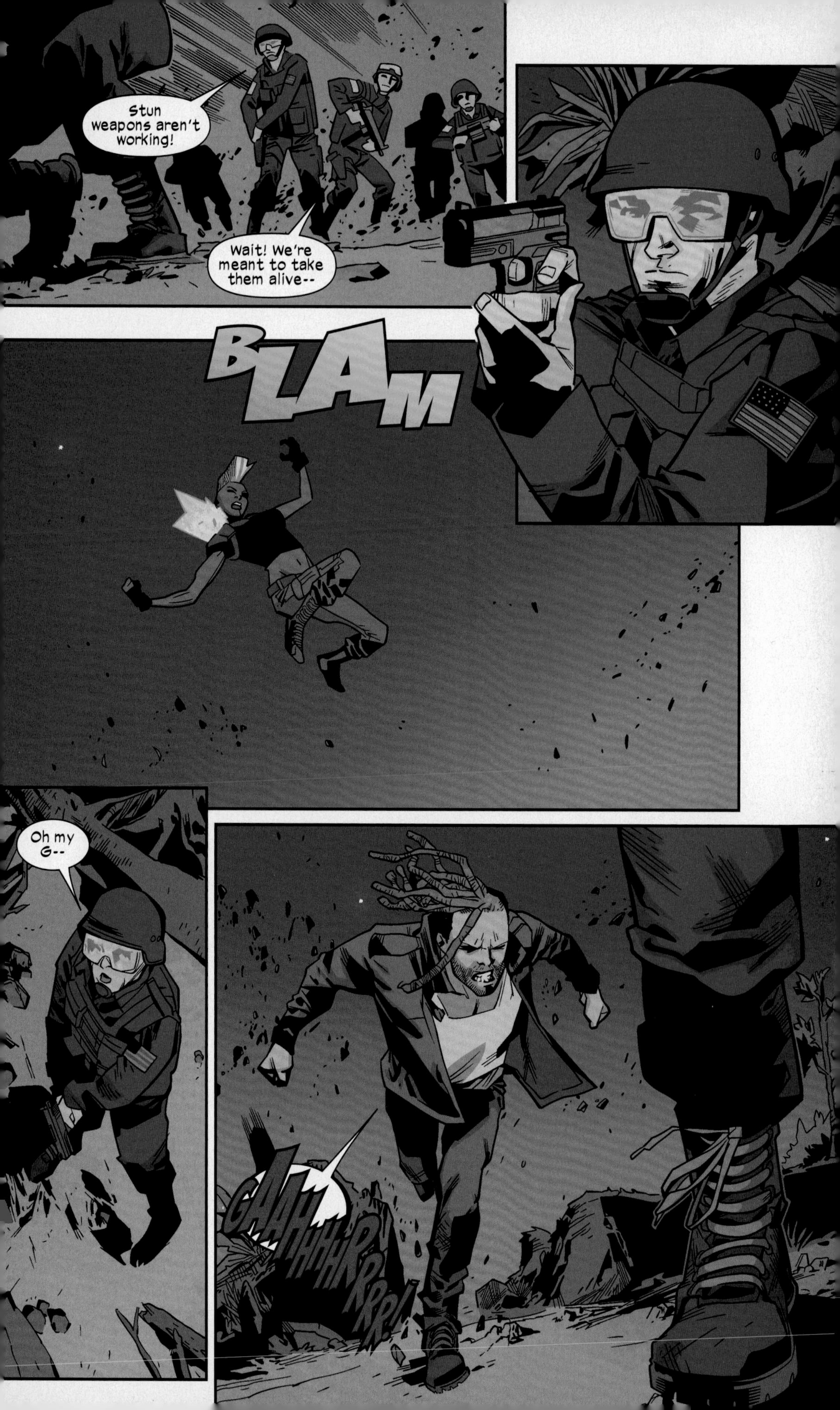
Stun weapons aren't working!
Wait! We're meant to take them alive--
BLAM
Oh my G--
GAHHHHRRRR!

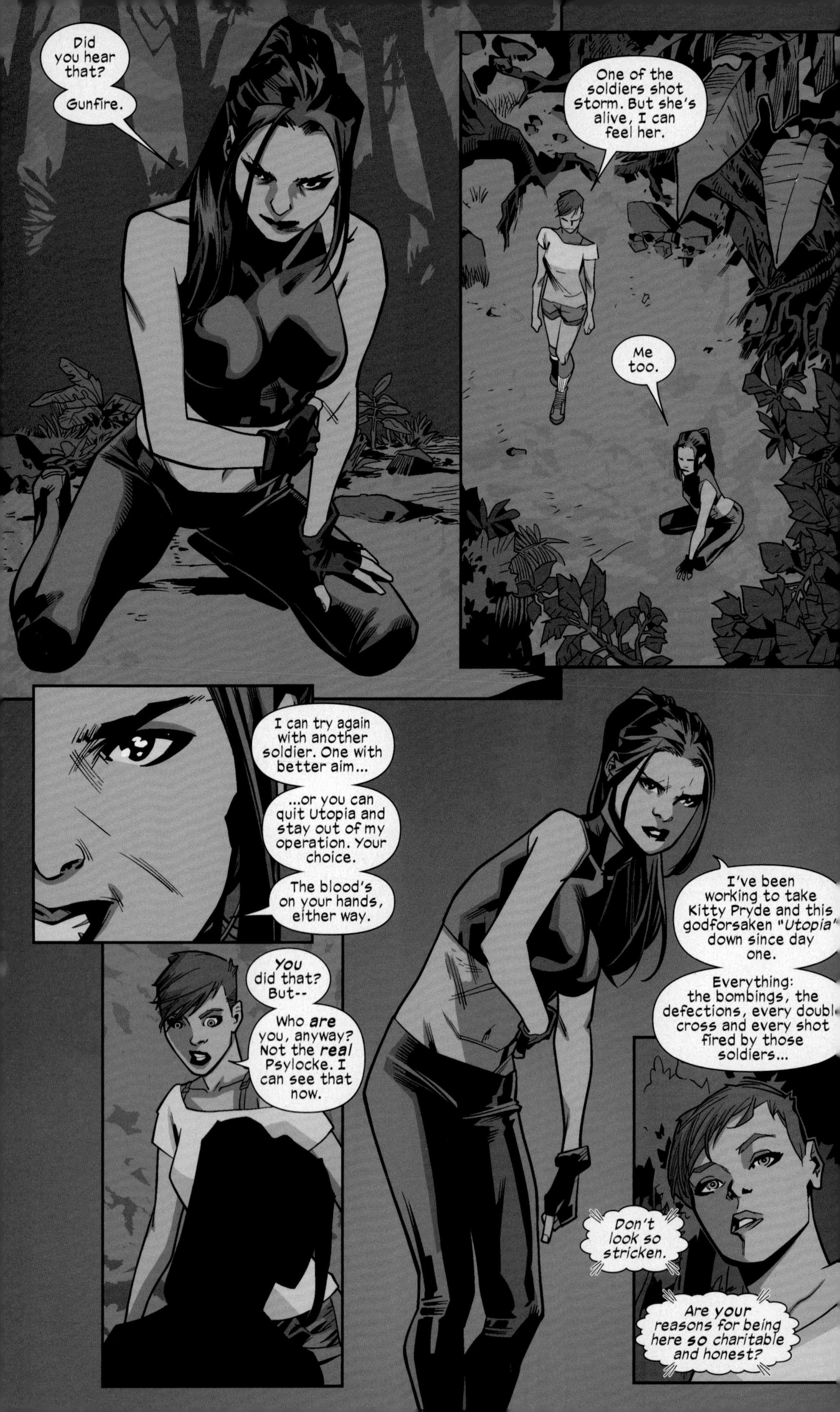

Did you hear that?
Gunfire.
One of the soldiers shot Storm. But she's alive, I can feel her.
Me too.
I can try again with another soldier. One with better aim...
...or you can quit Utopia and stay out of my operation. Your choice.
The blood's on your hands, either way.
You did that? But--
Who *are* you, anyway? Not the *real* Psylocke. I can see that now.
I've been working to take Kitty Pryde and this godforsaken *"Utopia"* down since day one.
Everything: the bombings, the defections, every doubl cross and every shot fired by those soldiers...
Don't look so stricken.
Are *your* reasons for being here *so* charitable and honest?

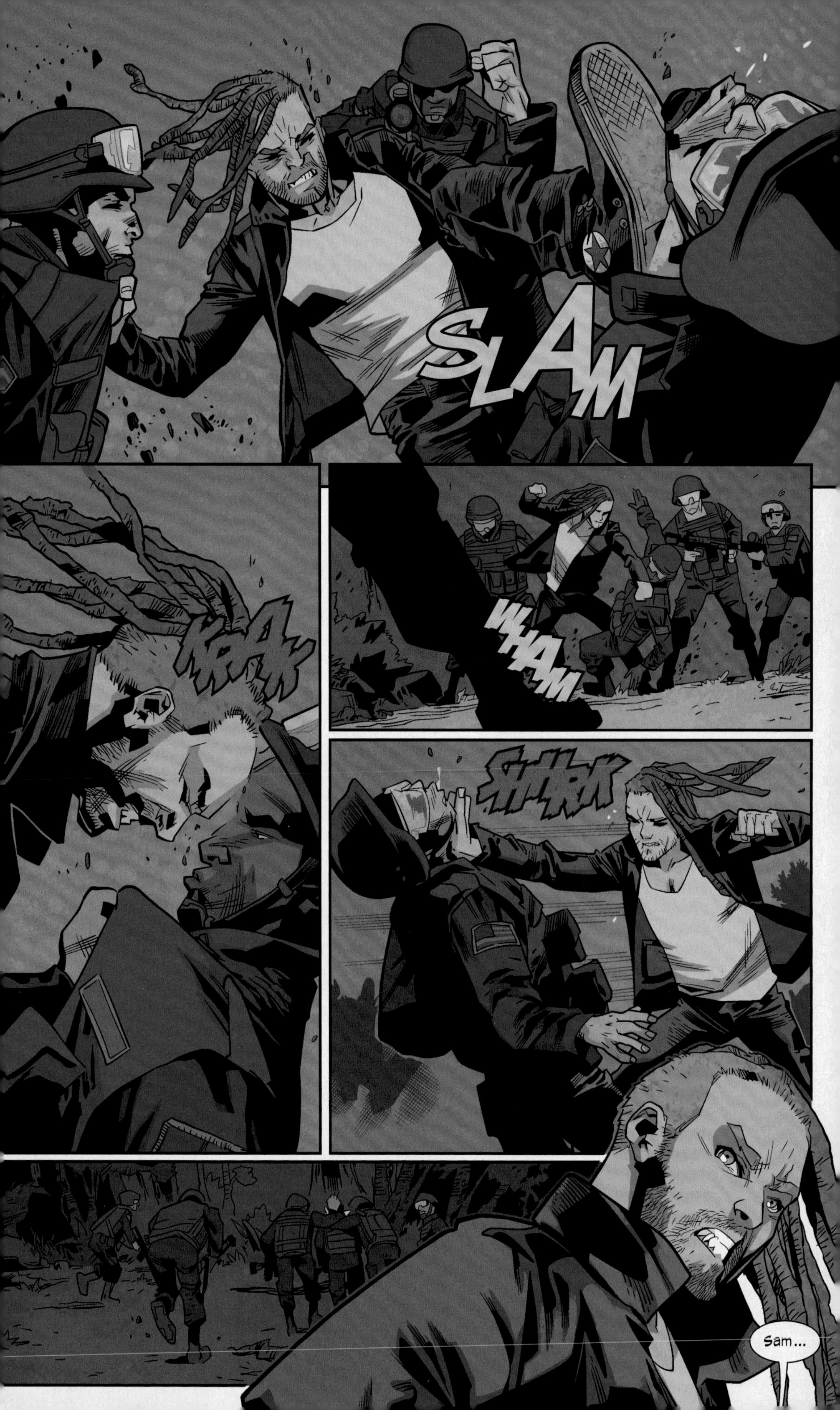

SLAM
KRAK
WHAM
SHHRK
Sam...

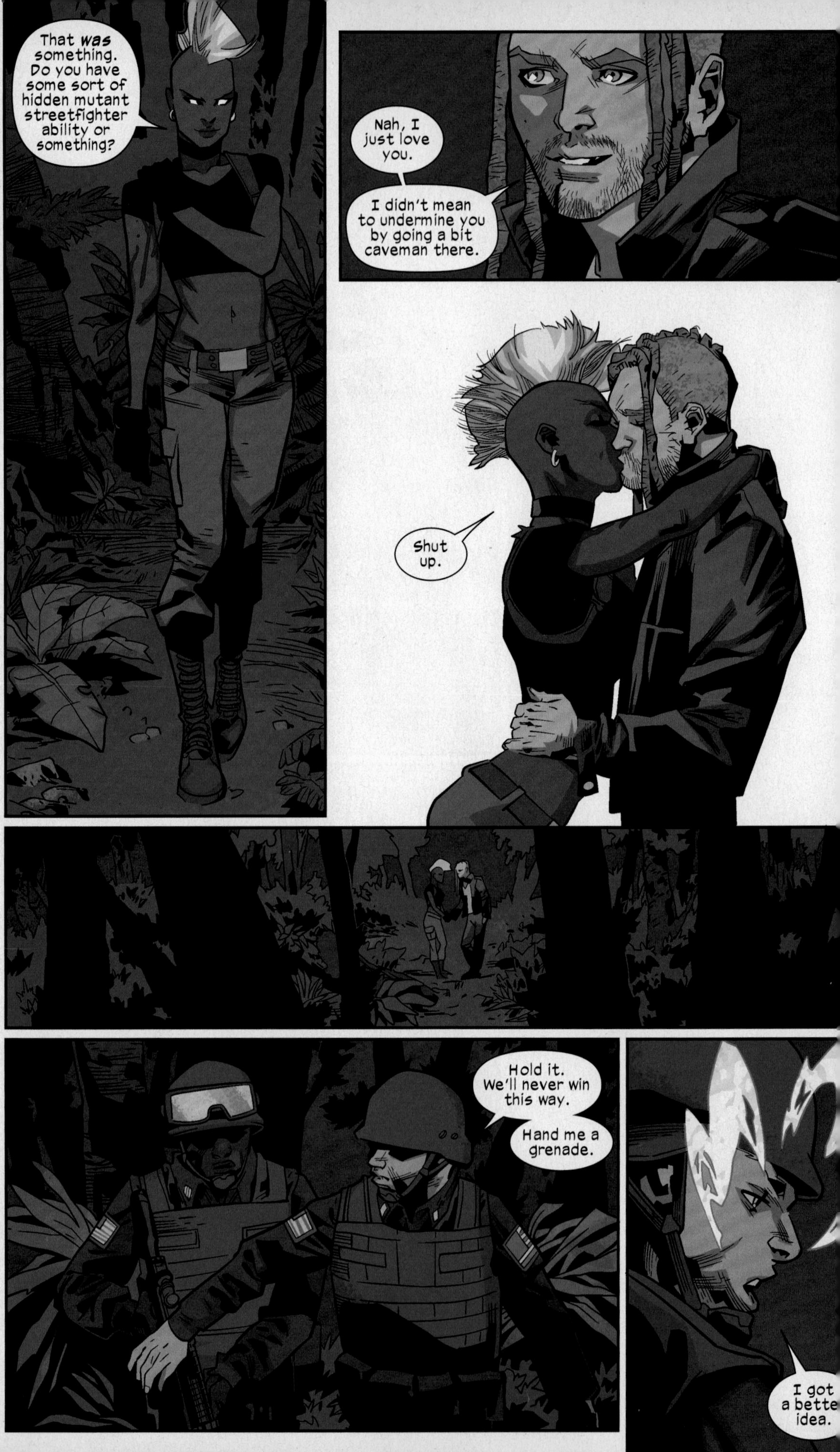
That *was* something. Do you have some sort of hidden mutant streetfighter ability or something?
Nah, I just love you.
I didn't mean to undermine you by going a bit caveman there.
Shut up.
Hold it. We'll never win this way.
Hand me a grenade.
I got a bette idea.

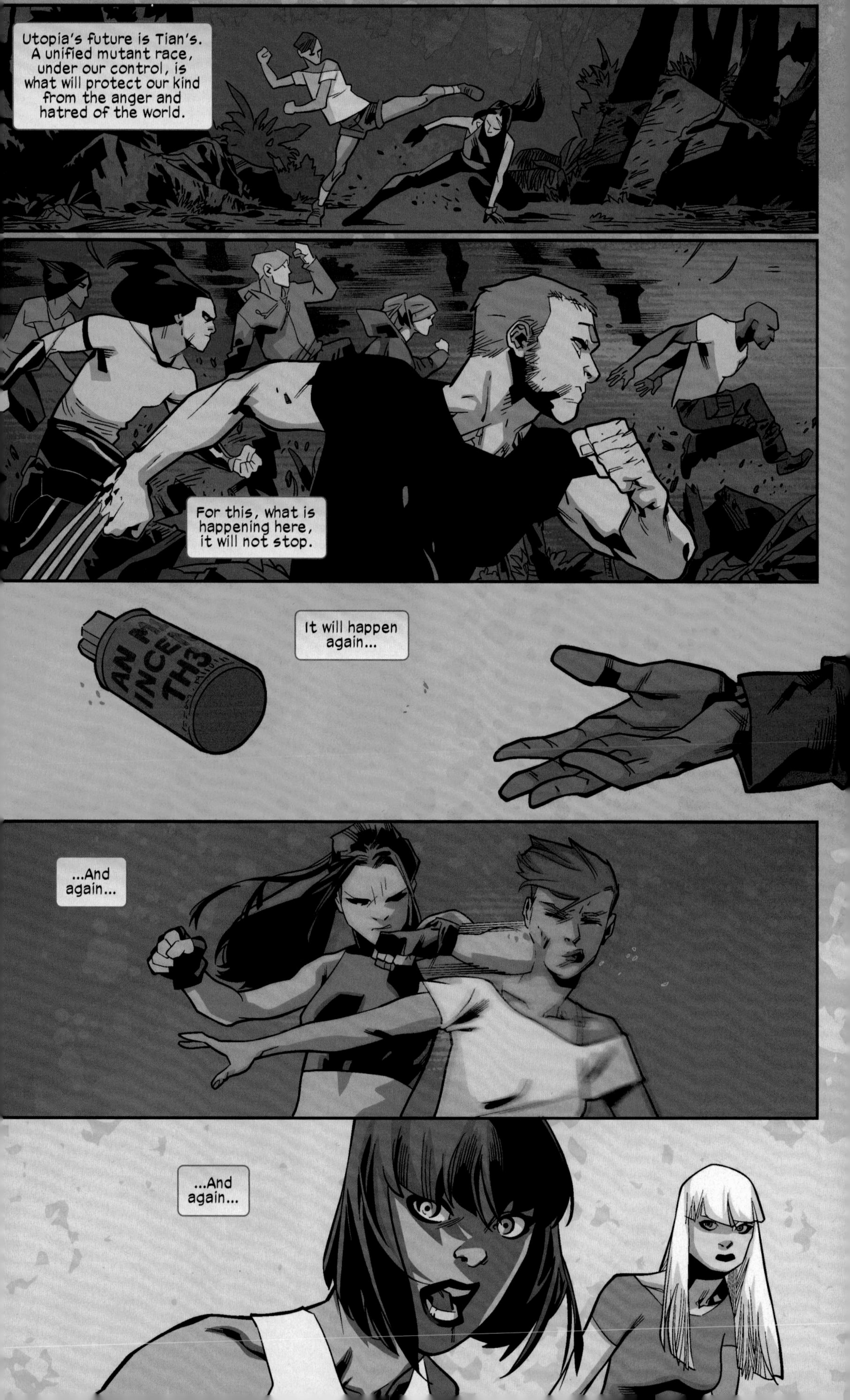
Utopia's future is Tian's. A unified mutant race, under our control, is what will protect our kind from the anger and hatred of the world.
For this, what is happening here, it will not stop.
It will happen again...
...And again...
...And again...

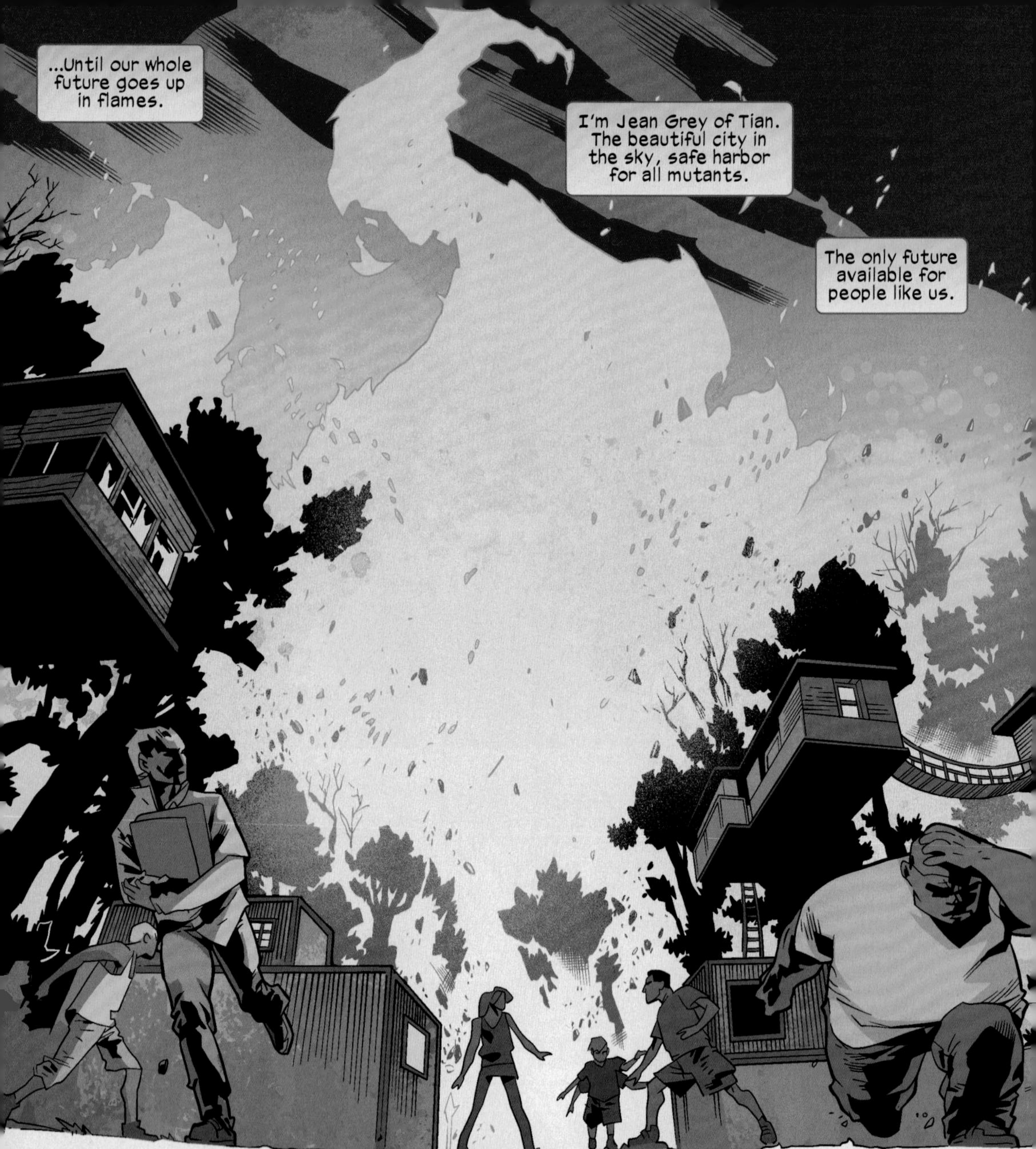
...Until our whole future goes up in flames.
I'm Jean Grey of Tian. The beautiful city in the sky, safe harbor for all mutants.
The only future available for people like us.

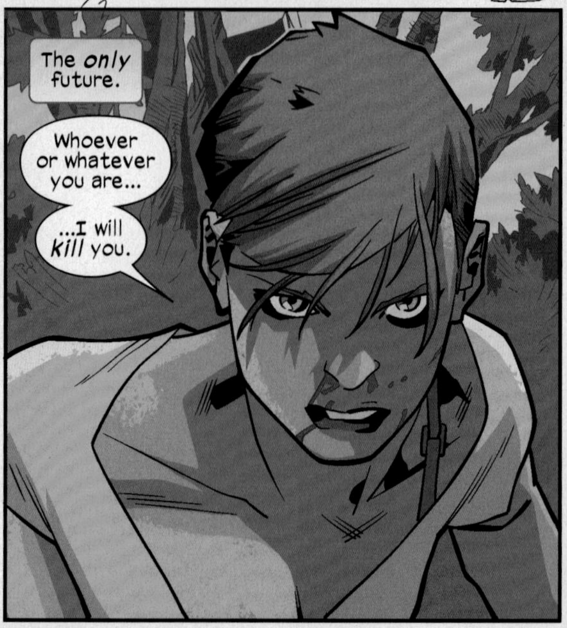
The *only* future.
Whoever or whatever you are...
...I will *kill* you.

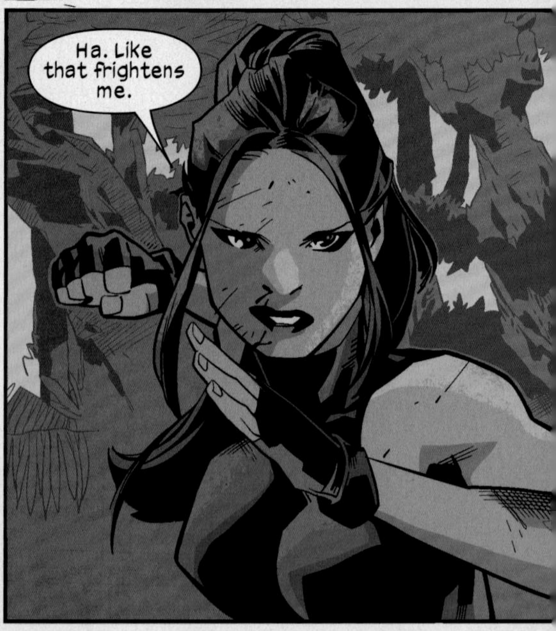
Ha. Like that frightens me.

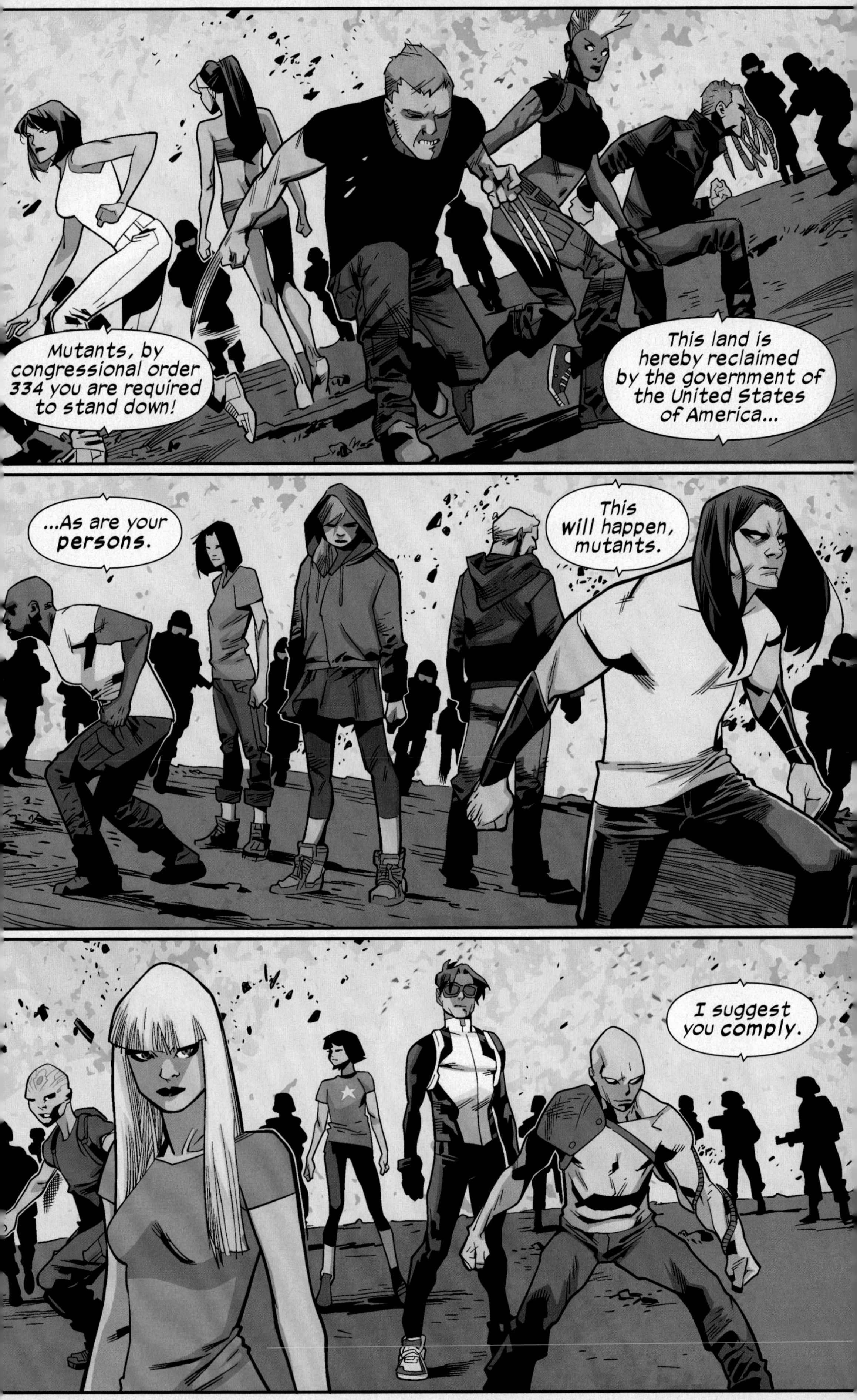
Mutants, by congressional order 334 you are required to stand down!
This land is hereby reclaimed by the government of the United States of America...
...As are your **persons.**
This will happen, mutants.
I suggest you **comply.**

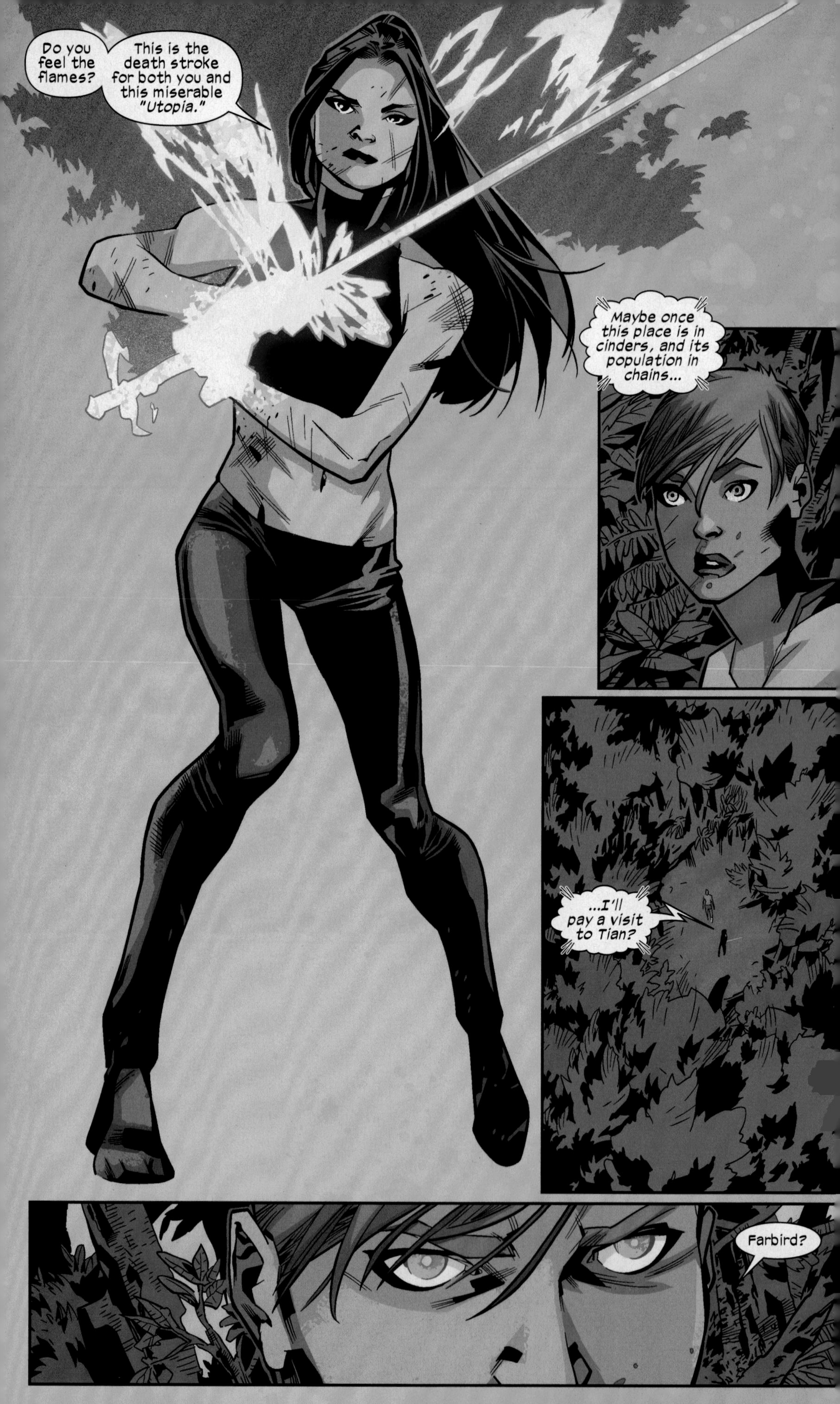

Do you feel the flames?
This is the death stroke for both you and this miserable "Utopia."
Maybe once this place is in cinders, and its population in chains...
...I'll pay a visit to Tian?
Farbird?

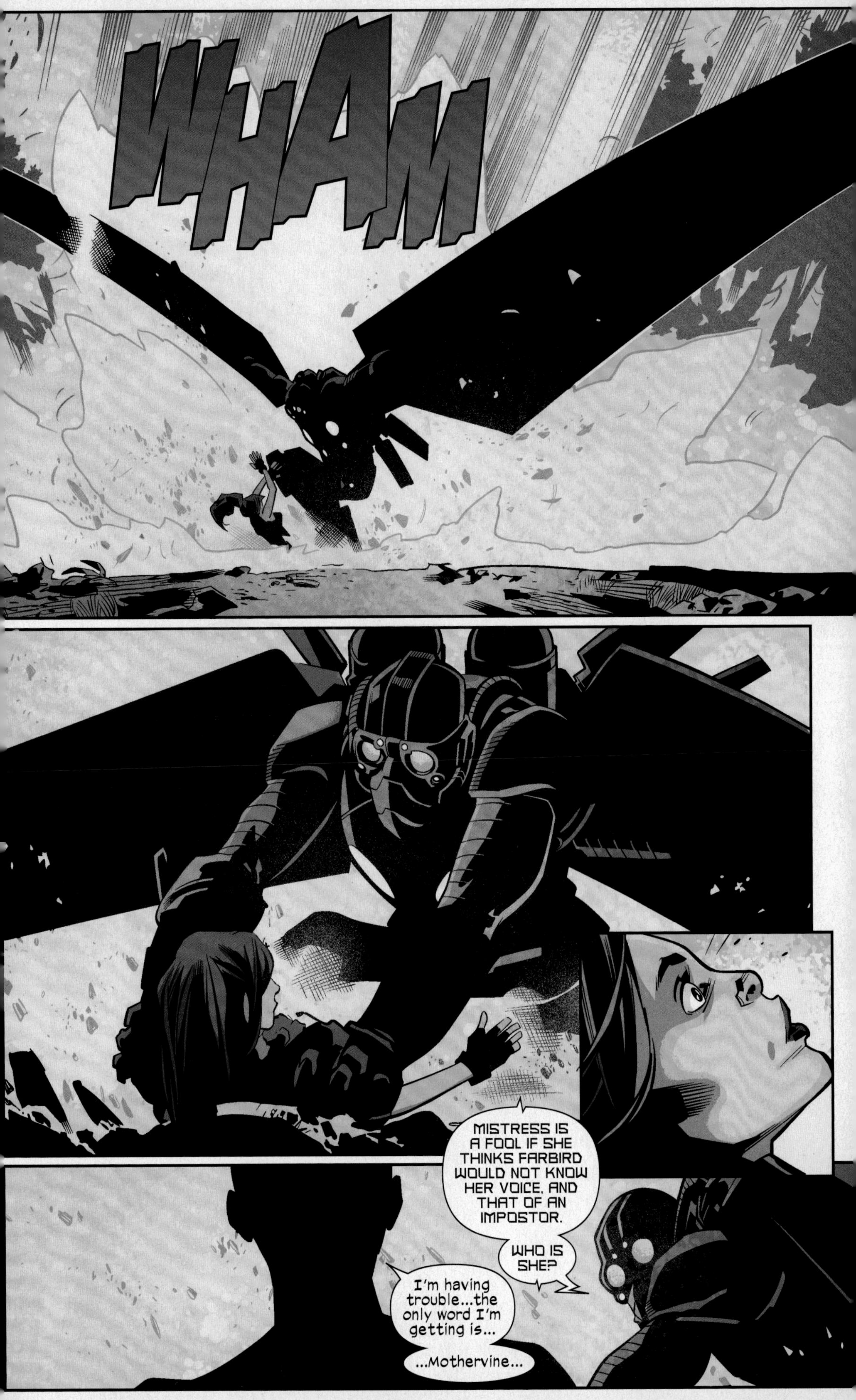
WHAM
MISTRESS IS A FOOL IF SHE THINKS FARBIRD WOULD NOT KNOW HER VOICE, AND THAT OF AN IMPOSTOR.
WHO IS SHE?
I'm having trouble...the only word I'm getting is...
...Mothervine...

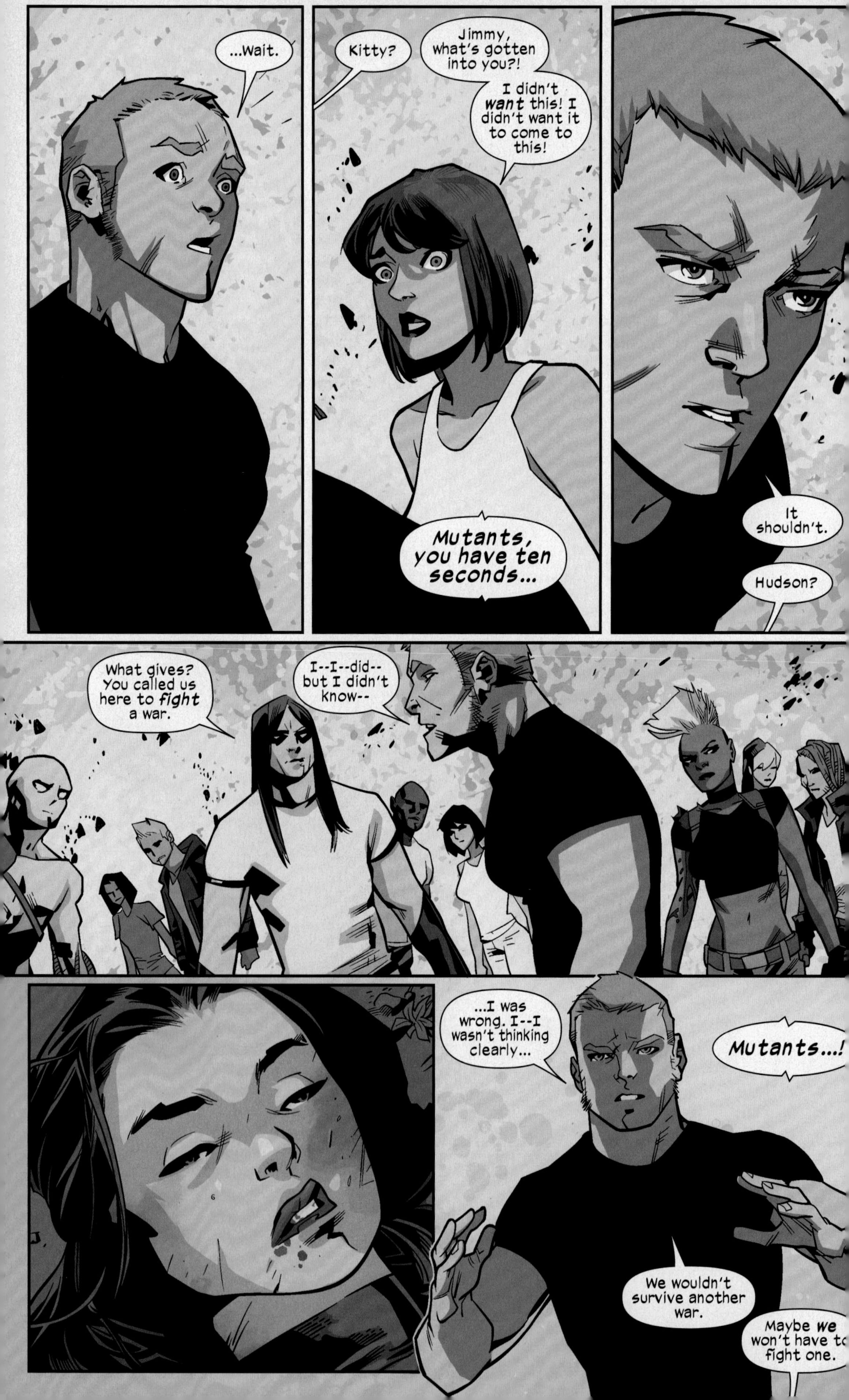
...Wait.
Kitty?
Jimmy, what's gotten into you?!
I didn't *want* this! I didn't want it to come to this!
Mutants, you have ten seconds...
It shouldn't.
Hudson?
What gives? You called us here to *fight* a war.
I--I--did-- but I didn't know--
...I was wrong. I--I wasn't thinking clearly...
Mutants...!
We wouldn't survive another war.
Maybe *we* won't have to fight one.

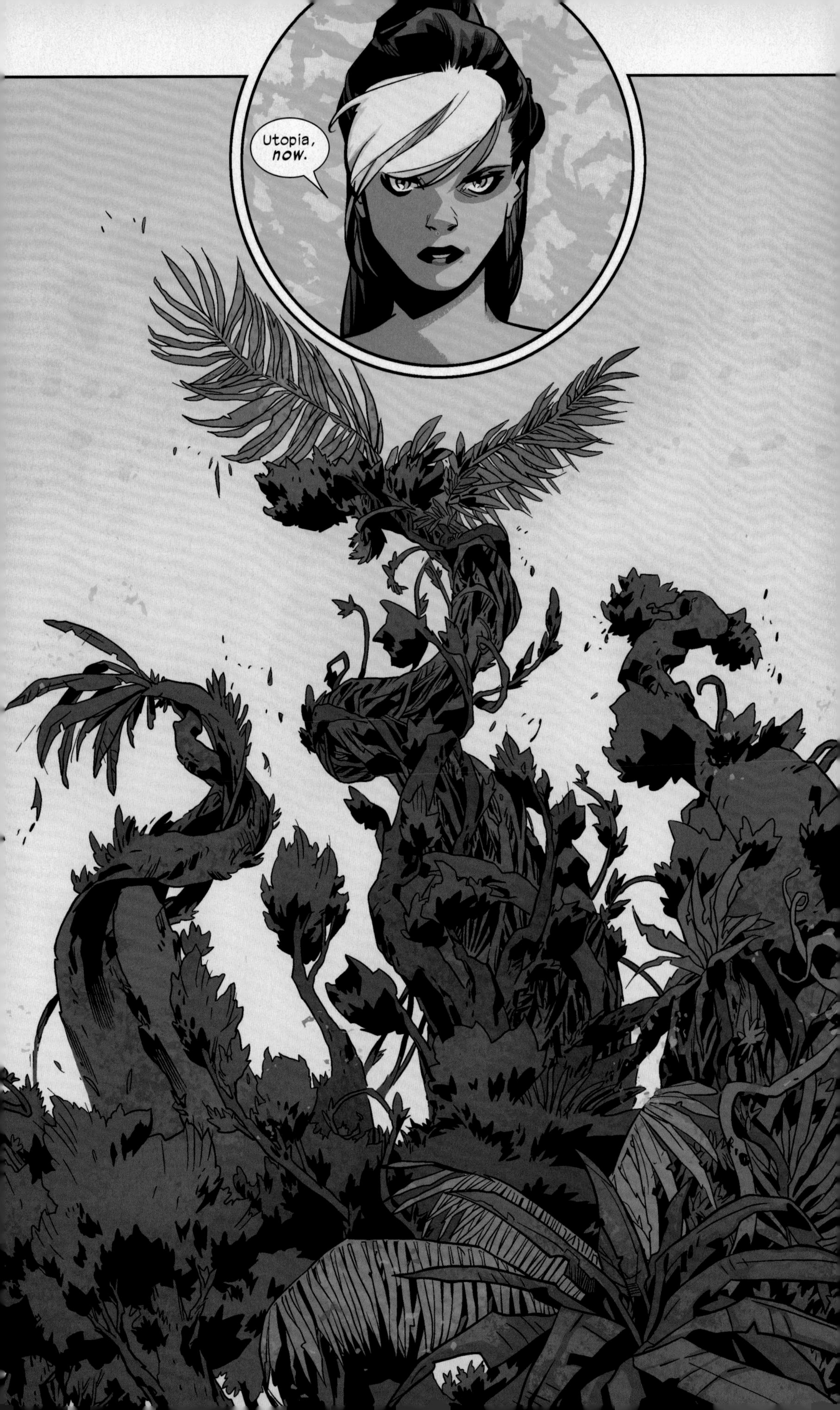
Utopia, now.

28

NATURAL RESOURCES

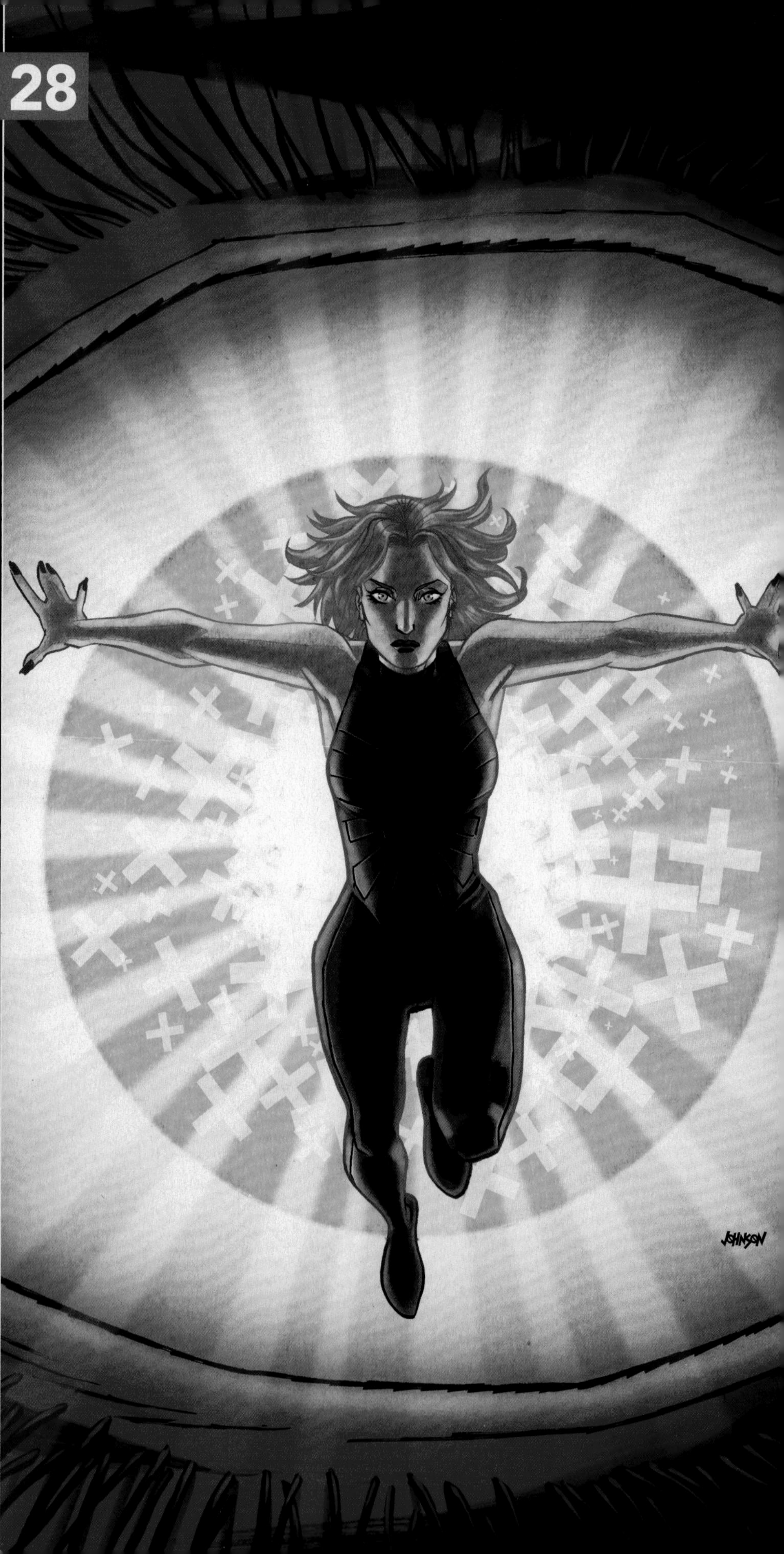

JOHNSON

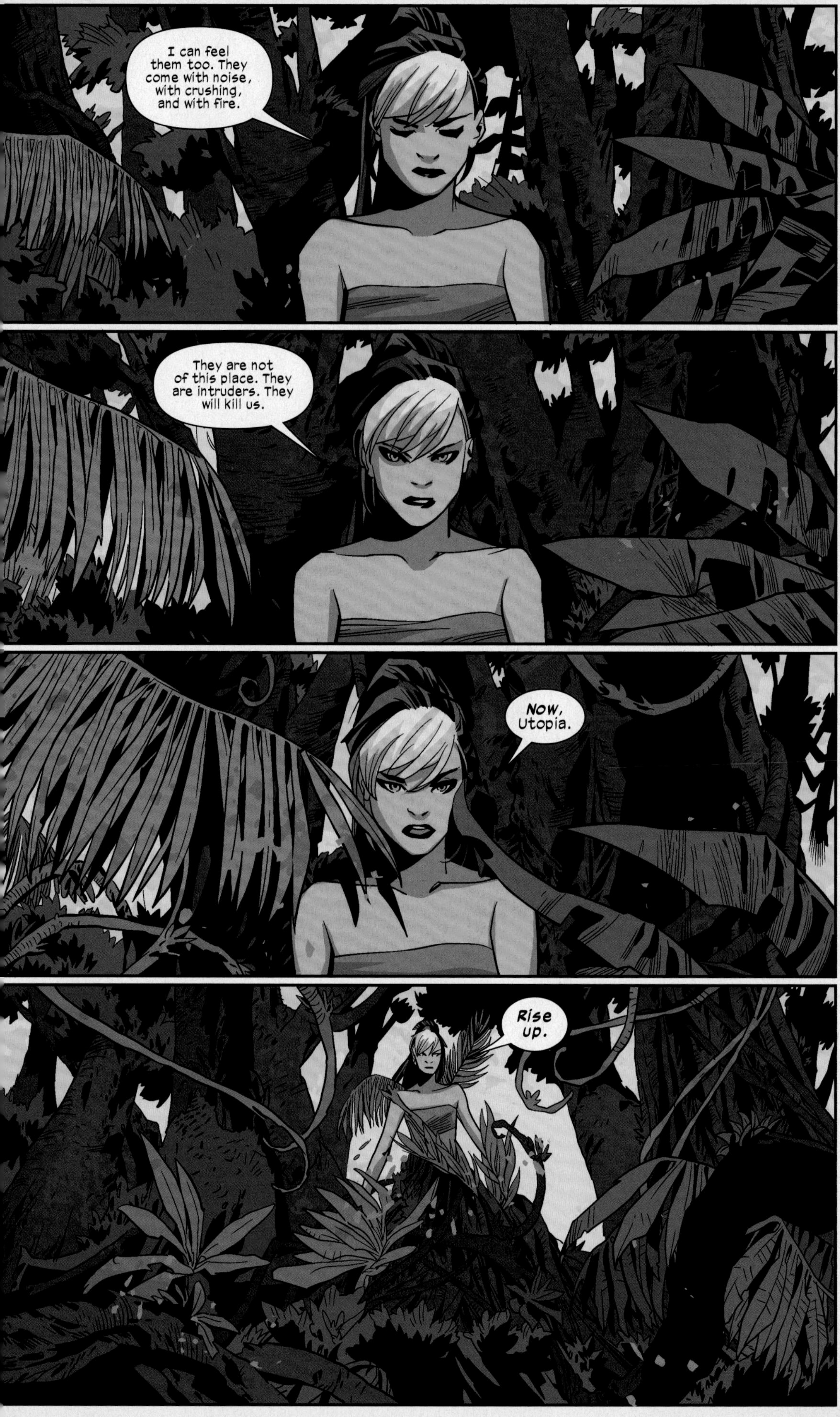
I can feel them too. They come with noise, with crushing, and with fire.
They are not of this place. They are intruders. They will kill us.
NOW, Utopia.
Rise up.

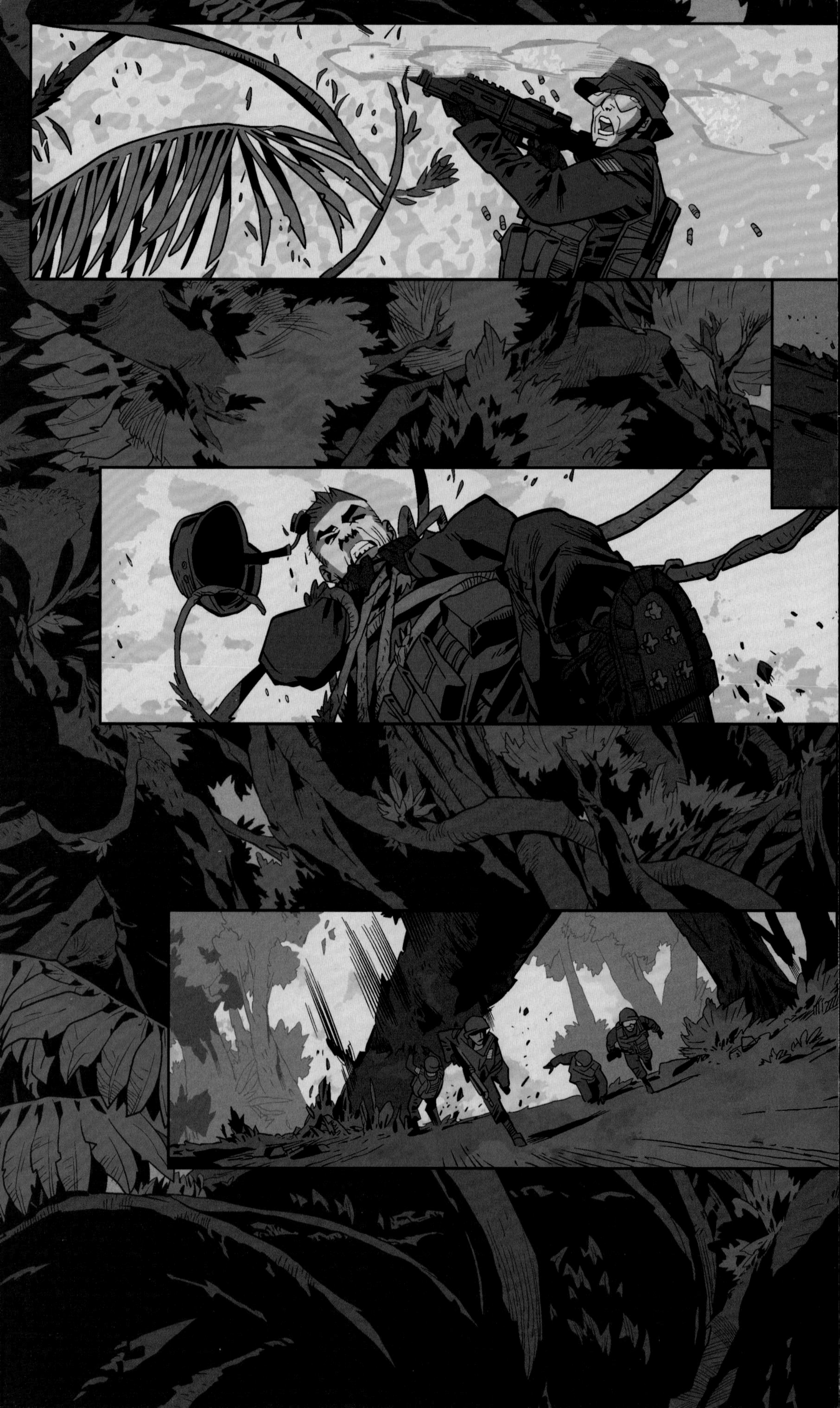

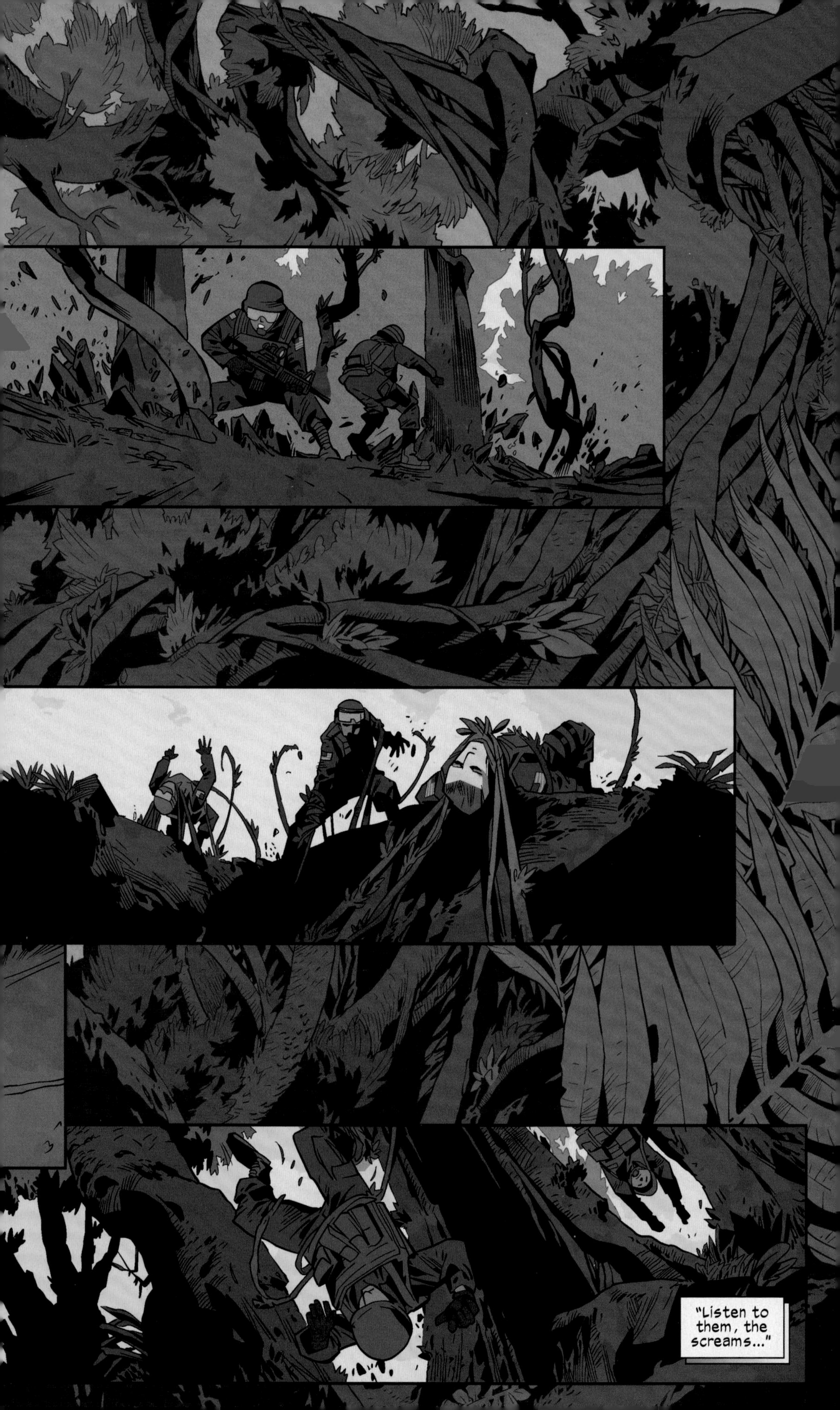
"Listen to them, the screams..."

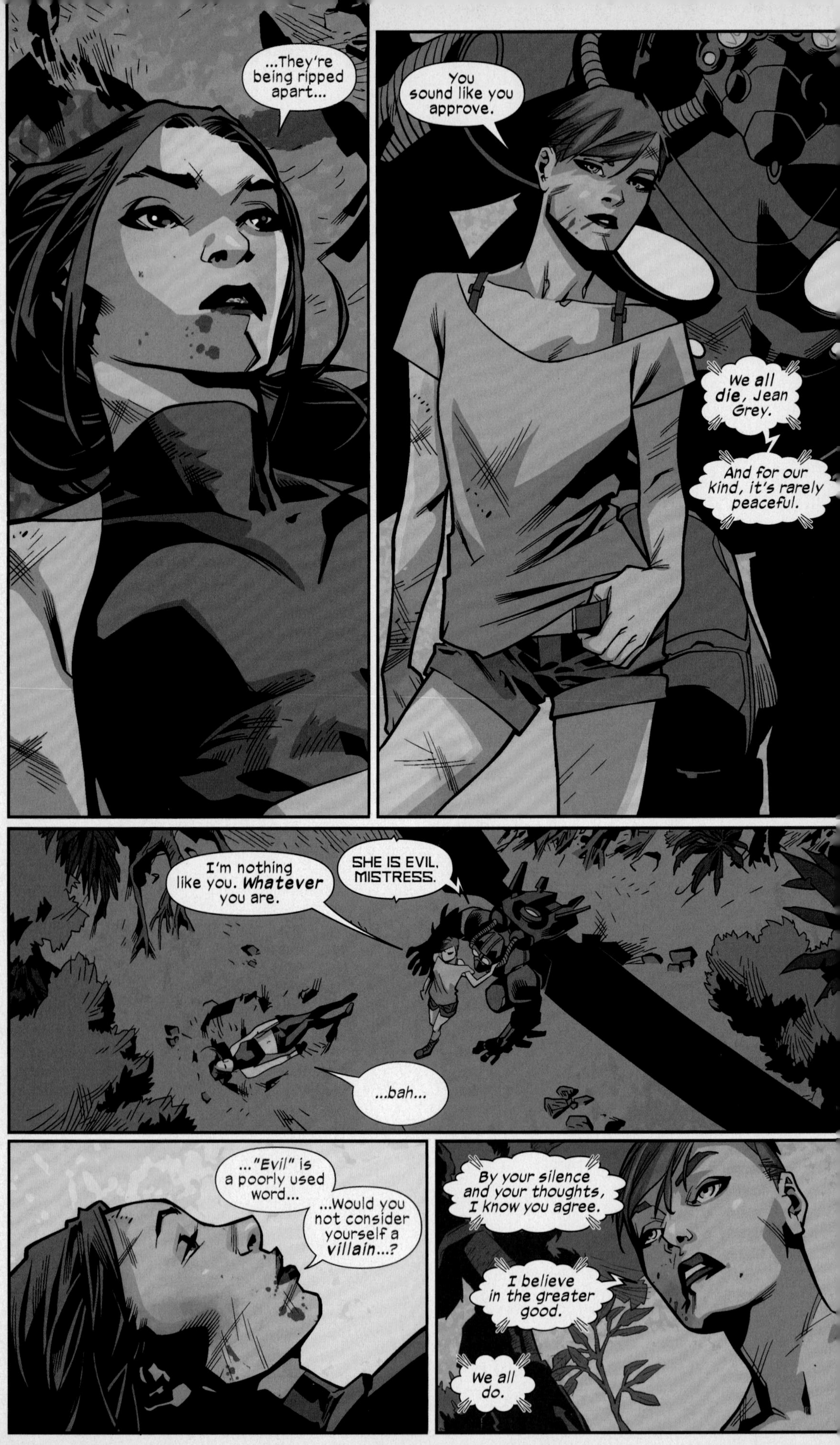

...They're being ripped apart...
You sound like you approve.
We all die, Jean Grey.
And for our kind, it's rarely peaceful.
I'm nothing like you. Whatever you are.
SHE IS EVIL, MISTRESS.
...bah...
..."Evil" is a poorly used word...
...Would you not consider yourself a villain...?
By your silence and your thoughts, I know you agree.
I believe in the greater good.
We all do.

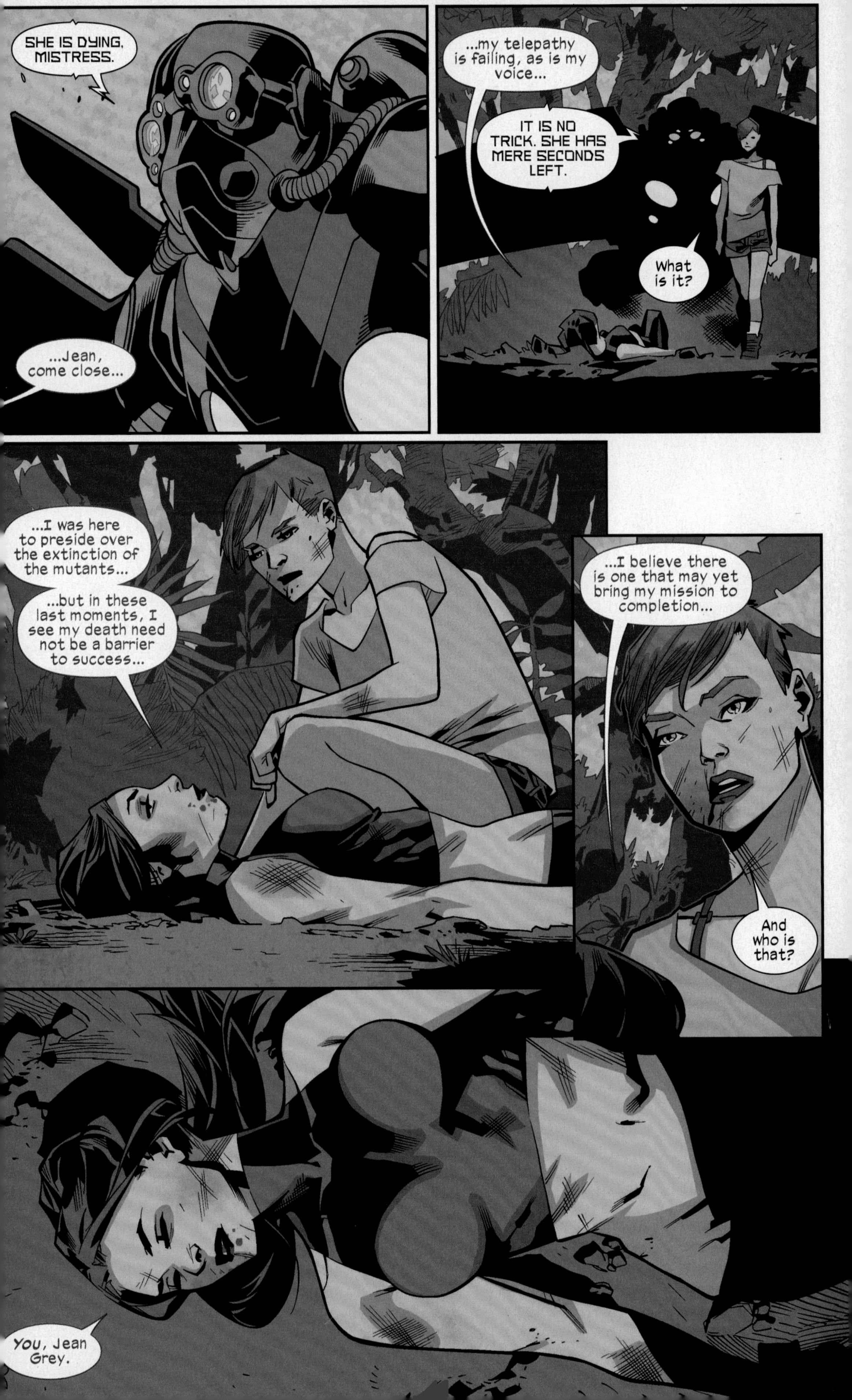
SHE IS DYING, MISTRESS.
...Jean, come close...
...my telepathy is failing, as is my voice...
IT IS NO TRICK. SHE HAS MERE SECONDS LEFT.
What is it?
...I was here to preside over the extinction of the mutants...
...but in these last moments, I see my death need not be a barrier to success...
...I believe there is one that may yet bring my mission to completion...
And who is that?
YOU, Jean Grey.

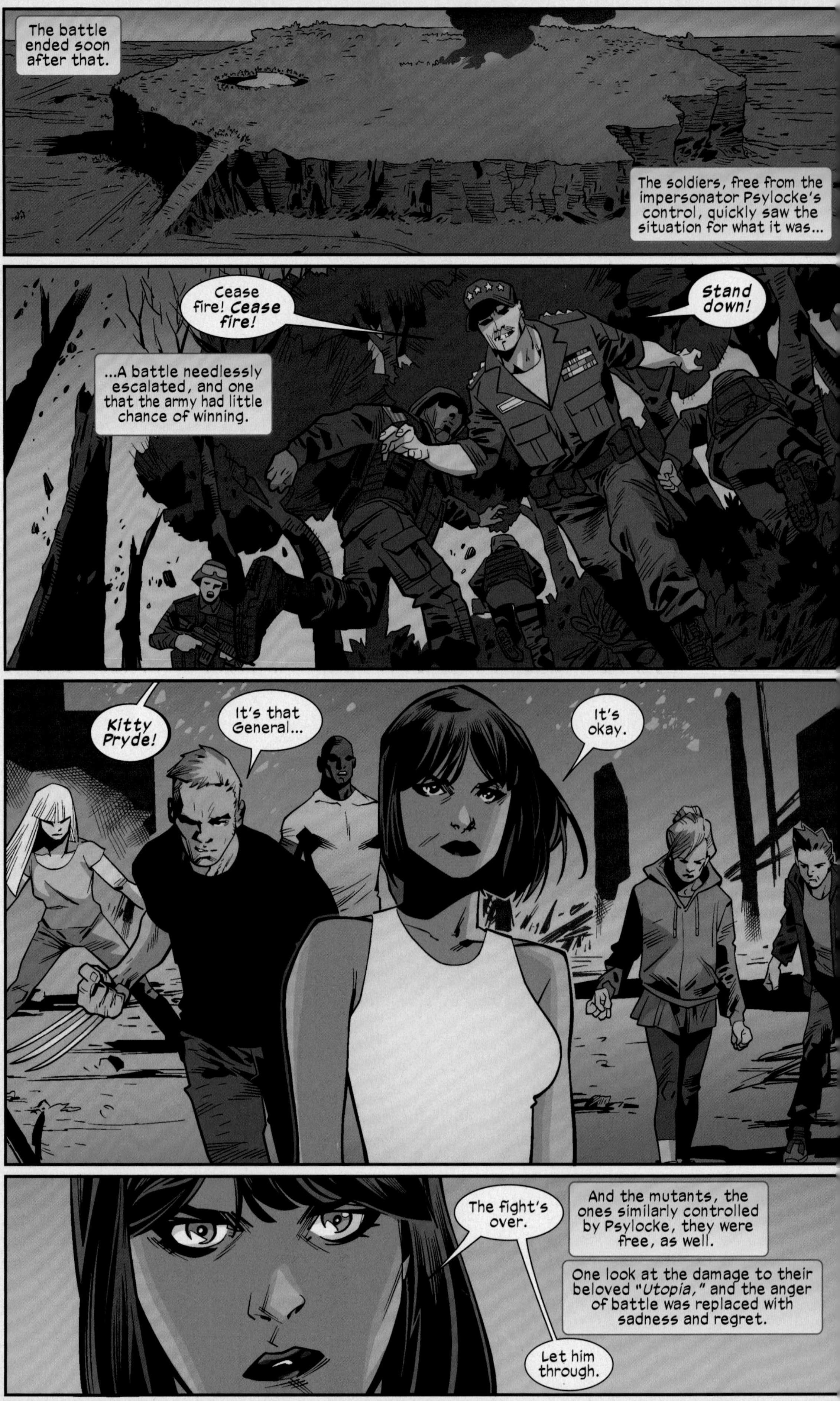

The battle ended soon after that.
The soldiers, free from the impersonator Psylocke's control, quickly saw the situation for what it was...
Cease fire! *Cease fire!*
Stand down!
...A battle needlessly escalated, and one that the army had little chance of winning.
Kitty Pryde!
It's that General...
It's okay.
The fight's over.
And the mutants, the ones similarly controlled by Psylocke, they were free, as well.
One look at the damage to their beloved "*Utopia,*" and the anger of battle was replaced with sadness and regret.
Let him through.

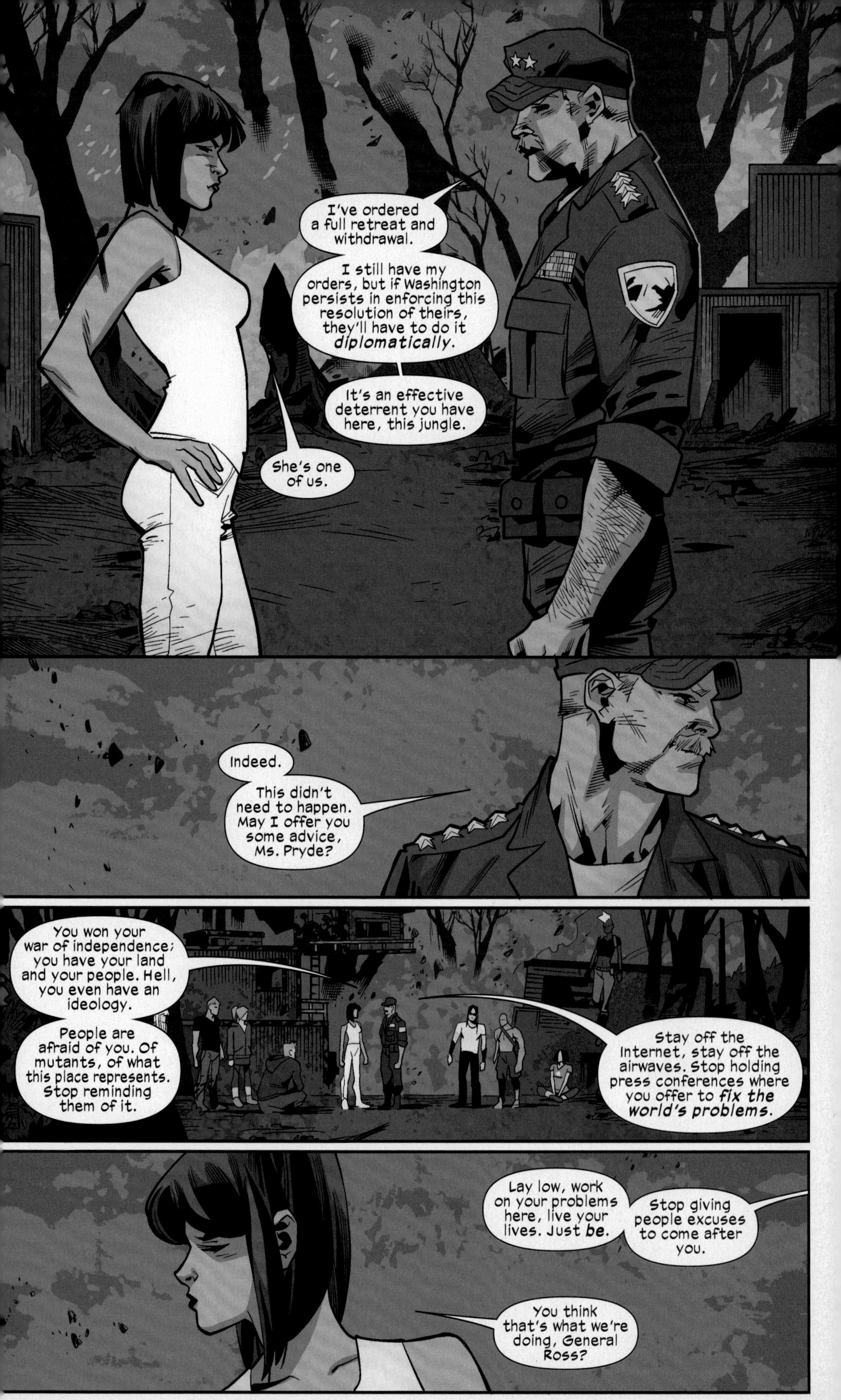
I've ordered a full retreat and withdrawal.
I still have my orders, but if Washington persists in enforcing this resolution of theirs, they'll have to do it *diplomatically*.
It's an effective deterrent you have here, this jungle.
She's one of us.
Indeed.
This didn't need to happen. May I offer you some advice, Ms. Pryde?
You won your war of independence; you have your land and your people. Hell, you even have an ideology.
People are afraid of you. Of mutants, of what this place represents. Stop reminding them of it.
Stay off the Internet, stay off the airwaves. Stop holding press conferences where you offer to *fix the world's problems*.
Lay low, work on your problems here, live your lives. Just *be*.
Stop giving people excuses to come after you.
You think that's what we're doing, General Ross?

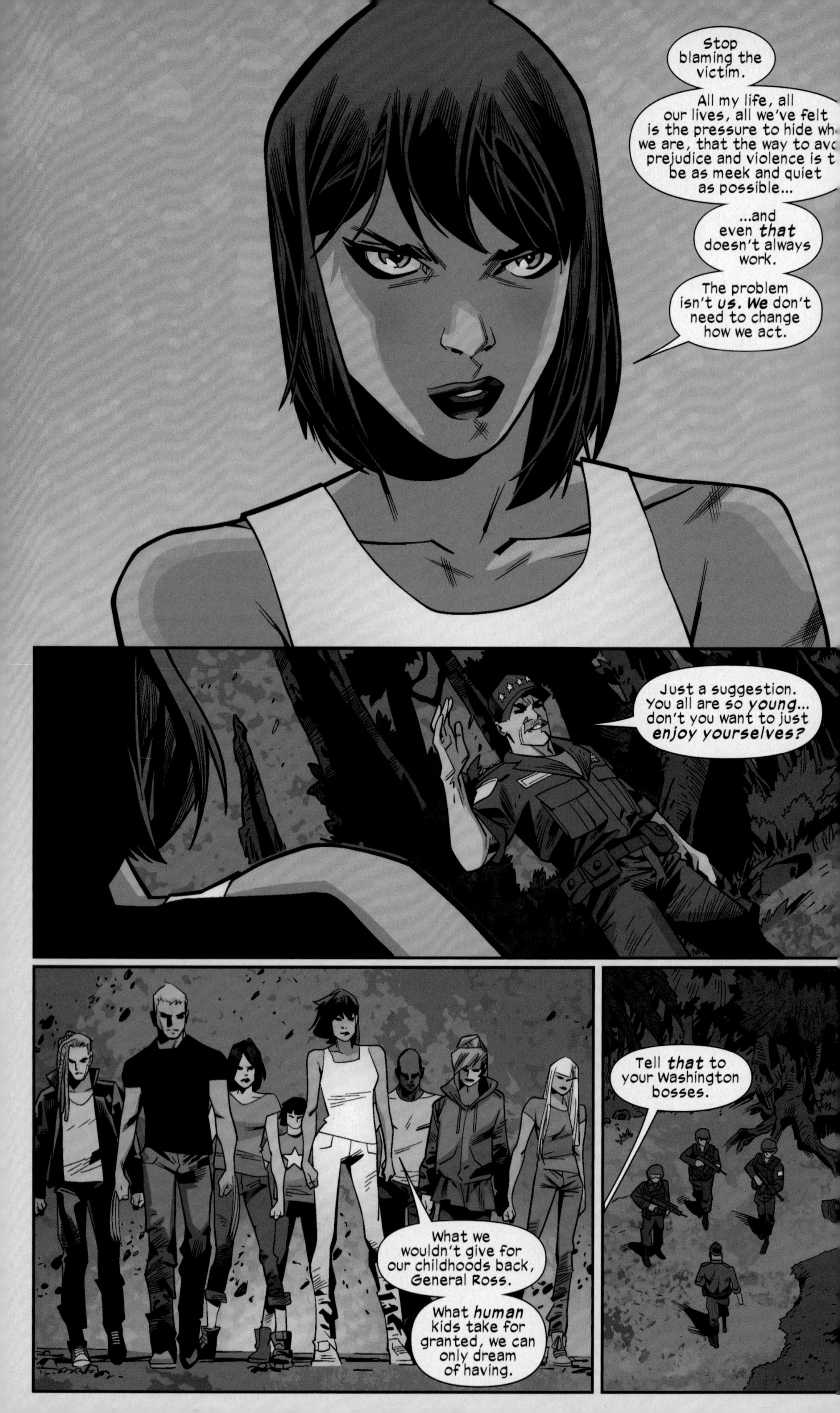
Stop blaming the victim.
All my life, all our lives, all we've felt is the pressure to hide wh we are, that the way to av prejudice and violence is t be as meek and quiet as possible...
...and even *that* doesn't always work.
The problem isn't *us. We* don't need to change how we act.
Just a suggestion. You all are so *young*... don't you want to just *enjoy yourselves?*
What we wouldn't give for our childhoods back, General Ross.
What *human* kids take for granted, we can only dream of having.
Tell *that* to your Washington bosses.

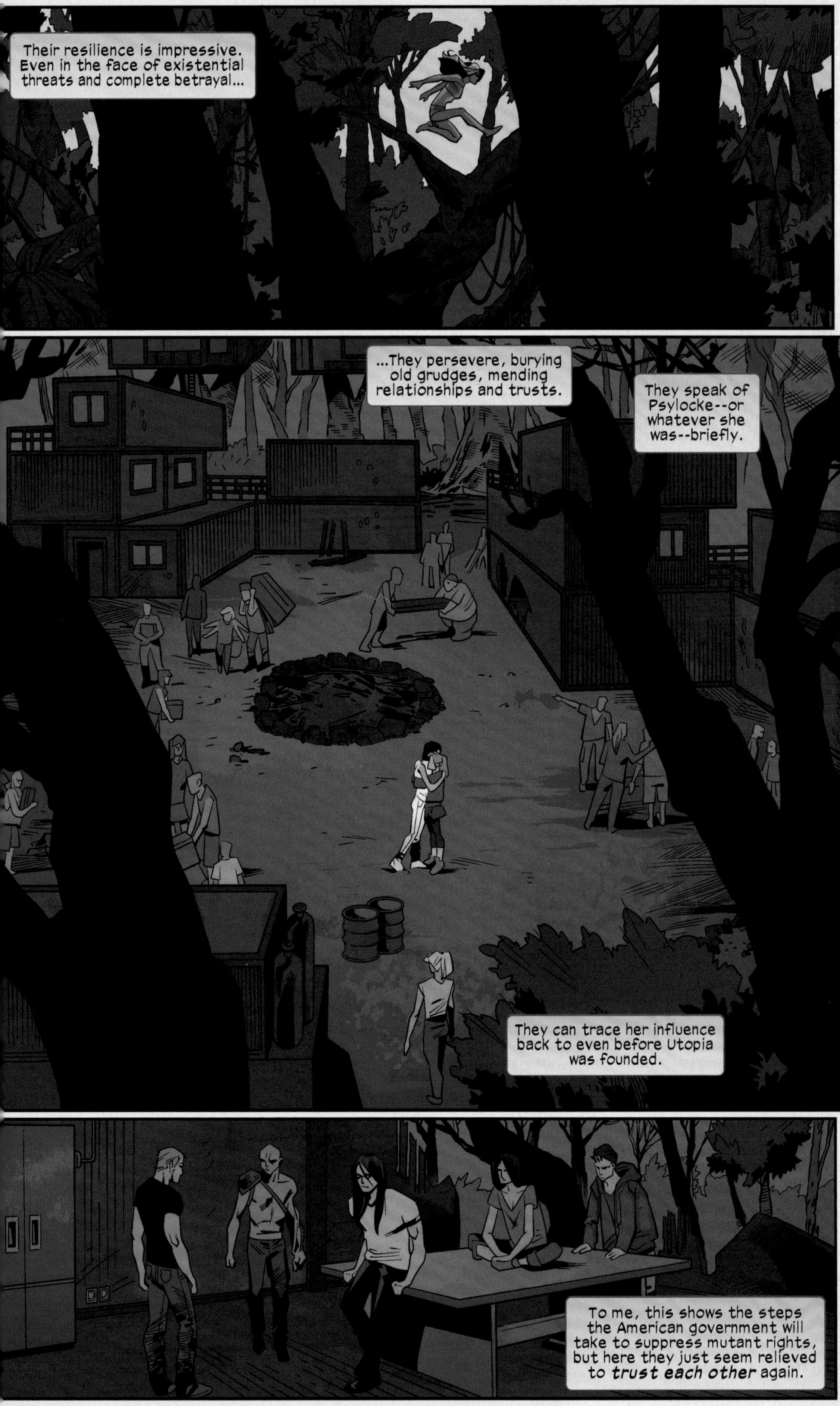
Their resilience is impressive. Even in the face of existential threats and complete betrayal...
...They persevere, burying old grudges, mending relationships and trusts.
They speak of Psylocke--or whatever she was--briefly.
They can trace her influence back to even before Utopia was founded.
To me, this shows the steps the American government will take to suppress mutant rights, but here they just seem relieved to *trust each other* again.

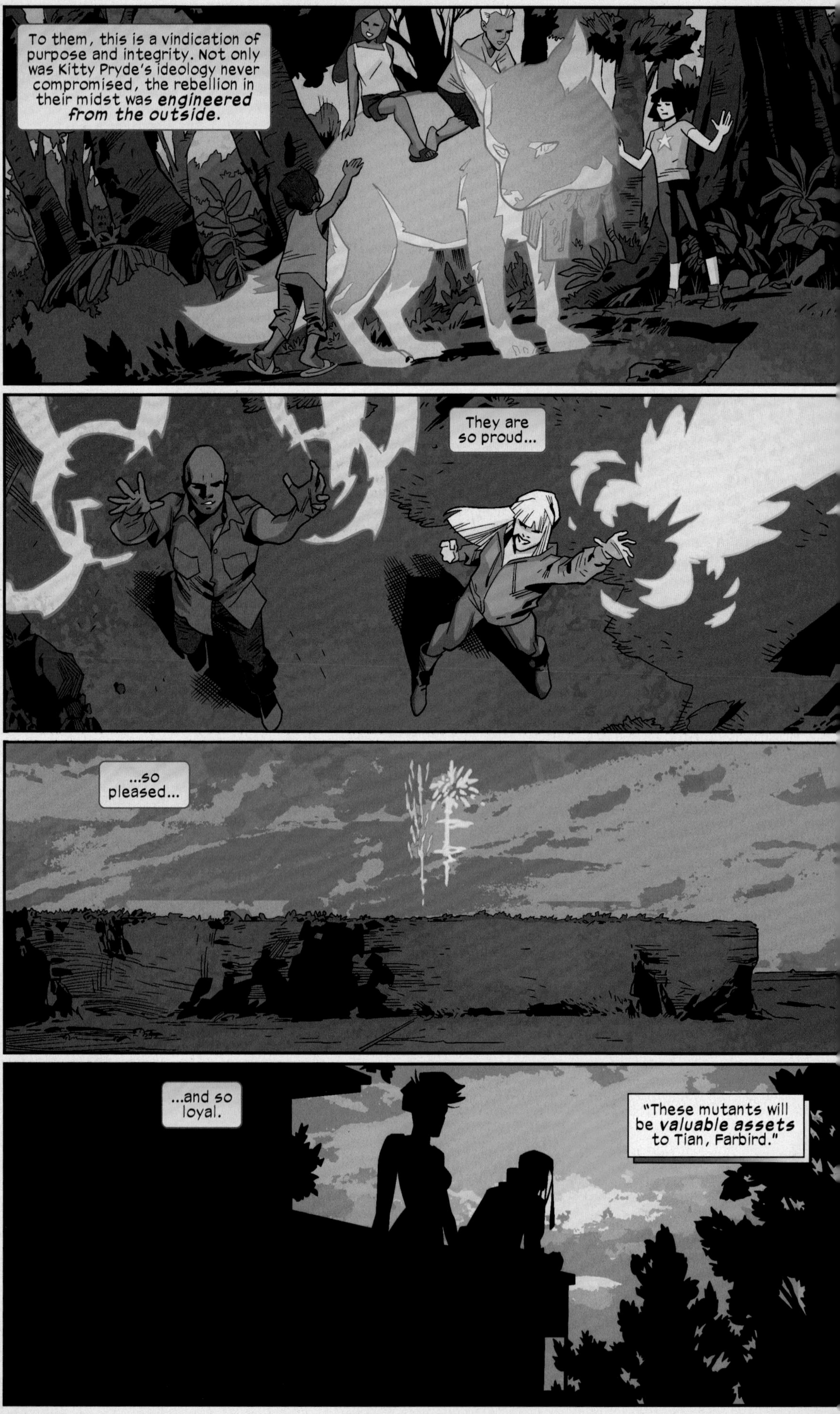
To them, this is a vindication of purpose and integrity. Not only was Kitty Pryde's ideology never compromised, the rebellion in their midst was *engineered from the outside.*
They are so proud...
...so pleased...
...and so loyal.
"These mutants will be *valuable assets* to Tian, Farbird."

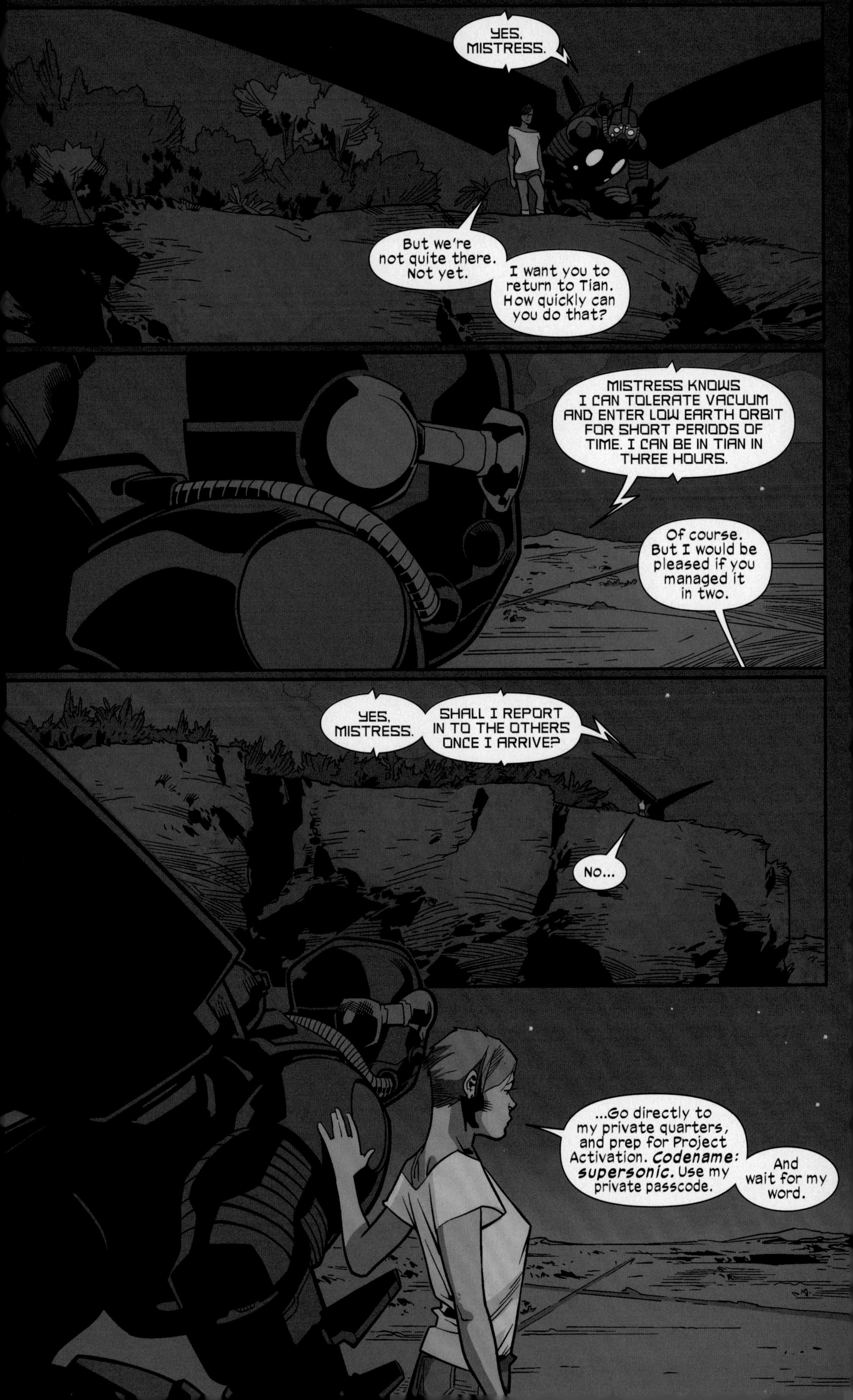

YES, MISTRESS.
But we're not quite there. Not yet.
I want you to return to Tian. How quickly can you do that?
MISTRESS KNOWS I CAN TOLERATE VACUUM AND ENTER LOW EARTH ORBIT FOR SHORT PERIODS OF TIME. I CAN BE IN TIAN IN THREE HOURS.
Of course. But I would be pleased if you managed it in two.
YES, MISTRESS.
SHALL I REPORT IN TO THE OTHERS ONCE I ARRIVE?
No...
...Go directly to my private quarters, and prep for Project Activation. ***Codename: supersonic.*** Use my private passcode.
And wait for my word.

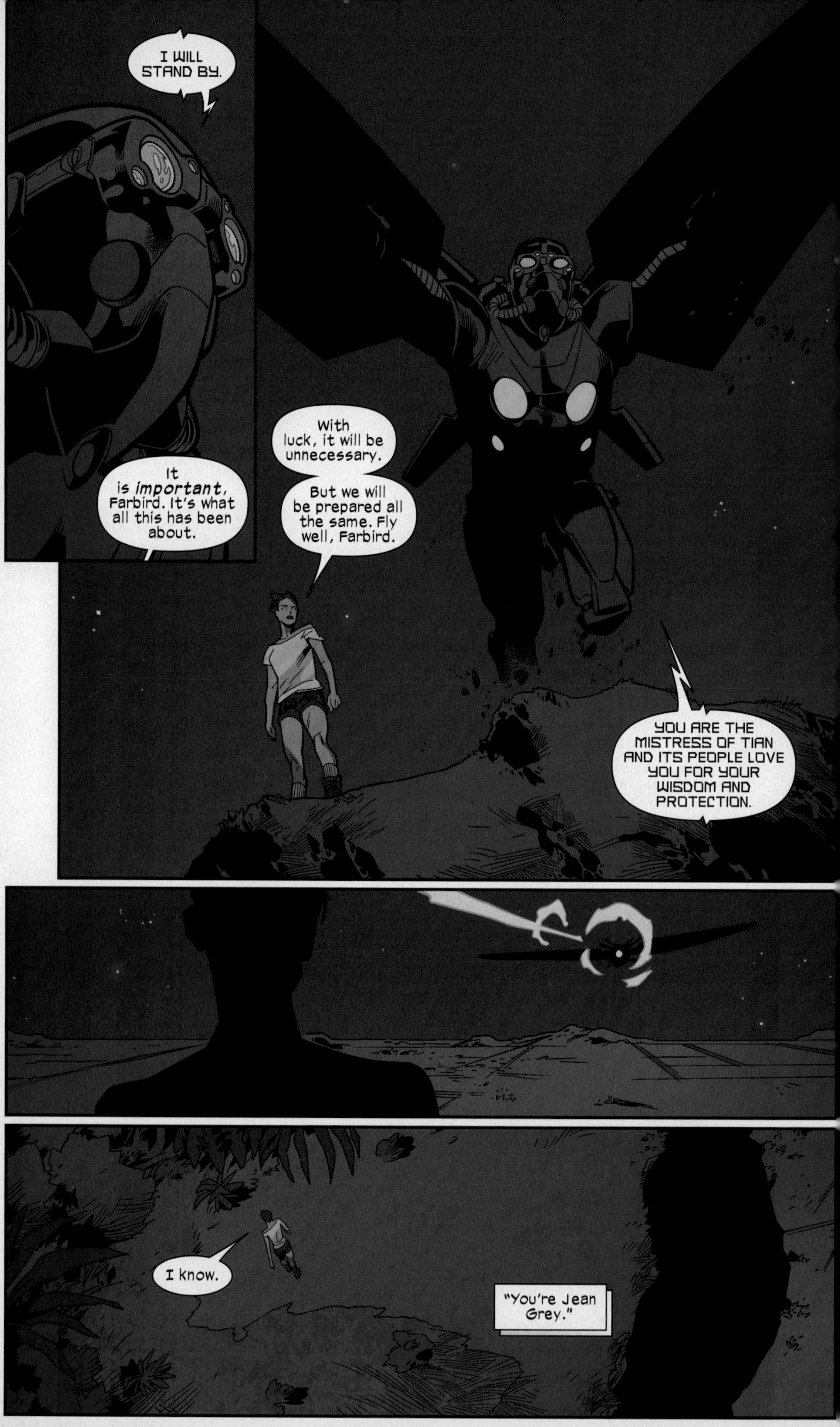
I WILL STAND BY.
It is *important*, Farbird. It's what all this has been about.
With luck, it will be unnecessary.
But we will be prepared all the same. Fly well, Farbird.
YOU ARE THE MISTRESS OF TIAN AND ITS PEOPLE LOVE YOU FOR YOUR WISDOM AND PROTECTION.
I know.
"You're Jean Grey."

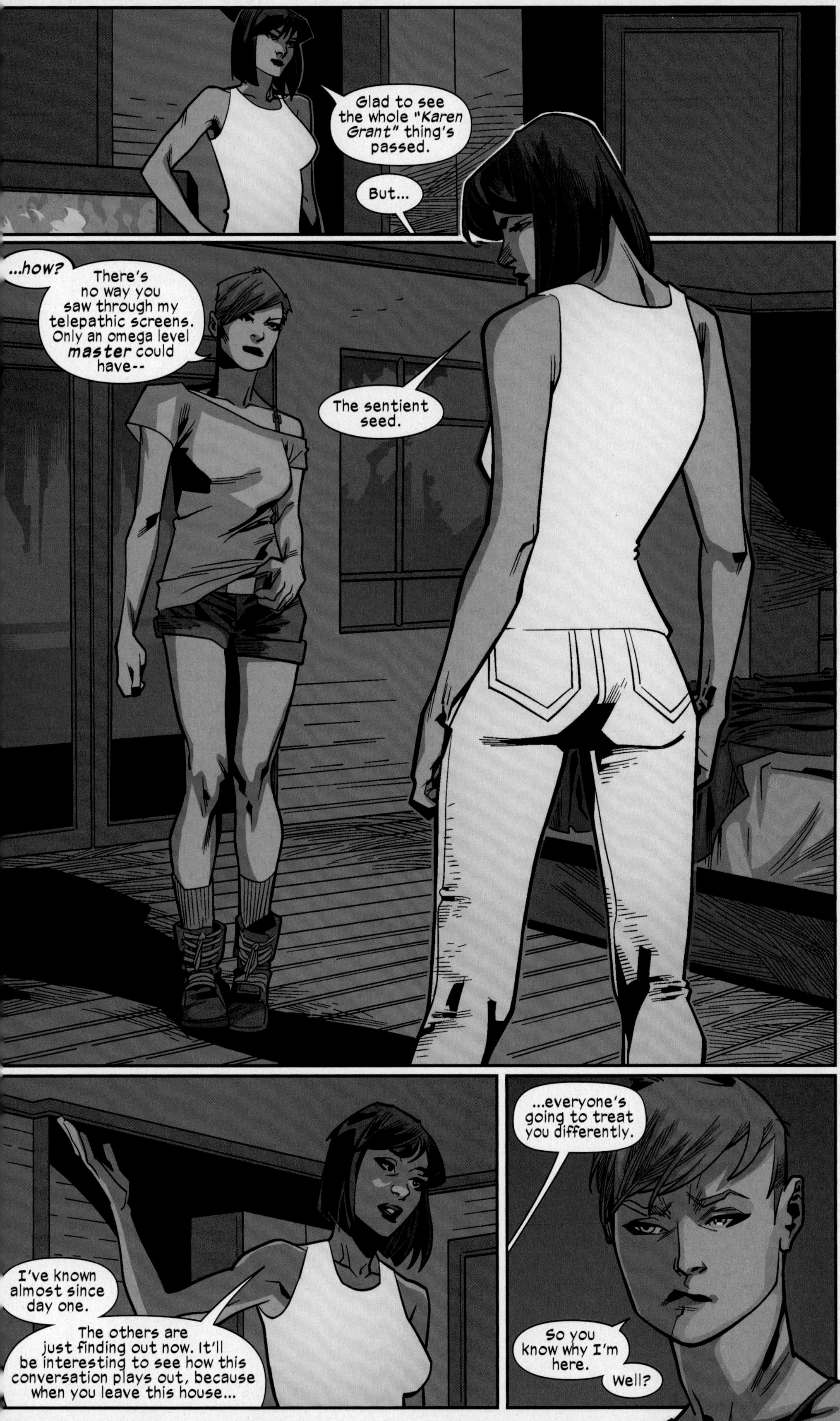
Glad to see the whole "Karen Grant" thing's passed.
But...
...how?
There's no way you saw through my telepathic screens. Only an omega level master could have--
The sentient seed.
I've known almost since day one.
The others are just finding out now. It'll be interesting to see how this conversation plays out, because when you leave this house...
...everyone's going to treat you differently.
So you know why I'm here.
Well?

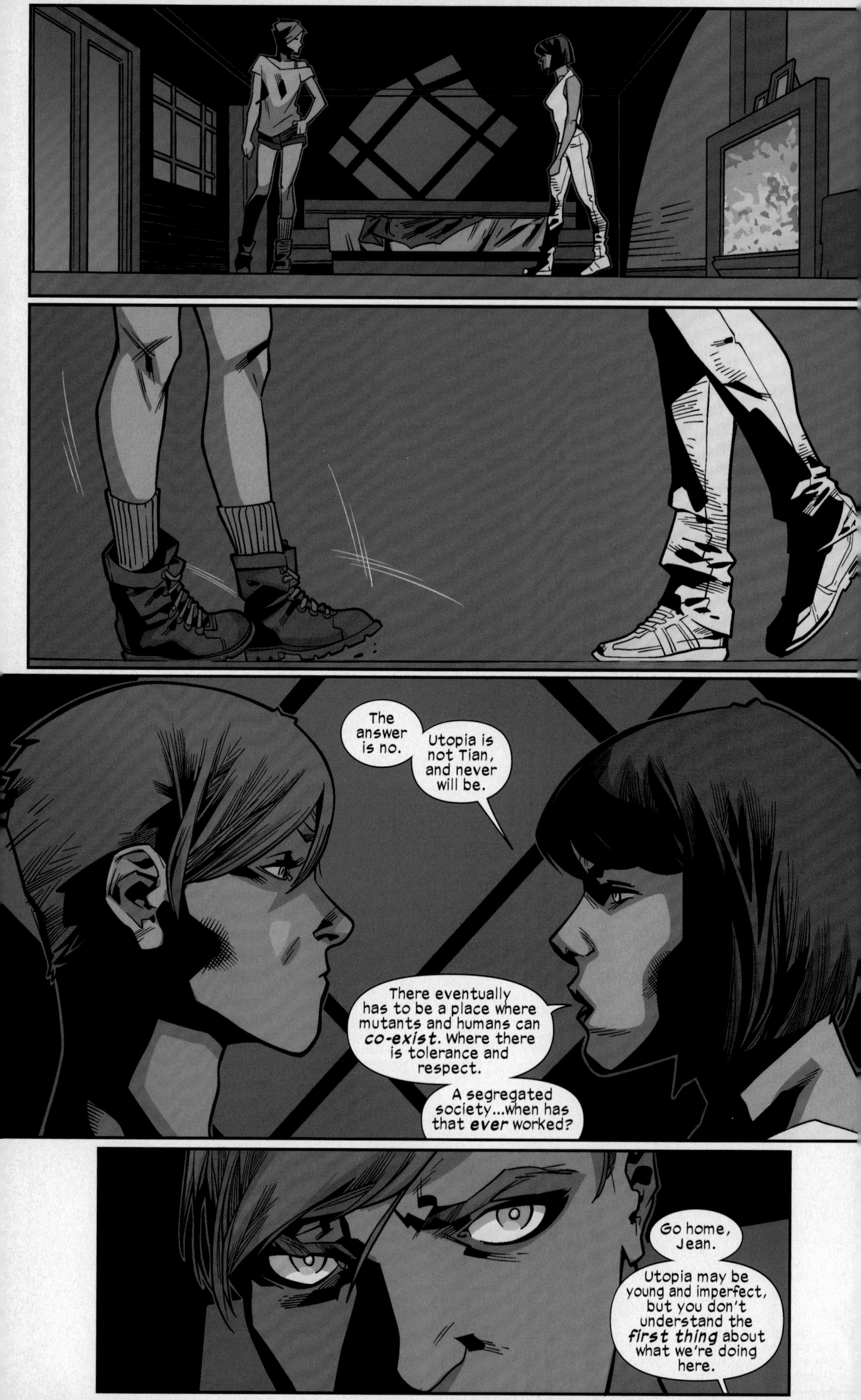

The answer is no.
Utopia is not Tian, and never will be.
There eventually has to be a place where mutants and humans can *co-exist*. Where there is tolerance and respect.
A segregated society...when has that *ever* worked?
Go home, Jean.
Utopia may be young and imperfect, but you don't understand the *first thing* about what we're doing here.

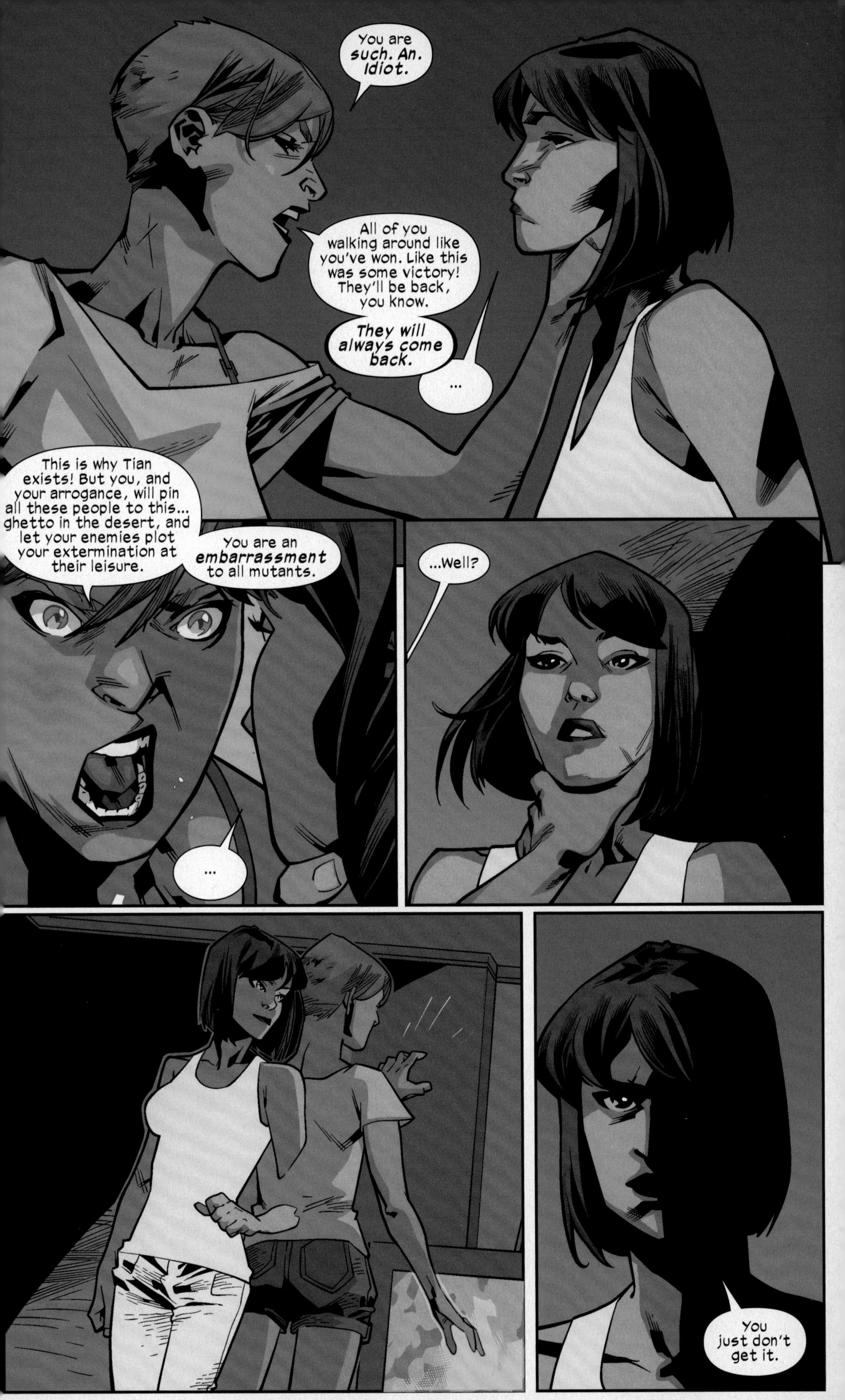
You are such. An. Idiot.
All of you walking around like you've won. Like this was some victory! They'll be back, you know.
They will always come back.
...
This is why Tian exists! But you, and your arrogance, will pin all these people to this... ghetto in the desert, and let your enemies plot your extermination at their leisure.
You are an embarrassment to all mutants.
...
...Well?
You just don't get it.

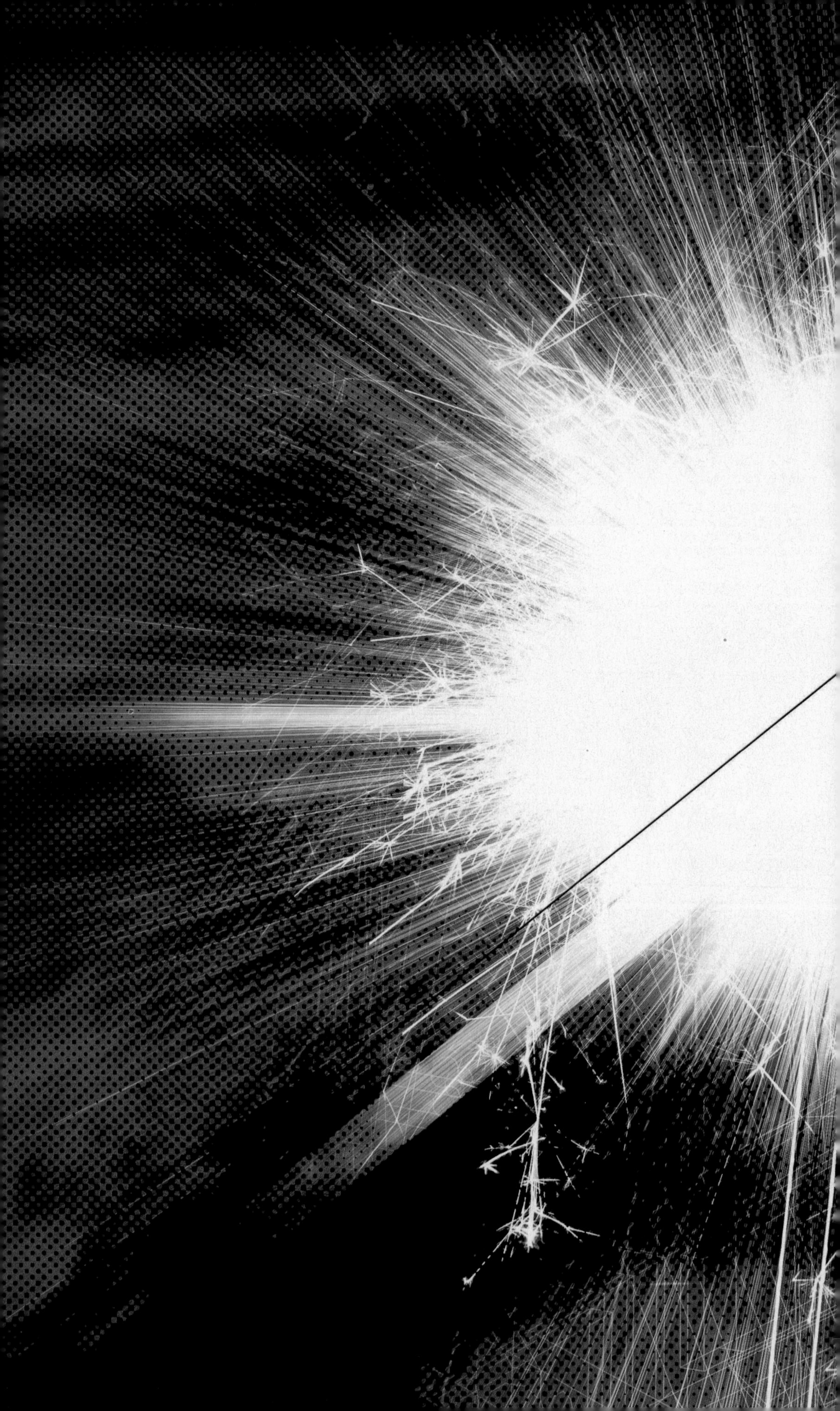

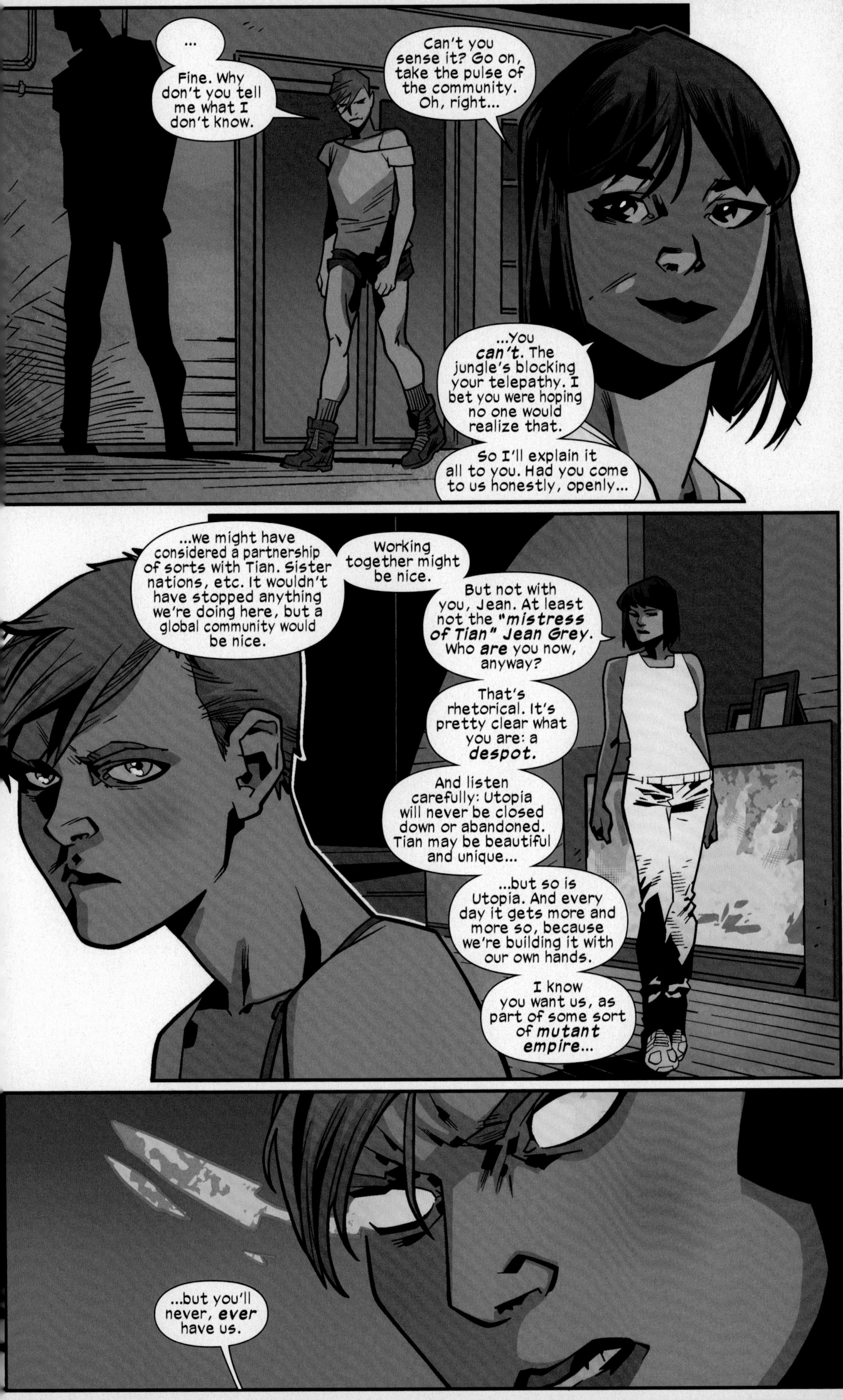
...
Fine. Why don't you tell me what I don't know.
Can't you sense it? Go on, take the pulse of the community. Oh, right...
...You *can't*. The jungle's blocking your telepathy. I bet you were hoping no one would realize that.
So I'll explain it all to you. Had you come to us honestly, openly...
...we might have considered a partnership of sorts with Tian. Sister nations, etc. It wouldn't have stopped anything we're doing here, but a global community would be nice.
Working together might be nice.
But not with you, Jean. At least not the *"mistress of Tian" Jean Grey*. Who *are* you now, anyway?
That's rhetorical. It's pretty clear what you are: a *despot.*
And listen carefully: Utopia will never be closed down or abandoned. Tian may be beautiful and unique...
...but so is Utopia. And every day it gets more and more so, because we're building it with our own hands.
I know you want us, as part of some sort of *mutant empire*...
...but you'll never, *ever* have us.

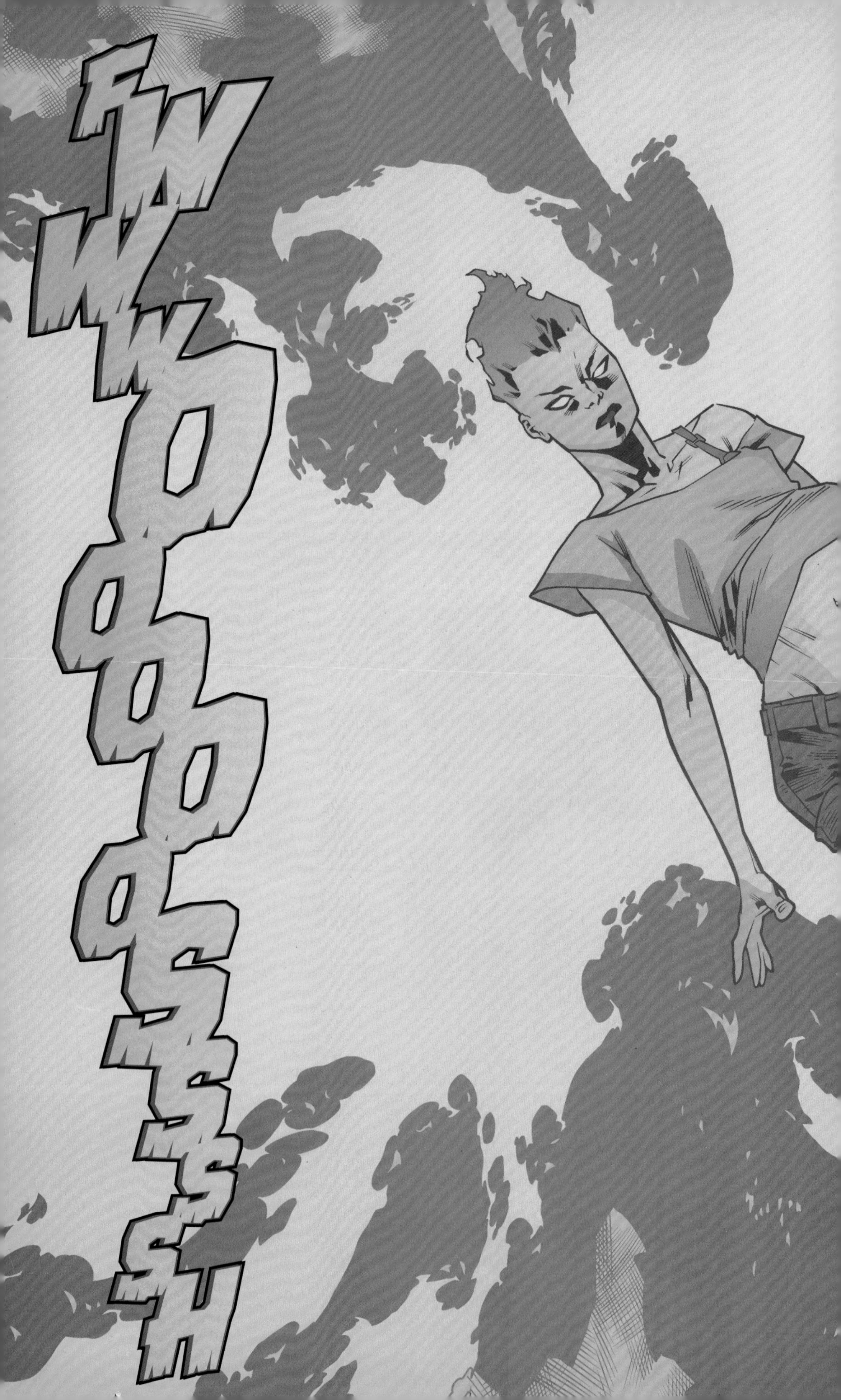
FWOOOOSSSH

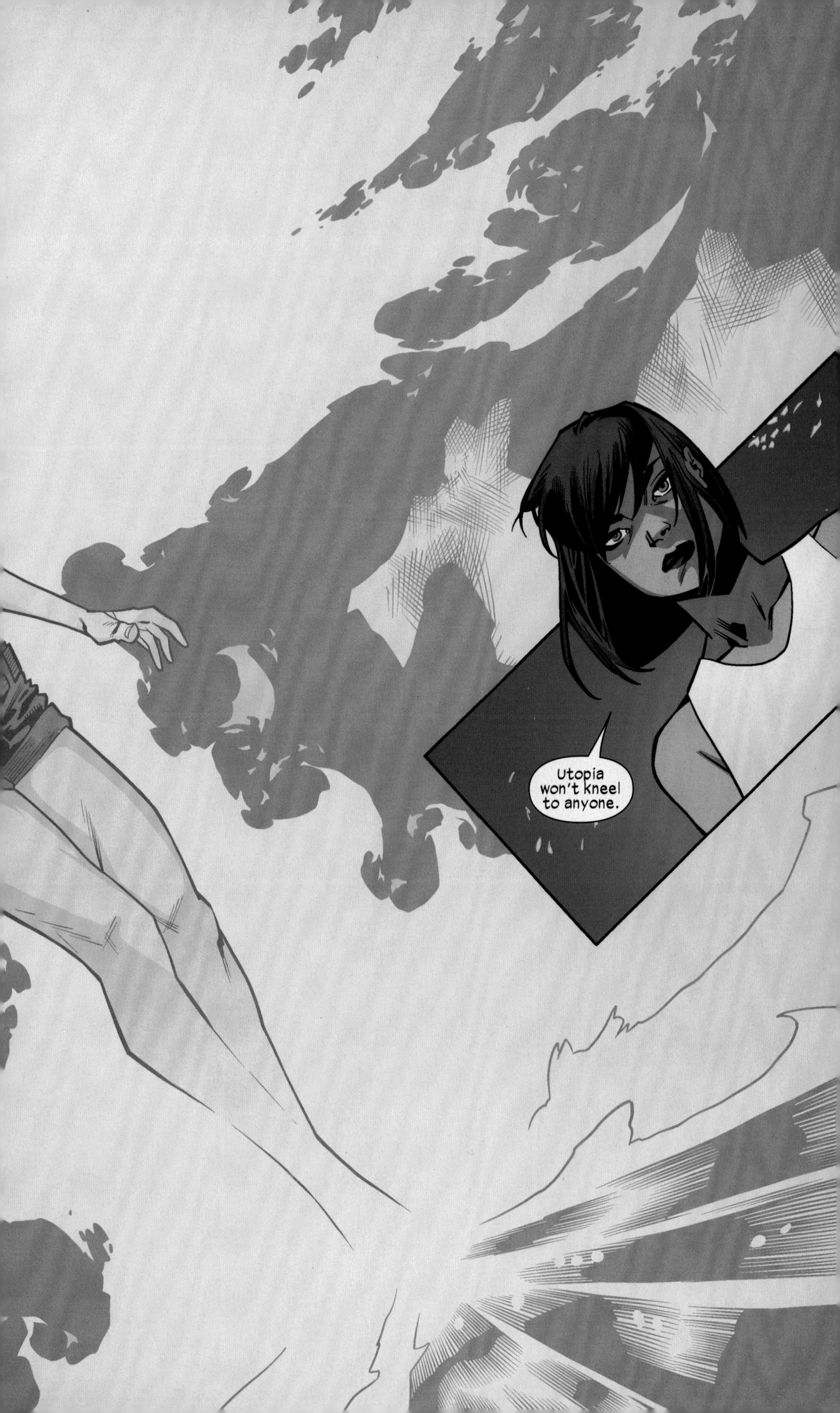
Utopia won't kneel to anyone.

Whoa!

We're safe.

She promised me.

What are we seeing, then?

A Utopia that's learned how to *win*...

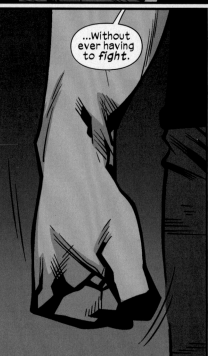

...Without ever having to *fight*.

Did you *hear what I said?*

Go home...

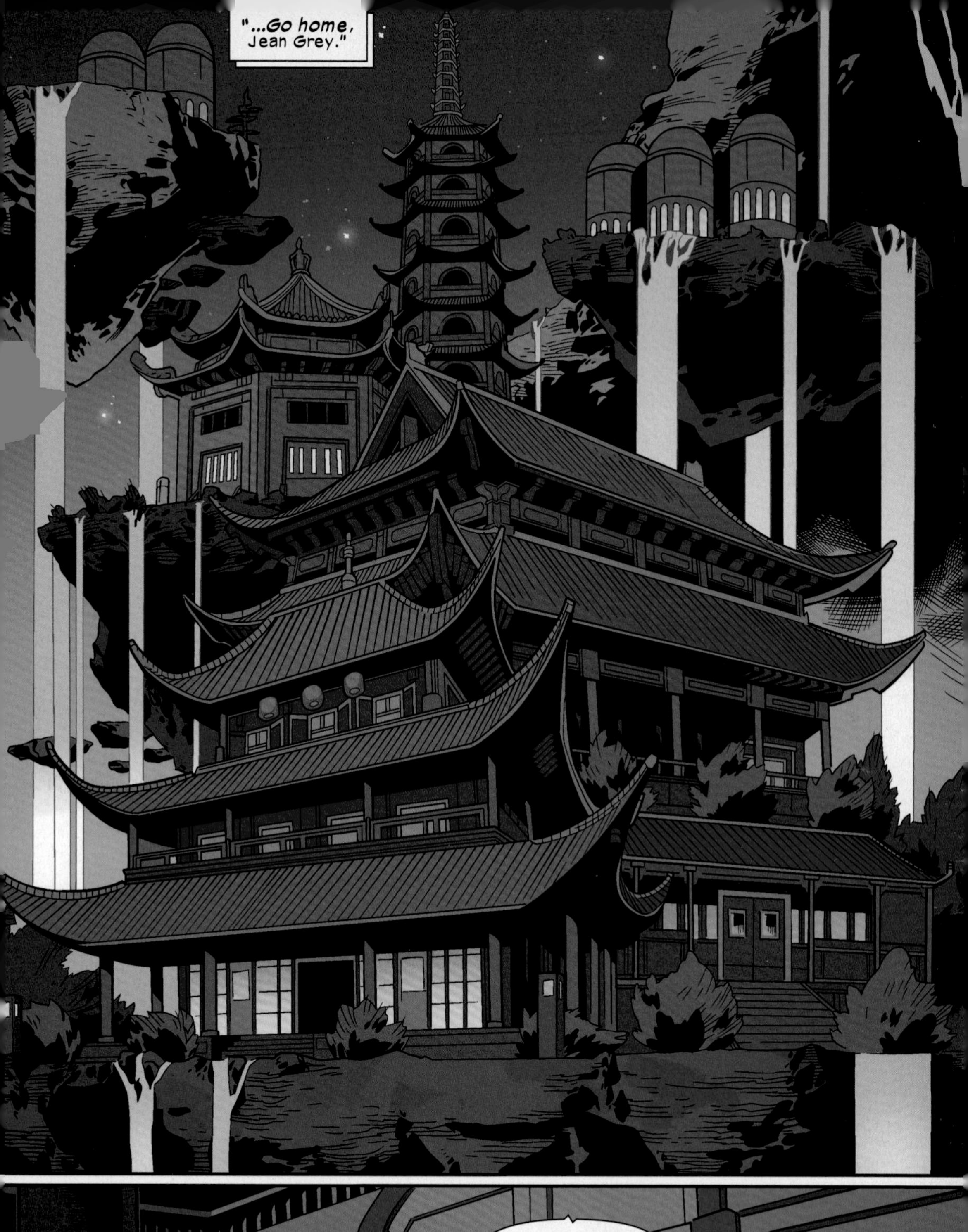
"...Go home, Jean Grey."

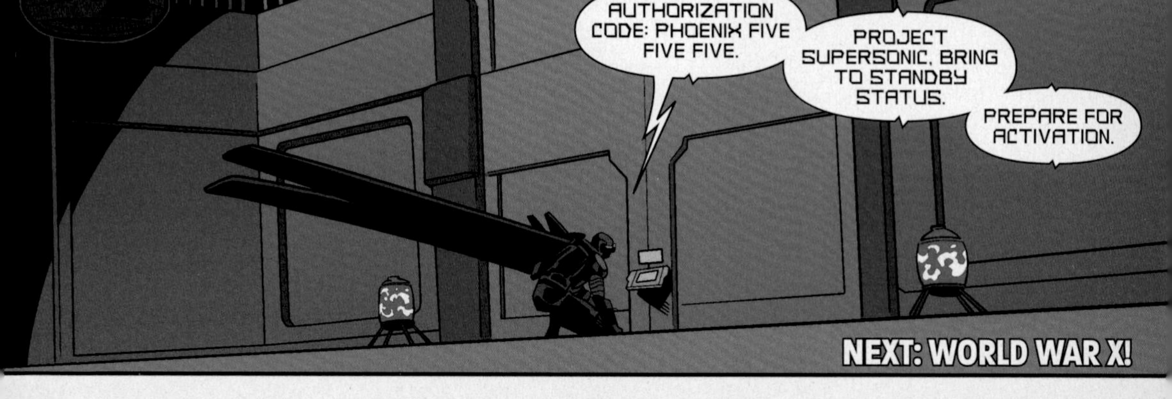
AUTHORIZATION CODE: PHOENIX FIVE FIVE FIVE.
PROJECT SUPERSONIC, BRING TO STANDBY STATUS.
PREPARE FOR ACTIVATION.
NEXT: WORLD WAR X!

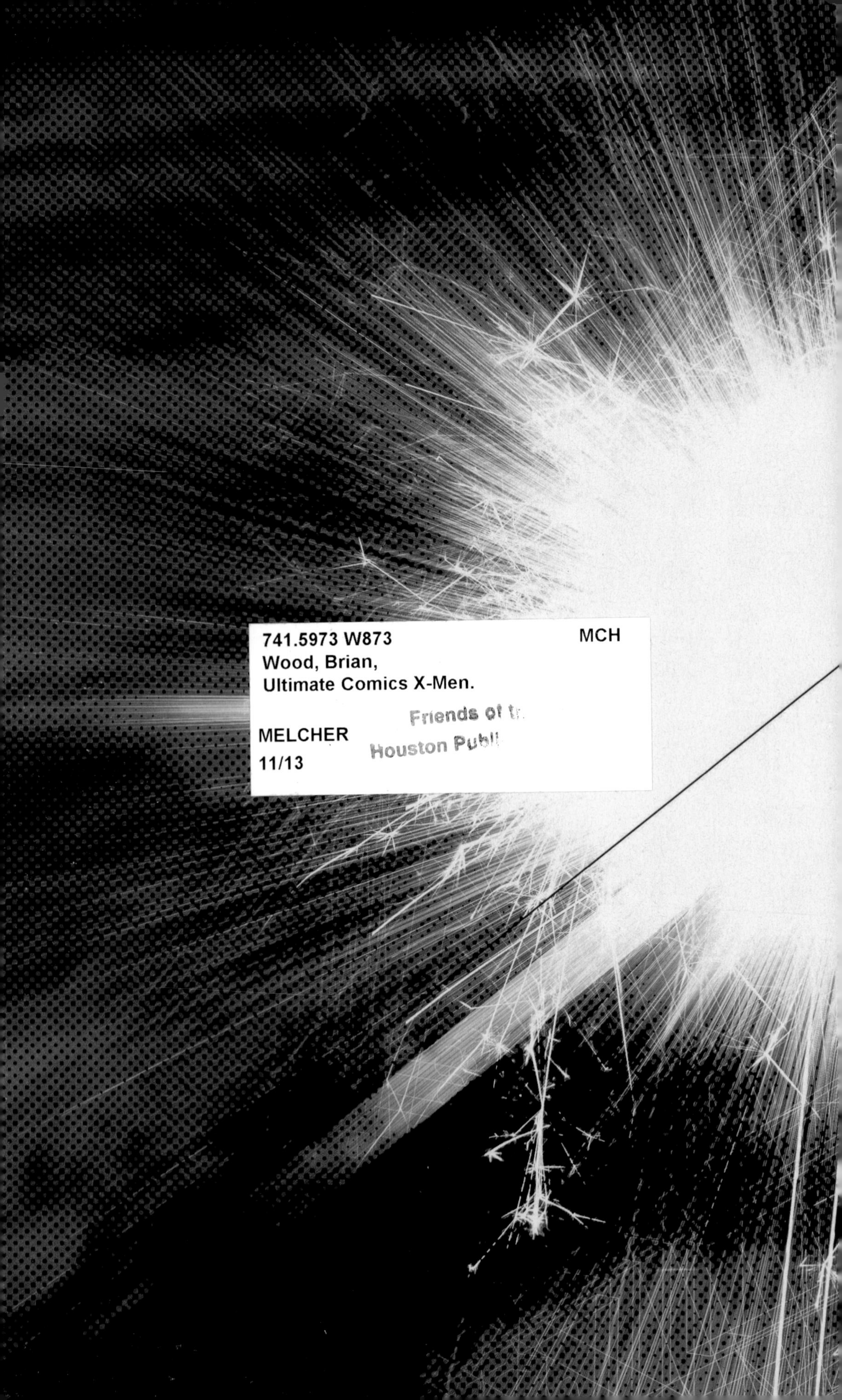